菲迪克(FIDIC)文献译丛

施工合同条件

Conditions of Contract
for Construction

国际咨询工程师联合会
中国工程咨询协会 编译

朱锦林 翻译　　徐礼章 校译
王　川　徐礼章　唐　萍　审订

（1999年第1版）
（中英文对照本）

（译者对译文的准确度承担全部责任，
正式使用发生争端时，以英文原版为准）

机械工业出版社

本《施工合同条件》(中文版)是对照国际咨询工程师联合会(FIDIC 即菲迪克)编写的最新英文版本，由 FIDIC 在中国的成员协会——中国工程咨询协会组织专家编译。

本《施工合同条件》1999 英文版不是在菲迪克以往合同版本基础上修改，而是进行了重新编写。它继承了原有合同条件的优点，并根据多年来在实践中取得的经验以及专家、学者和相关各方的意见和建议，作出了重大的调整。

本书内容包括施工合同的通用条件和专用条件，附有争端裁决协议书一般条件、各担保函格式以及投标函、合同协议书和争端裁决协议书格式。

本书推荐用于由雇主或其代表工程师设计的建筑或工程项目。这种合同的通常情况是，由承包商按照雇主提供的设计进行工程施工。但该工程可以包含由承包商设计的土木、机械、电气和(或)构筑物的某些部分。

读者对象：工程咨询单位，从事投资、金融和工程项目管理的部门和组织、各类项目业主、建筑施工监理企业、工程承包企业、环保企业、会计/律师事务所、保险公司以及有关高等院校等单位和人员。

北京市版权局著作权合同登记号：图字：01-2002-1264 号

图书在版编目(CIP)数据

施工合同条件/中国工程咨询协会编译. —北京：机械工业出版社，2002.5(2021.5 重印)

(菲迪克(FIDIC)文献译丛)

书名原文：Conditions of Contract for Construction

ISBN 978-7-111-10243-4

Ⅰ. 施… Ⅱ. 中… Ⅲ. 建筑工程—工程施工—合同—基本知识 Ⅳ. TU723.1

中国版本图书馆 CIP 数据核字(2002)第 028532 号

机械工业出版社(北京市百万庄大街 22 号 邮政编码 100037)

责任编辑：何文军 责任校对：刘志文

封面设计：姚 毅 责任印制：李 昂

北京铭成印刷有限公司印刷

2021 年 5 月第 1 版·第 20 次印刷

210mm×297mm ·16 印张·508 千字

标准书号：ISBN 978-7-111-10243-4

本书定价：110.00 元(全套 360 元)

凡购本书，如有缺页、倒页、脱页，由本社发行部调换

电话服务　　　　　　　　　网络服务

服务咨询热线：010-88361066　机 工 官 网：www.cmpbook.com

读者购书热线：010-68326294　机 工 官 博：weibo.com/cmp1952

　　　　　　　010-88379203　金 书 网：www.golden-book.com

封面无防伪标均为盗版　　　教育服务网：www.cmpedu.com

菲迪克(FIDIC)授权书

I herewith authorize CNAEC to translate FIDIC's publications (but not the publications as edited by other organizations)into Chinese and publish them.

I agree with your statement, as part of the agreement, that you will:

a) provide FIDIC with 10 copies of the translation per document, and

b) make a statement on the inside cover of the translation that the translator takes full responsibility for the accuracy of the translation and that in case of dispute, the original version in English shall prevail.

Peter van der TOGT

Publications manager

[译文]

在此，我授权中国工程咨询协会把 FIDIC 出版物译成中文并出版(但是,不包括其他组织编写的出版物)。

我同意你们的意见，作为协议的一部分，你们应:

a) 向 FIDIC 提供每份文件中译本 10 本;

b) 在译文的扉页上注明译者对译文的准确度承担全部责任，如果发生争端，以英文原版为准。

出版经理: Peter van der TOGT

FIDIC is the French acronym for the International Federation of Consulting Engineers.

FIDIC was founded in 1913 by three national associations of consulting engineers within Europe. The objectives of forming the federation were to promote in common the professional interests of the member associations and to disseminate information of interest to members of its component national associations.

Today FIDIC membership numbers more than 60 countries from all parts of the globe and the federation represents most of the private practice consulting engineers in the world.

FIDIC arranges seminars, conferences and other events in the furtherance of its goals: maintenance of high ethical and professional standards; exchange of views and information; discussion of problems of mutual concern among member associations and representatives of the international financial institutions; and development of the consulting engineering industry in developing countries.

FIDIC publications include proceedings of various conferences and seminars, information for consulting engineers, project owners and international development agencies, standard pre-qualification forms, contract documents and client/consultant agreements. They are available from the secretariat in Switzerland.

FIDIC（中译"菲迪克"）是国际咨询工程师联合会的法文首字母缩写。

菲迪克（FIDIC）是由欧洲三个国家的咨询工程师协会于 1913 年成立的。组建联合会的目的是共同促进成员协会的职业利益，以及向其成员协会会员传播有益信息。

今天，菲迪克（FIDIC）已有来自于全球各地 60 多个国家的成员协会，代表着世界上大多数私人执业的咨询工程师。

菲迪克（FIDIC）举办各类研讨会、会议及其他活动，以促进其目标：维护高的道德和职业标准；交流观点和信息；讨论成员协会和国际金融机构代表共同关心的问题；以及发展中国家工程咨询业的发展。

菲迪克（FIDIC）的出版物包括：各类会议和研讨会的文件，为咨询工程师、项目业主和国际开发机构提供的信息，资格预审标准格式，合同文件、以及客户与工程咨询单位协议书。这些资料可以从设在瑞士的菲迪克（FIDIC）秘书处得到。

"菲迪克(FIDIC)文献译丛" 出版前言

世界工程咨询业已有上百年的发展历史,成为各国投资建设领域重要的智力服务行业。国际咨询工程师联合会(按其法文缩写 FIDIC,通称菲迪克)成立已有 90 多年,是国际工程咨询业的权威性行业组织,与世界银行等国际金融组织有着密切的联系。菲迪克的各种文献出版物,包括各种合同、协议标准范本、各项工作指南、以及工作惯例建议等,得到世界各有关组织的广泛承认和实施,是工程咨询行业的重要指导性文献。

我国工程咨询业是改革开放以来,在原有工程设计和建设管理队伍基础上发展起来的,承担着为各级投资决策部门和各类建设项目提供战略规划、项目决策、工程设计、以及项目实施管理等投资建设全过程的咨询服务。今后随着我国建设事业的发展,项目的决策与实施要求提供咨询服务的工作量将会大量增长,咨询服务质量要求也将越来越高。特别是我国已加入世界贸易组织(WTO),投资建设领域既有新的机遇,也有新的挑战。借鉴国外工程咨询的成功经验,努力提高我国工程咨询服务水平,已成为当务之急。

中国工程咨询协会于 1996 年正式加入菲迪克组织,并取得在我国翻译出版菲迪克文献的授权。为了系统介绍菲迪克有关出版物,协会成立了菲迪克文献编译委员会,将以"菲迪克文献译丛"形式,陆续翻译出版菲迪克有关文献。

我们相信"译丛"的出版,将为我国广大工程咨询单位和人员、从事投资、金融和工程项目管理的部门和组织、各类项目业主、建筑施工监理企业、工程承包企业、环保企业、会计/律师事务所、保险公司以及有关高等院校学习国际经验,提供重要帮助。

中国工程咨询协会

编者的话

本书由国际咨询工程师联合会(FIDIC 即菲迪克)编写，于 1999 年出版的新合同标准格式第 1 版。新版《施工合同条件》继承了菲迪克以往合同条件的优点，并根据多年来在实践中取得的经验以及专家、学者和相关各方的意见和建议，作出了重大的调整。在结构、布局和措辞等方面做了重大的修改：统一了条款、定义和措辞；条款数目统一为二十条。此次出版的《施工合同条件》，不是在原有合同基础上修改，而是进行了重新编写。1998 年菲迪克在成员协会中推出了试用本，在全世界范围内收集建议和意见，并在一些国家进行试点使用，在经过 1 年多的试用后，于 1999 年才正式出版了重新改写的《施工合同条件》。

希望此译本的出版，对我国从事工程咨询、投资、金融和项目管理的部门和组织、各类项目业主、建筑施工监理企业、工程承包企业、环保企业、会计/律师事务所、保险公司以及有关高等院校等人员在学习和运用菲迪克合同条件，有效地解决在国际、国内工程咨询和工程承包活动中的合同管理问题，更好地开拓国内外工程咨询和工程承包市场，促进我国工程咨询业与国际惯例接轨，推动我国工程咨询事业的发展会有所帮助。

翻译过程中，我们虽然尽力想使译文准确通顺，但限于专业知识与语言水平，译文中可能出现不妥乃至错误之处，敬请读者指正。

本书由朱锦林翻译，徐礼章校译，王川、徐礼章、唐萍审校，刘菡、邓冰茹、莫伟平、李莉萍、申小丹、刘毅、张平、胡仲翔、张甲英、张芳芳、时小军、杨海昆、郑海燕、陈雄、曾家平、王新之、唐璐璐、郑海萍等参加了部分章节的编译工作。

中国工程咨询协会 FIDIC 文献编译委员会

ACKNOWLEDGEMENTS

Fédération Internationale des Ingénieurs-Conseils (FIDIC) extends special thanks to the following members of its Update Task Group: Christopher Wade (Group Leader), SWECO-VBB, Sweden; Peter L Booen (Principal Drafter), GIBB Ltd, UK; Hermann Bayerlein, Fichtner, Germany; Christopher R Seppala (Legal Adviser), White & Case, France; and José F Speziale, IATASA, Argentina.

The preparation was carried out under the general direction of the FIDIC Contracts Committee which comprised John B Bowcock, Consulting Engineer, UK (Chairman); Michael Mortimer-Hawkins, SwedPower, Sweden; and Axel-Volkmar Jaeger, Schmidt Reuter Partner, Germany; together with K B (Tony) Norris as Special Adviser.

Drafts were reviewed by many persons and organisations, including those listed below. Their comments were duly studied by the Update Task Group and, where considered appropriate, have influenced the wording of the clauses. Ihab Abu-Zahra, CRC – Hassan Dorra, Egypt; Mushtaq Ahmad, NESPAK, Pakistan; Peter Batty, Post Buckley International, USA; Roeland Bertrams, Clifford Chance, Netherlands; Bosen He, Tianjin University, China; Manfred Breege, Lahmeyer International, Germany; Pablo Bueno, TYPSA, Spain; Nael G Bunni, Consulting Engineer, Ireland; Peter H J Chapman, Engineer & Barrister, UK; Ian Fraser, Beca Carter Hollings & Ferner, New Zealand; Roy Goode, Oxford University, UK; Dan W Graham, Bristows Cooke & Carpmael, UK; Mark Griffiths, Griffiths & Armour, UK; Geoffrey F Hawker, Consulting Engineer, UK; Hesse & Steinberger, VDMA, Germany; Poul E Hvilsted, Elsamprojekt, Denmark; Gordon L Jaynes, Whitman Breed Abbott & Morgan, UK; Tonny Jensen (Chairman of FIDIC Quality Management Committee), COWI, Denmark; David S Khalef, Jordan; Philip Loots & Associates, South Africa; Neil McCole, Merz and McLellan, UK; Matthew Needham-Laing, Victoria Russell & Paul J Taylor, Berrymans Lace Mawer, UK; Brian W Totterdill, Consulting Engineer, UK; David R Wightman & Gerlando Butera, Nabarro Nathanson, UK; the Association of Japanese Consulting Engineers; the Construction Industry Authority of the Philippines; European International Contractors; Organisme de Liaison Industries Métalliques Européennes ("ORGALIME"); the International Association of Dredging Contractors; the International Bar Association; the Asian Development Bank; and the World Bank. Acknowledgement of reviewers does not mean that such persons or organizations approve of the wording of all clauses.

FIDIC wishes to record its appreciation of the time and effort devoted by all the above.

The ultimate decision on the form and content of the document rests with FIDIC.

致谢

国际咨询工程师联合会（FIDIC 即菲迪克）向其新版工作组的以下成员特致谢意：瑞典 SWE-CO-VBB 公司的 Christopher Wade（组长），英国 GIBB 有限公司的 Peter L Booen（主要起草人），德国 Fichtner 公司的 Hermann Bayerlein；法国 White & Case 公司的 Christopher R Seppala（法律顾问），及阿根廷 IATASA 公司的 Jose F Speziale。

本书是在 FIDIC 合同委员会指导下编写的，该委员会成员包括：英国咨询工程师 John B Bowcock（主席）、瑞典 SwedPower 公司的 Michael Mortimer – Hawkins、德国 Schmidt Reuter Partner 公司的 Axel – Volkmar Jaeger；还有特别顾问 K B（Tony）Norris。

书稿曾经下列许多人员和组织审阅，他们的意见已由新版工作组充分研究，认为适宜的意见已反映在条款措辞中。这些人员和组织包括：埃及 CRC – Hassan Dorra 公司的 Ihab Abu – Zahra、巴基斯坦 NESPAK 公司的 Mushtaq Ahmad、美国 Post Buckley International 公司的 Peter Batty、荷兰 Clifford Chance 公司的 Roeland Bertrams、中国天津大学的何伯森、德国 Lahmeyer International 公司的 Manfred Breege、西班牙 TYPSA 公司的 Pablo Bueno、爱尔兰咨询工程师 Nael G Bunni、英国 Engineer & Barrister 公司的 Peter H J Chapman、新西兰 Beca Carter Hollings & Ferner 公司的 Ian Fraser、英国牛津大学的 Roy Goode、英国 Bristows Cooke & Carpmael 公司的 Dan W Graham、英国 Griffiths & Armour 公司的 Mark Griffiths、英国咨询工程师 Geoffrey F Hawker、德国 VDMA 的 Hesse & Steinberger、丹麦 Elsamprojekt 公司的 Poul E Hvilsted、英国 Whitman Breed Abbott & Morgan 公司的 Gordon L Jaynes、丹麦 COWI 公司的 Tony Jensen（FIDIC 质量管理委员会主席）、约旦的 David S Khalef、南非的 Philip Loots & Associates、英国 Merz and McLellan 公司的 Neil McCole、英国 Berrymans Lace Mawer 的 Victoria Russell & Paul J Taylor 公司的 Matthew Needham – Laing、英国咨询工程师 Brian W Totterdill、英国 Nabarro Nathanson 公司的 David R Wightman 和 Gerlando Butera、日本咨询工程师协会、菲律宾建设工业局、欧洲国际承包商组织、欧洲金属工业联络组织（ORGALIME）、国际疏浚承包商协会、国际律师协会、亚洲开发银行以及世界银行。对审稿人的致谢，并不表示审稿人和审稿组织对所有条款措辞的赞同。

菲迪克（FIDIC）对所有上述人员和组织付出的时间和精力表示感谢。

本文件格式和内容的最终确定由菲迪克（FIDIC）负责。

FOREWORD

The Fédération Internationale des Ingénieurs-Conseils (FIDIC) published, in 1999, First Editions of four new standard forms of contract:

Conditions of Contract for Construction,
> which are recommended for building or engineering works designed by the Employer or by his representative, the Engineer. Under the usual arrangements for this type of contract, the Contractor constructs the works in accordance with a design provided by the Employer. However, the works may include some elements of Contractor-designed civil, mechanical, electrical and/or construction works.

Conditions of Contract for Plant and Design-Build,
> which are recommended for the provision of electrical and/or mechanical plant, and for the design and execution of building or engineering works. Under the usual arrangements for this type of contract, the Contractor designs and provides, in accordance with the Employer's requirements, plant and/or other works; which may include any combination of civil, mechanical, electrical and/or construction works.

Conditions of Contract for EPC/Turnkey Projects,
> which may be suitable for the provision on a turnkey basis of a process or power plant, of a factory or similar facility, or of an infrastructure project or other type of development, where (i) a higher degree of certainty of final price and time is required, and (ii) the Contractor takes total responsibility for the design and execution of the project, with little involvement of the Employer. Under the usual arrangements for turnkey projects, the Contractor carries out all the Engineering, Procurement and Construction (EPC), providing a fully-equipped facility, ready for operation (at the "turn of the key").

Short Form of Contract,
> which is recommended for building or engineering works of relatively small capital value. Depending on the type of work and the circumstances, this form may also be suitable for contracts of greater value, particularly for relatively simple or repetitive work or work of short duration. Under the usual arrangements for this type of contract, the Contractor constructs the works in accordance with a design provided by the Employer or by his representative (if any), but this form may also be suitable for a contract which includes, or wholly comprises, Contractor-designed civil, mechanical, electrical and/or construction works.

The forms are recommended for general use where tenders are invited on an international basis. Modifications may be required in some jurisdictions, particularly if the Conditions are to be used on domestic contracts. FIDIC considers the official and authentic texts to be the versions in the English language.

In the preparation of these Conditions of Contract for Construction, it was recognised that, while there are many sub-clauses which will be generally applicable, there are some sub-clauses which must necessarily vary to take account of the circumstances

前言

国际咨询工程师联合会(FIDIC 即菲迪克)于 1999 年出版了 4 本新的合同标准格式第一版:

《施工合同条件》,

推荐用于由**雇主**或其代表**工程师**设计的建筑或工程项目。这种合同的通常情况是,由**承包商**按照**雇主**提供的设计进行工程施工。但该工程可以包含由**承包商**设计的土木、机械、电气和(或)构筑物的某些部分。

《生产设备和设计-施工合同条件》,

推荐用于电气和(或)机械设备供货和建筑或工程的设计与施工。这种合同的通常情况是,由**承包商**按照**雇主**要求,设计和提供生产设备和(或)其他工程;可以包括土木、机械、电气和(或)构筑物的任何组合。

《设计采购施工(EPC)/交钥匙工程合同条件》,

可适用于以交钥匙方式提供加工或动力设备、工厂或类似设施、或基础设施工程或其他类型开发项目,这种方式(i)项目的最终价格和要求的工期具有更大程度的确定性,(ii)由**承包商**承担项目的设计和实施的全部职责,**雇主**介入很少。交钥匙工程的通常情况是,由**承包商**进行全部**设计、采购**和**施工(EPC)**,提供一个配备完善的设施,("转动钥匙"时)即可运行。

《简明合同格式》,

推荐用于资本金额较小的建筑或工程项目。根据工程的类型和具体情况,这种格式也可用于较大资本金额的合同,特别是适用于简单或重复性的工程或工期较短的工程。这种合同的通常情况是,由**承包商**按照**雇主**或其代表(如果有)提供的设计进行工程施工,但这种格式也可适用于包括或全部是由**承包商**设计的土木、机械、电气和(或)构筑物的合同。

这些合同格式是推荐在国际招标中通用的。在某些司法管辖范围,特别是用于国内合同的条件,可能需要做些修改。菲迪克(FIDIC)认为,正式的、权威性的文本应为英文版。

在编写本《施工合同条件》中感到,虽有许多条款可以通用,但有些条款必须考虑特定合同的有关情况做出必要的变更。我们认为可以用于多数(但非全部)合同的

relevant to the particular contract. The sub-clauses which were considered to be applicable to many (but not all) contracts have been included in the General Conditions, in order to facilitate their incorporation into each contract.

The General Conditions and the Particular Conditions will together comprise the Conditions of Contract governing the rights and obligations of the parties. It will be necessary to prepare the Particular Conditions for each individual contract, and to take account of those sub-clauses in the General Conditions which mention the Particular Conditions.

For this publication, the General Conditions were prepared on the following basis:

(i)   interim and final payments will be determined by measurement, applying the rates and prices in a Bill of Quantities;

(ii)   if the wording in the General Conditions necessitates further data, then (unless it is so descriptive that it would have to be detailed in the Specification) the sub-clause makes reference to this data being contained in the Appendix to Tender, the data either being prescribed by the Employer or being inserted by the Tenderer;

(iii)   where a sub-clause in the General Conditions deals with a matter on which different contract terms are likely to be applicable for different contracts, the principles applied in writing the sub-clause were:

     (a)   users would find it more convenient if any provisions which they did not wish to apply could simply be deleted or not invoked, than if additional text had to be written (in the Particular Conditions) because the General Conditions did not cover their requirements; or

     (b)   in other cases, where the application of (a) was thought to be inappropriate, the sub-clause contains the provisions which were considered applicable to most contracts.

For example, Sub-Clause 14.2 [*Advance Payment*] is included for convenience, not because of any FIDIC policy in respect of advance payments. This Sub-Clause becomes inapplicable (even if it is not deleted) if it is disregarded by not specifying the amount of the advance. It should therefore be noted that some of the provisions contained in the General Conditions may not be appropriate for an apparently-typical contract.

Further information on these aspects, example wording for other arrangements, and other explanatory material and example wording to assist in the preparation of the Particular Conditions and the other tender documents, are included within this publication as Guidance for the Preparation of the Particular Conditions. Before incorporating any example wording, it must be checked to ensure that it is wholly suitable for the particular circumstances; if not, it must be amended.

Where example wording is amended, and in all cases where other amendments or additions are made, care must be taken to ensure that no ambiguity is created, either with the General Conditions or between the clauses in the Particular Conditions. It is essential that all these drafting tasks, and the entire preparation of the tender

条款已包括进**通用条件**中，以便纳入每项合同。

通用条件和**专用条件**共同组成管理合同各方权利和义务的合同条件。对每个具体的合同，都需要编制其**专用条件**，并要考虑提到**专用条件**的那些**通用条件**条款。

本文本中**通用条件**根据以下原则编写：

(i)期中付款和最终付款的金额，将按工程量测量，采用**工程量表**中的费率和价格进行计算。

(ii)如果**通用条件**中的措辞需要进一步的资料(除非这些资料具有过多描述，需在规范中详加说明)，这时，条款指明该资料将包含在**投标书附录**中，这些资料或由**雇主**规定，或由**投标人**填入。

(iii)当**通用条件**中处理某一事项的条款，在不同的合同中对该事项可能采用不同的合同条款时，编写此类条款采用的原则是：

(a)使用户感到能够简单地删除或不动用任何他们不想采用的规定，要比因为**通用条件**中没有包括他们的要求，而必须(在**专用条件**中)编写附加条款要方便得多；或

(b)在采用(a)项办法被认为不适宜的情况下，使该条款包含经考虑认为对大多数合同都能适用的规定。

例如，列入**第 14.2 款 [预付款]** 是为了方便，而不是因为**菲迪克(FIDIC)**关于预付款的任何政策。如果该条款由于没有做出预付款额的规定而未被理会，则该款(即使未被删除)也将变为无用。因此应注意到**通用条件**中包含的一些规定对明显典型的合同可能不适宜。

这些方面的进一步资料、其他规定的范例措辞，以及帮助编写**专用条件**和其他招标文件的其他说明性材料和范例措辞，都包括在本文本**专用条件编写指南**中。在引用任何范例措辞前，必须认真核对，确保其完全适合特定的情况，否则必须进行修改。

当对范例措辞进行修改，以及所有其他修改或补充的情况下，必须注意确保与其**通用条件**之间，或在**专用条件**各条款间避免产生歧义。重要的是，所有这些起草工作，以及整个招标文件的编写，要委托具有相关专门知识的人员，包括合同、

documents, are entrusted to personnel with the relevant expertise, including the contractual, technical and procurement aspects.

This publication concludes with example forms for the Letter of Tender, the Appendix to Tender (providing a check-list of the sub-clauses which refer to it), the Contract Agreement, and alternatives for the Dispute Adjudication Agreement. This Dispute Adjudication Agreement provides text for the agreement between the Employer, the Contractor and the person appointed to act either as sole adjudicator or as a member of a three-person dispute adjudication board; and incorporates (by reference) the terms in the Appendix to the General Conditions.

FIDIC intends to publish a guide to the use of its Conditions of Contract for Construction, for Plant and Design-Build, and for EPC/Turnkey Projects. Another relevant FIDIC publication is "Tendering Procedure", which presents a systematic approach to the selection of tenderers and the obtaining and evaluation of tenders.

In order to clarify the sequence of Contract activities, reference may be made to the charts on the next two pages and to the Sub-Clauses listed below (some Sub-Clause numbers are also stated in the charts). The charts are illustrative and must not be taken into consideration in the interpretation of the Conditions of Contract.

1.1.3.1	&	13.7	Base Date
1.1.3.2	&	8.1	Commencement Date
1.1.6.6	&	4.2	Performance Security
1.1.4.7	&	14.3	Interim Payment Certificate
1.1.3.3	&	8.2	Time for Completion (as extended under 8.4)
1.1.3.4	&	9.1	Tests on Completion
1.1.3.5	&	10.1	Taking-Over Certificate
1.1.3.7	&	11.1	Defects Notification Period (as extended under 11.3)
1.1.3.8	&	11.9	Performance Certificate
1.1.4.4	&	14.13	Final Payment Certificate

技术和采购方面的专家进行。

本文本最后附有**投标函**、**投标书附录**(提供有关条款涉及内容的核查表)、**合同协议书**和备选**争端裁决协议书**的范例格式。该**争端裁决协议书**提供了**雇主**、**承包商**和被任命为唯一裁决人或三人争端裁决委员会中的一名成员之间的协议书文本,并(通过引用)体现了**通用条件附录**的条款。

菲迪克(FIDIC)准备出版一本《**施工合同条件**》、《**生产设备和设计-施工合同条件**》,以及《**设计采购施工(EPC)/交钥匙工程合同条件**》的应用指南。另一个有关的菲迪克(FIDIC)出版物是《**招标程序**》,为选择投标人和招标、评标提供了一套系统的办法。

为了澄清各项**合同**活动的顺序,可参考下面两页的**图**和下列各个**条款**(有些**条款**序号也在图中标出)。这些图只是说明性的,不应作为**合同条件**的解释。

1.1.3.1 和 13.7	基准日期
1.1.3.2 和 8.1	开工日期
1.1.6.6 和 4.2	履约担保
1.1.4.7 和 14.3	期中付款证书
1.1.3.3 和 8.2	竣工时间(及根据第 8.4 款的延长)
1.1.3.4 和 9.1	竣工试验
1.1.3.5 和 10.1	接收证书
1.1.3.7 和 11.1	缺陷通知期限(及根据第 11.3 款的延长)
1.1.3.8 和 11.9	履约证书
1.1.4.4 和 14.13	最终付款证书

Issue of   Submission   Issue of the   8.1   10.1 Issue of   11.9 Issue of the
Tender   of the   Letter of   Commencement   Taking-Over   Performance
Documents   Tender   Acceptance   Date   Certificate   Certificate

                  Base   Defects
                  Date   8.2 Time for   Notification
                                                            Completion [1]   Period [3]

                  28d   <28d   Delay attributable   11 Notifying →   <21d
                                                                                     to the   of Defects
                                                                                     Contractor [2]

        Tender   4.2 Issue of   9.1 Tests on →   Remedying →
        period   Performance Security   Completion [2]   of Defects

                                                                                                          4.2 Return of
                                                                                                          the Performance
                                                                                                          Security

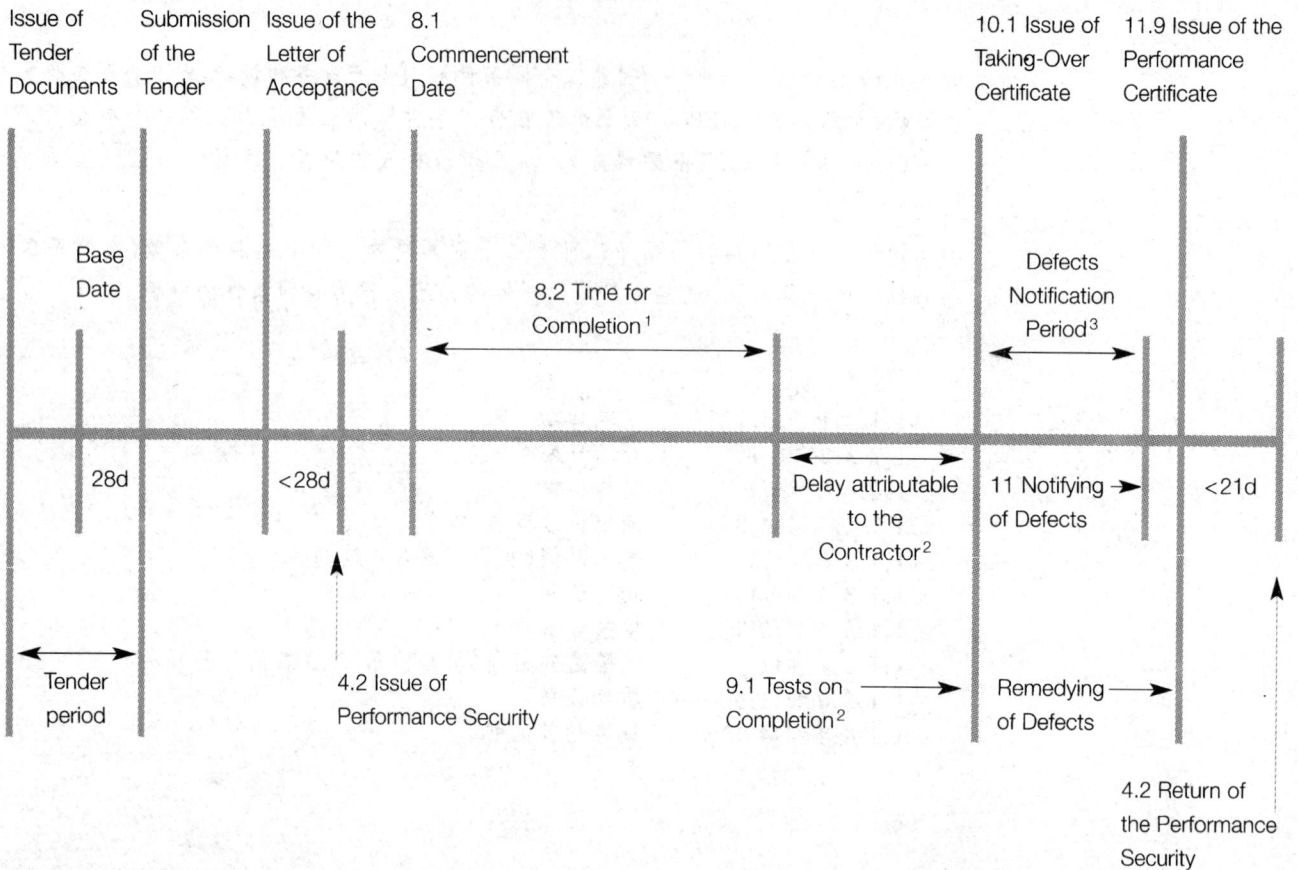

Typical sequence of Principal Events during Contracts for Construction

1.   The Time for Completion is to be stated (in the Appendix to Tender) as a number of days, to which is added
      any extensions of time under Sub-Clause 8.4.
2.   In order to indicate the sequence of events, the above diagram is based upon the example of the Contractor
      failing to comply with Sub-Clause 8.2.
3.   The Defects Notification Period is to be stated (in the Appendix to Tender) as a number of days, to which is
      added any extensions under Sub-Clause 11.3

颁发 招标 文件　提交 投标 书　颁发 中标 函　8.1 开工 日期　　　10.1 颁发 接收证书　11.9 颁发 履约证书

基准 日期

8.2 竣工时间 [1]

缺陷通 知期限 [3]

28 天　<28 天　承包商 造成的 延误 [2]　11 缺陷 通知　<21天

投标期限　4.2 发出履 约担保函　9.1 竣工试验 [2] → 修补缺陷 →

4.2 退还履 约担保函

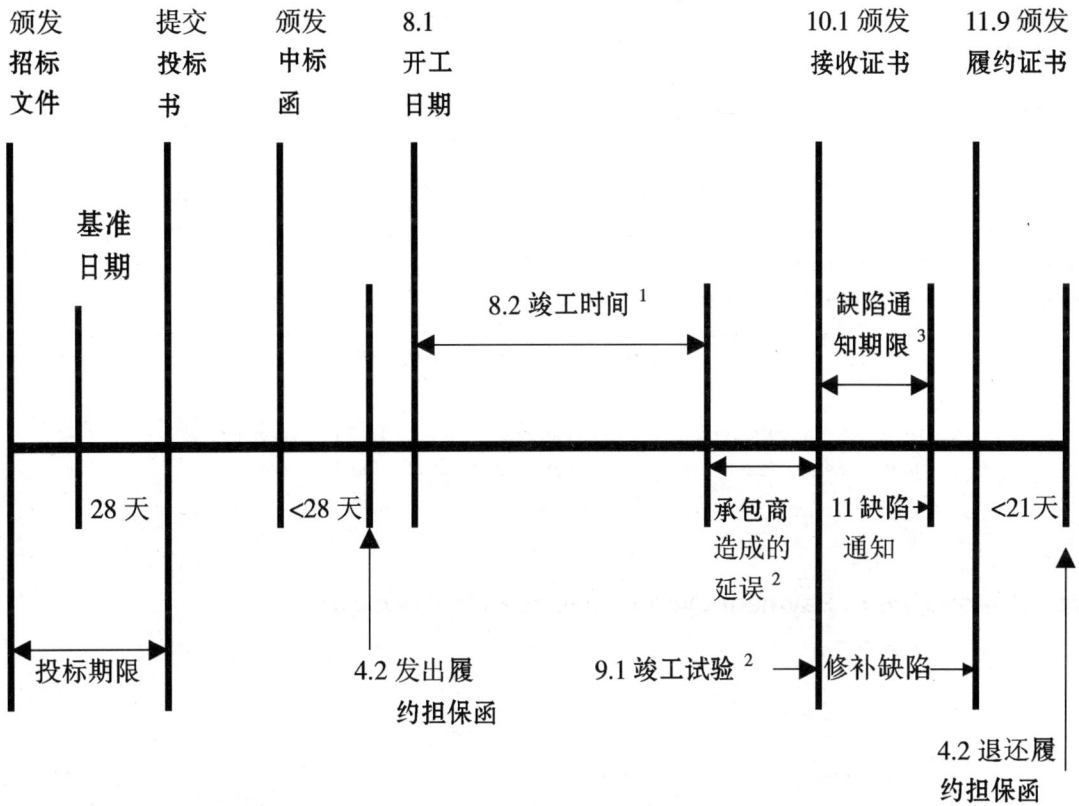

施工合同中主要事项的典型顺序

1. **竣工时间**(在**投标书附录**中)用天数表示，加上根据**第 8.4 款**规定的任何延长期。

2. 为了表示事项的顺序，上图以**承包商**未能遵守**第 8.2 款**的规定为例。

3. **缺陷通知期限**(在**投标书附录**中)用天数表示，加上根据**第 11.3 款**规定的任何延长期。

Each of the monthly (or otherwise) interim payments

14.3 Contractor submits Statement to the Engineer	14.6 Engineer issues Interim Payment Certificate	14.7 Employer makes the payment to the Contractor

<56d

<28d

The final payment

Engineer verifies the statement, Contractor submits information

<28d

<56d

14.11 Contractor submits draft final statement to the Engineer	14.11 Contractor submits Final Statement and the 14.12 discharge	14.13 Engineer issues Final Payment Certificate	14.7 Employer makes payment

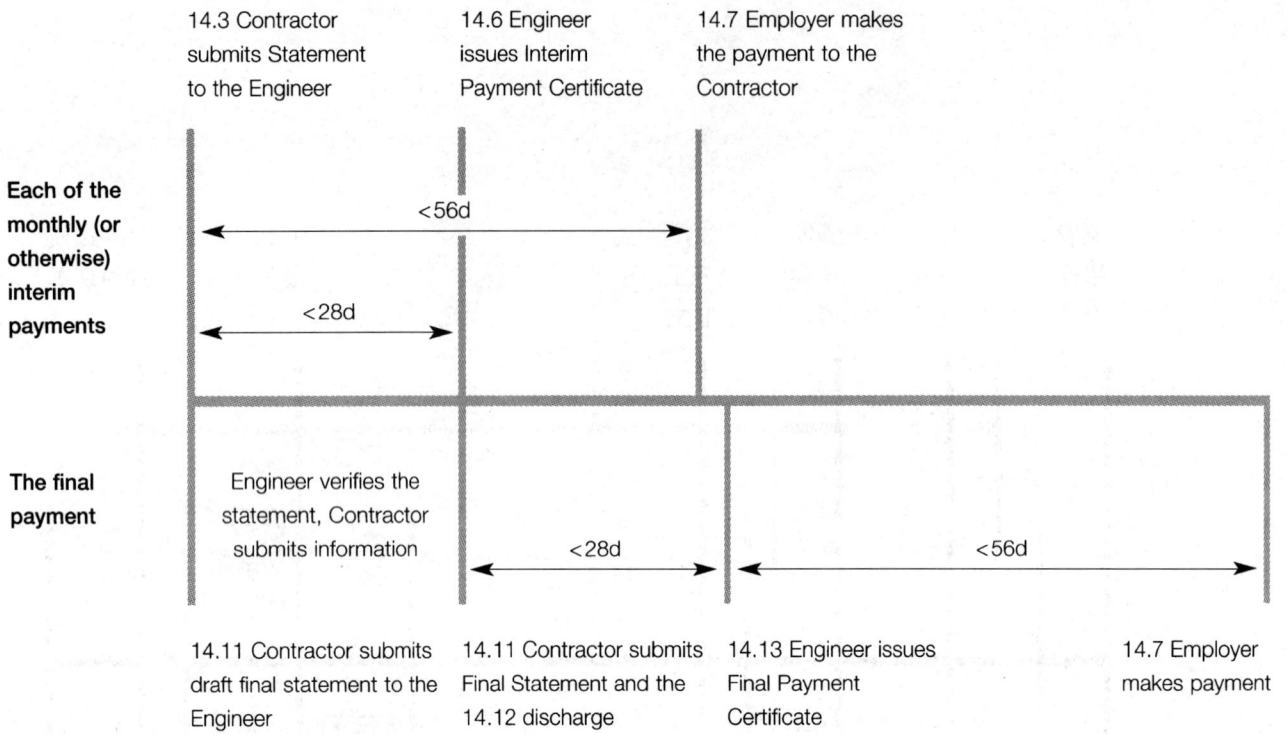

Typical sequence of Payment Events envisaged in Clause 14

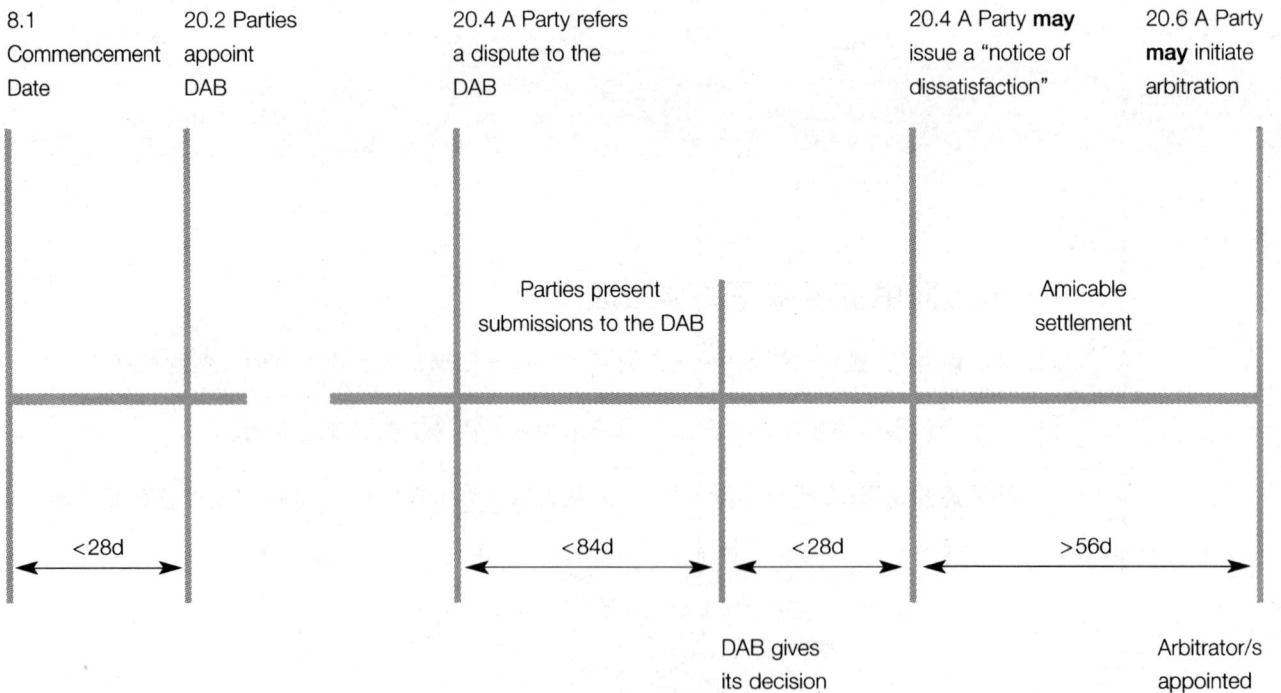

8.1 Commencement Date	20.2 Parties appoint DAB	20.4 A Party refers a dispute to the DAB	20.4 A Party **may** issue a "notice of dissatisfaction"	20.6 A Party **may** initiate arbitration

Parties present submissions to the DAB

Amicable settlement

<28d

<84d

<28d

>56d

DAB gives its decision

Arbitrator/s appointed

Typical sequence of Dispute Events envisaged in Clause 20

14.3 承包商
向工程师提
交报表

14.6 工程师
颁发期中付
款证书

14.7 雇主向
承包商付款

每月（或
其他时间
间隔）期
中付款

<56 天

<28 天

最终付款

工程师核实报表，
承包商提交有关
资料

<28 天

<56 天

14.11 承包商向工
程师提交最终报
表草案

14.11 承包商发出
最终报表及
14.12 结清证明

14.13 工程师发出
最终付款证书

14.7 雇主付款

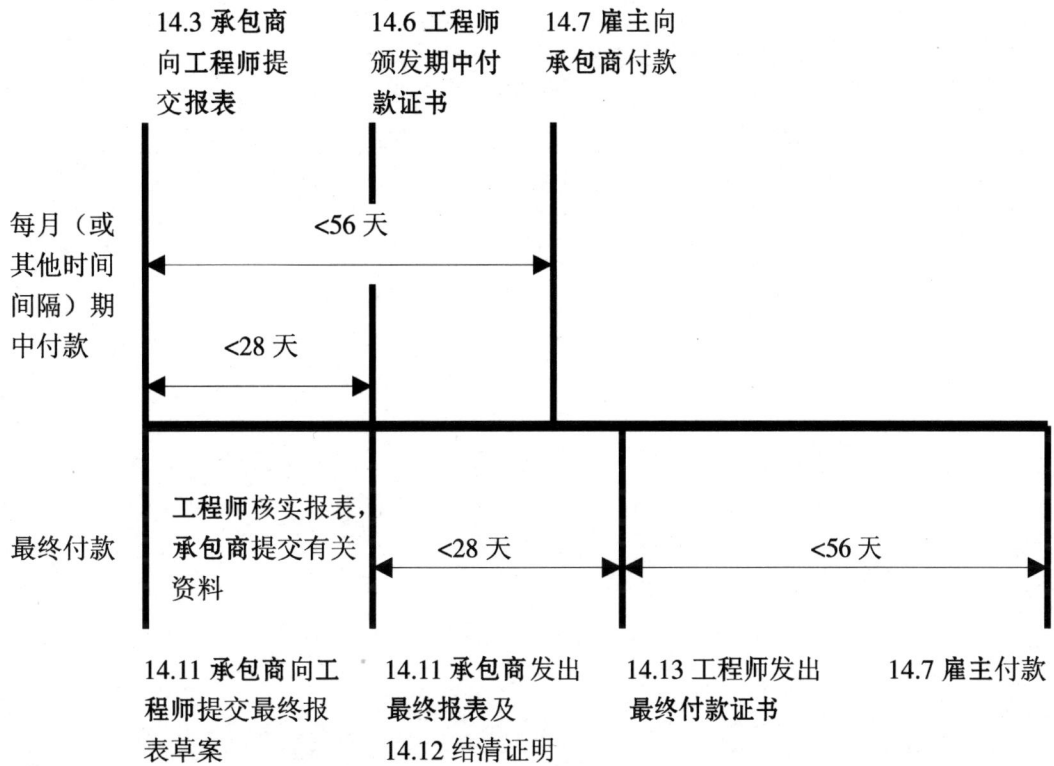

第 14 条中设想的付款事项的典型顺序

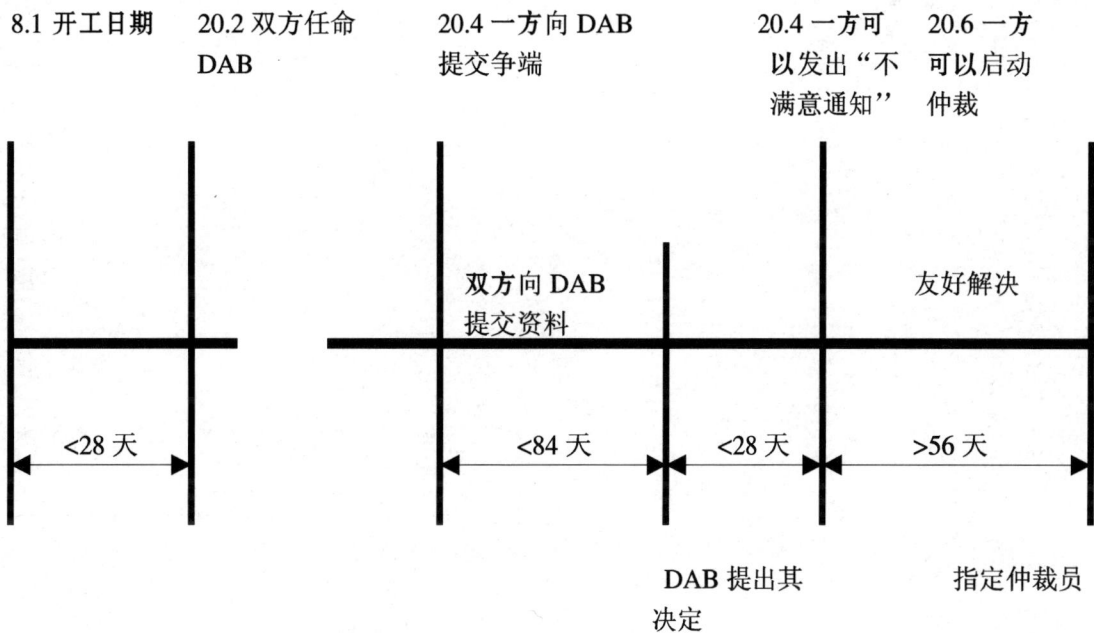

8.1 开工日期

20.2 双方任命
DAB

20.4 一方向 DAB
提交争端

20.4 一方可
以发出"不
满意通知"

20.6 一方
可以启动
仲裁

双方向 DAB
提交资料

友好解决

<28 天

<84 天

<28 天

>56 天

DAB 提出其
决定

指定仲裁员

第 20 条中设想的解决争端事项的典型顺序

施工合同条件

Conditions of Contract
for CONSTRUCTION

用于由雇主设计的建筑和工程
FOR BUILDING AND ENGINEERING WORKS
DESIGNED BY THE EMPLOYER

通用条件
General Conditions

专用条件编写指南
GUIDANCE FOR THE
PREPARATION OF
PARTICULAR CONDITIONS

投标函、合同协议书和
争端裁决协议书格式
FORMS OF LETTER OF
TENDER, CONTRACT
AGREEMENT AND
DISPUTE ADJUDICATION
AGREEMENT

国 际 咨 询 工 程 师 联 合 会
FEDERATION INTERNATIONALE DES INGENIEURS-CONSEILS
INTERNATIONAL FEDERATION OF CONSULTING ENGINEERS
INTERNATIONALE VEREINIGUNG BERATENDER INGENIEURE
FEDERACION INTERNACIONAL DE INGENIEROS CONSOLTORES

FIDIC

General Conditions

CONTENTS

通 用 条 件

目 录

5

6

Definitions listed alphabetically

按字母顺序排列的定义词语表

(原文按英文字母顺序排列,中译文按汉语拼音字母顺序排列)

保留金	1.1.4.11	货物	1.1.5.2
报表	1.1.4.12	基准日期	1.1.3.1
变更	1.1.6.9	计日工作计划表	1.1.1.10
不可抗力	1.1.6.4	接收证书	1.1.3.5
不可预见	1.1.6.8	竣工后试验	1.1.3.6
材料	1.1.5.3	竣工时间	1.1.3.3
成本(费用)	1.1.4.3	竣工试验	1.1.3.4
承包商	1.1.2.3	开工日期	1.1.3.2
承包商代表	1.1.2.5	临时工程	1.1.5.7
承包商人员	1.1.2.7	履约担保	1.1.6.6
承包商设备	1.1.5.1	履约证书	1.1.3.8
承包商文件	1.1.6.1	年	1.1.3.9
单位工程	1.1.5.6	期中付款证书	1.1.4.7
当地货币	1.1.4.8	缺陷通知期限	1.1.3.7
当事方(一方)	1.1.2.1	日(天)	1.1.3.9
法律	1.1.6.5	生产设备	1.1.5.5
菲迪克(FIDIC)	1.1.2.10	投标函	1.1.1.4
分包商	1.1.2.8	投标书	1.1.1.8
付款证书	1.1.4.9	投标书附录	1.1.1.9
工程	1.1.5.8	图纸	1.1.1.6
工程量表	1.1.1.10	外币	1.1.4.6
工程师	1.1.2.4	现场	1.1.6.7
工程所在国	1.1.6.2	永久工程	1.1.5.4
雇主	1.1.2.2	暂列金额	1.1.4.10
雇主人员	1.1.2.6	争端裁决委员会	1.1.2.9
雇主设备	1.1.6.3	中标函	1.1.1.3
规范要求	1.1.1.5	中标合同金额	1.1.4.1
合同	1.1.1.1	资料表	1.1.1.7
合同价格	1.1.4.2	最终报表	1.1.4.5
合同协议书	1.1.1.2	最终付款证书	1.1.4.4

General Conditions

1 General Provisions

**1.1
Definitions**

In the Conditions of Contract ("these Conditions"), which include Particular Conditions and these General Conditions, the following words and expressions shall have the meanings stated. Words indicating persons or parties include corporations and other legal entities, except where the context requires otherwise.

**1.1.1
The Contract**

1.1.1.1 **"Contract"** means the Contract Agreement, the Letter of Acceptance, the Letter of Tender, these Conditions, the Specification, the Drawings, the Schedules, and the further documents (if any) which are listed in the Contract Agreement or in the Letter of Acceptance.

1.1.1.2 **"Contract Agreement"** means the contract agreement (if any) referred to in Sub-Clause 1.6 [*Contract Agreement*].

1.1.1.3 **"Letter of Acceptance"** means the letter of formal acceptance, signed by the Employer, of the Letter of Tender, including any annexed memoranda comprising agreements between and signed by both Parties. If there is no such letter of acceptance, the expression "Letter of Acceptance" means the Contract Agreement and the date of issuing or receiving the Letter of Acceptance means the date of signing the Contract Agreement.

1.1.1.4 **"Letter of Tender"** means the document entitled letter of tender, which was completed by the Contractor and includes the signed offer to the Employer for the Works.

1.1.1.5 **"Specification"** means the document entitled specification, as included in the Contract, and any additions and modifications to the specification in accordance with the Contract. Such document specifies the Works.

1.1.1.6 **"Drawings"** means the drawings of the Works, as included in the Contract, and any additional and modified drawings issued by (or on behalf of) the Employer in accordance with the Contract.

1.1.1.7 **"Schedules"** means the document(s) entitled schedules, completed by the Contractor and submitted with the Letter of Tender, as included in the Contract. Such document may include the Bill of Quantities, data, lists, and schedules of rates and/or prices.

1.1.1.8 **"Tender"** means the Letter of Tender and all other documents which the Contractor submitted with the Letter of Tender, as included in the Contract.

1.1.1.9 **"Appendix to Tender"** means the completed pages entitled appendix to tender which are appended to and form part of the Letter of Tender.

1.1.1.10 **"Bill of Quantities"** and **"Daywork Schedule"** mean the documents so named (if any) which are comprised in the Schedules.

14

通 用 条 件

1 一般规定

1.1
定义

在包括**专用条件**和本**通用条件**的合同条件（"**本条件**"）中，下列词语和措辞应具有以下所述的含义。除上下文另有要求外，人员或当事各方等词语包括 公司和其他合法实体。

1.1.1
合同

1.1.1.1 "**合同**"系指**合同协议书**、**中标函**、**投标函**、本**条件**、**规范要求**、**图纸**、**资料表**以及**合同协议书**或**中标函**中列出的添加文件（如果有）。

1.1.1.2 "**合同协议书**"系指根据**第 1.6 款**[**合同协议书**]所述的**合同协议书**（如果有）。

1.1.1.3 "**中标函**"系指**雇主**签署的正式接受**投标函**的信件，包括其所附的含有双方间签署的协议的任何备忘录。如无此类**中标函**，则"**中标函**"一词系指**合同协议书**，发出或收到**中标函**的日期系指签署**合同协议书**的日期。

1.1.1.4 "**投标函**"系指由**承包商**填写的名为投标函的文件，包括其签署的向**雇主**的工程报价。

1.1.1.5 "**规范要求**"系指包含在**合同**中名为规范要求的文件，以及按照**合同**对规范要求所作的任何补充和修改。此类文件规定对**工程**的要求。

1.1.1.6 "**图纸**"系指包含在**合同**中的工程图纸，以及由**雇主**（或其代表）按照**合同**发出的任何补充和修改的图纸。

1.1.1.7 "**资料表**"系指**合同**中名为各种表的文件，由**承包商**填写并随**投标函**一起提交。此类文件可包括**工程量表**、数据、表册、费率和（或）价格表。

1.1.1.8 "**投标书**"系指**投标函**和**合同**中包括的由**承包商**随**投标函**一起提交的所有其他文件。

1.1.1.9 "**投标书附录**"系指填写的名为投标书附录的文件，附在**投标函**后作为其一部分。

1.1.1.10 "**工程量表**"和"**计日工作计划表**"系指包含在**资料表**中如此命名的文件（如果有）。

1.1.2
Parties and Persons

1.1.2.1   **"Party"** means the Employer or the Contractor, as the context requires.

1.1.2.2   **"Employer"** means the person named as employer in the Appendix to Tender and the legal successors in title to this person.

1.1.2.3   **"Contractor"** means the person(s) named as contractor in the Letter of Tender accepted by the Employer and the legal successors in title to this person(s).

1.1.2.4   **"Engineer"** means the person appointed by the Employer to act as the Engineer for the purposes of the Contract and named in the Appendix to Tender, or other person appointed from time to time by the Employer and notified to the Contractor under Sub-Clause 3.4 [*Replacement of the Engineer*].

1.1.2.5   **"Contractor's Representative"** means the person named by the Contractor in the Contract or appointed from time to time by the Contractor under Sub-Clause 4.3 [*Contractor's Representative*], who acts on behalf of the Contractor.

1.1.2.6   **"Employer's Personnel"** means the Engineer, the assistants referred to in Sub-Clause 3.2 [*Delegation by the Engineer*] and all other staff, labour and other employees of the Engineer and of the Employer; and any other personnel notified to the Contractor, by the Employer or the Engineer, as Employer's Personnel.

1.1.2.7   **"Contractor's Personnel"** means the Contractor's Representative and all personnel whom the Contractor utilises on Site, who may include the staff, labour and other employees of the Contractor and of each Subcontractor; and any other personnel assisting the Contractor in the execution of the Works.

1.1.2.8   **"Subcontractor"** means any person named in the Contract as a subcontractor, or any person appointed as a subcontractor, for a part of the Works; and the legal successors in title to each of these persons.

1.1.2.9   **"DAB"** means the person or three persons so named in the Contract, or other person(s) appointed under Sub-Clause 20.2 [*Appointment of the Dispute Adjudication Board*] or Sub-Clause 20.3 [*Failure to Agree Dispute Adjudication Board*]

1.1.2.10   **"FIDIC"** means the Fédération Internationale des Ingénieurs-Conseils, the international federation of consulting engineers.

1.1.3
Dates, Tests, Periods and Completion

1.1.3.1   **"Base Date"** means the date 28 days prior to the latest date for submission of the Tender.

1.1.3.2   **"Commencement Date"** means the date notified under Sub-Clause 8.1 [*Commencement of Works*].

1.1.3.3   **"Time for Completion"** means the time for completing the Works or a Section (as the case may be) under Sub-Clause 8.2 [*Time for Completion*], as stated in the Appendix to Tender (with any extension under Sub-Clause 8.4 [*Extension of Time for Completion*]), calculated from the Commencement Date.

1.1.3.4   **"Tests on Completion"** means the tests which are specified in the Contract or agreed by both Parties or instructed as a Variation, and which are carried

1.1.2
各方和人员

1.1.2.1 **"当事方(一方)"** 根据上下文需要，指**雇主**或**承包商**。

1.1.2.2 **"雇主"** 系指在**投标书附录**中称为雇主的当事人，及其财产所有权的合法继承人。

1.1.2.3 **"承包商"** 系指在**雇主**接受的**投标函**中称为承包商的当事人，及其财产所有权的合法继承人。

1.1.2.4 **"工程师"** 系指由**雇主**任命并在**投标书附录**中指名，为实施合同担任工程师的人员，或有时根据**第3.4款**[**工程师的替换**]的规定，由**雇主**任命并通知**承包商**的其他人员。

1.1.2.5 **"承包商代表"** 系指由**承包商**在合同中指名的人员，或有时根据**第4.3款**[**承包商代表**]的规定，由**承包商**任命为其代表的人员。

1.1.2.6 **"雇主人员"** 系指工程师、**第3.2款**[**由工程师付托**]的规定中提到的助手，以及工程师和雇主的所有其他职员、工人和其他雇员；以及由**雇主**或**工程师**通知**承包商**作为**雇主人员**的任何其他人员。

1.1.2.7 **"承包商人员"** 系指**承包商代表**和**承包商**在**现场**聘用的所有人员，包括**承包商**和每个**分包商**的职员、工人和其他雇员；以及所有其他帮助**承包商**实施工程的人员。

1.1.2.8 **"分包商"** 系指为完成部分工程，在**合同**中指名为分包商，或其后被任命为分包商的任何人员；以及这些人员各自财产所有权的合法继承人。

1.1.2.9 **"DAB(争端裁决委员会)"** 系指合同中如此指名的一名或三名人员，或根据**第20.2款**[**争端裁决委员会的任命**]或**第20.3款**[**对争端裁决委员会未能取得一致**]的规定任命的其他人员。

1.1.2.10 **"菲迪克"(FIDIC)** 系指国际咨询工程师联合会。

1.1.3
日期、试验、期限和竣工

1.1.3.1 **"基准日期"** 系指递交**投标书**截止日期前28天的日期。

1.1.3.2 **"开工日期"** 系指根据**第8.1款**[**工程的开工**]的规定通知的日期。

1.1.3.3 **"竣工时间"** 系指**投标书附录**中写明的，自开工日期算起至工程或某单位工程(视情况而定)根据**第8.2款**[**竣工时间**]规定的要求竣工(连同根据**第8.4款**[**竣工时间的延长**]的规定提出的任何延长期)的全部时间。

1.1.3.4 **"竣工试验"** 系指在合同中规定的，或双方商定的，或按指示作为一项**变更**的，在工程或某单位工程(视情况而定)被**雇主**接收

17

out under Clause 9 [*Tests on Completion*] before the Works or a Section (as the case may be) are taken over by the Employer.

1.1.3.5 **"Taking-Over Certificate"** means a certificate issued under Clause 10 [*Employer's Taking Over*].

1.1.3.6 **"Tests after Completion"** means the tests (if any) which are specified in the Contract and which are carried out in accordance with the provisions of the Particular Conditions after the Works or a Section (as the case may be) are taken over by the Employer.

1.1.3.7 **"Defects Notification Period"** means the period for notifying defects in the Works or a Section (as the case may be) under Sub-Clause 11.1 [*Completion of Outstanding Work and Remedying Defects*], as stated in the Appendix to Tender (with any extension under Sub-Clause 11.3 [*Extension of Defects Notification Period*]), calculated from the date on which the Works or Section is completed as certified under Sub-Clause 10.1 [*Taking Over of the Works and Sections*].

1.1.3.8 **"Performance Certificate"** means the certificate issued under Sub-Clause 11.9 [*Performance Certificate*].

1.1.3.9 **"day"** means a calendar day and **"year"** means 365 days.

**1.1.4
Money and Payments**

1.1.4.1 **"Accepted Contract Amount"** means the amount accepted in the Letter of Acceptance for the execution and completion of the Works and the remedying of any defects.

1.1.4.2 **"Contract Price"** means the price defined in Sub-Clause 14.1 [*The Contract Price*], and includes adjustments in accordance with the Contract.

1.1.4.3 **"Cost"** means all expenditure reasonably incurred (or to be incurred) by the Contractor, whether on or off the Site, including overhead and similar charges, but does not include profit.

1.1.4.4 **"Final Payment Certificate"** means the payment certificate issued under Sub-Clause 14.13 [*Issue of Final Payment Certificate*].

1.1.4.5 **"Final Statement"** means the statement defined in Sub-Clause 14.11 [*Application for Final Payment Certificate*].

1.1.4.6 **"Foreign Currency"** means a currency in which part (or all) of the Contract Price is payable, but not the Local Currency.

1.1.4.7 **"Interim Payment Certificate"** means a payment certificate issued under Clause 14 [*Contract Price and Payment*], other than the Final Payment Certificate.

1.1.4.8 **"Local Currency"** means the currency of the Country.

1.1.4.9 **"Payment Certificate"** means a payment certificate issued under Clause 14 [*Contract Price and Payment*].

1.1.4.10 **"Provisional Sum"** means a sum (if any) which is specified in the Contract as a provisional sum, for the execution of any part of the Works or for the supply of Plant, Materials or services under Sub-Clause 13.5 [*Provisional Sums*].

前，根据第9条[竣工试验]的要求进行的试验。

1.1.3.5　**"接收证书"** 系指根据第10条[**雇主的接收**]的规定颁发的证书。

1.1.3.6　**"竣工后试验"** 系指在合同中规定的，在工程或某单位工程（视情况而定）被雇主接收后，根据专用条件的规定进行的试验（如果有）。

1.1.3.7　**"缺陷通知期限"** 系指投标书附录中规定的，自工程或某单位工程（视情况而定）根据第10.1款[**工程和单位工程的接收**]的规定证明的竣工日期算起，至根据第11.1款[**完成扫尾工作和修补缺陷**]的规定，通知工程或单位工程（视情况而定）存在缺陷的期限（连同根据第11.3款[**缺陷通知期限的延长**]的规定提出的任何延长期）。

1.1.3.8　**"履约证书"** 系指根据第11.9款[**履约证书**]的规定颁发的证书。

1.1.4
款项和付款

1.1.3.9　**"日（天）"** 系指一个日历日，**"年"** 系指365天。

1.1.4.1　**"中标合同金额"** 系指在中标函中所认可的工程施工、竣工和修补任何缺陷所需的费用。

1.1.4.2　**"合同价格"** 系指第14.1款[**合同价格**]规定中确定的价格，包括按照合同所做的调整。

1.1.4.3　**"成本（费用）"** 系指承包商在现场内外发生的（或将发生的）所有合理开支，包括管理费用及类似的支出，但不包括利润。

1.1.4.4　**"最终付款证书"** 系指根据第14.13款[**最终付款证书的颁发**]的规定颁发的付款证书。

1.1.4.5　**"最终报表"** 系指第14.11款[**最终付款证书的申请**]中规定的报表。

1.1.4.6　**"外币"** 系指可用于支付合同价格中部分（或全部）款项的当地货币以外的某种货币。

1.1.4.7　**"期中付款证书"** 系指根据第14条[**合同价格和付款**]的规定颁发的最终付款证书以外的付款证书。

1.1.4.8　**"当地货币"** 系指工程所在国的货币。

1.1.4.9　**"付款证书"** 系指根据第14条[**合同价格和付款**]的规定颁发的付款证书。

1.1.4.10　**"暂列金额"** 系指合同中规定作为暂列金额的一笔款项（如果有），根据第13.5款[**暂列金额**]的规定，用于工程某一部分的实施，或用于提供生产设备、材料或服务。

1.1.4.11 **"Retention Money"** means the accumulated retention moneys which the Employer retains under Sub-Clause 14.3 [*Application for Interim Payment Certificates*] and pays under Sub-Clause 14.9 [*Payment of Retention Money*].

1.1.4.12 **"Statement"** means a statement submitted by the Contractor as part of an application, under Clause 14 [*Contract Price and Payment*], for a payment certificate.

1.1.5
Works and Goods

1.1.5.1 **"Contractor's Equipment"** means all apparatus, machinery, vehicles and other things required for the execution and completion of the Works and the remedying of any defects. However, Contractor's Equipment excludes Temporary Works, Employer's Equipment (if any), Plant, Materials and any other things intended to form or forming part of the Permanent Works.

1.1.5.2 **"Goods"** means Contractor's Equipment, Materials, Plant and Temporary Works, or any of them as appropriate.

1.1.5.3 **"Materials"** means things of all kinds (other than Plant) intended to form or forming part of the Permanent Works, including the supply-only materials (if any) to be supplied by the Contractor under the Contract.

1.1.5.4 **"Permanent Works"** means the permanent works to be executed by the Contractor under the Contract.

1.1.5.5 **"Plant"** means the apparatus, machinery and vehicles intended to form or forming part of the Permanent Works.

1.1.5.6 **"Section"** means a part of the Works specified in the Appendix to Tender as a Section (if any).

1.1.5.7 **"Temporary Works"** means all temporary works of every kind (other than Contractor's Equipment) required on Site for the execution and completion of the Permanent Works and the remedying of any defects.

1.1.5.8 **"Works"** mean the Permanent Works and the Temporary Works, or either of them as appropriate.

1.1.6
Other Definitions

1.1.6.1 **"Contractor's Documents"** means the calculations, computer programs and other software, drawings, manuals, models and other documents of a technical nature (if any) supplied by the Contractor under the Contract.

1.1.6.2 **"Country"** means the country in which the Site (or most of it) is located, where the Permanent Works are to be executed.

1.1.6.3 **"Employer's Equipment"** means the apparatus, machinery and vehicles (if any) made available by the Employer for the use of the Contractor in the execution of the Works, as stated in the Specification; but does not include Plant which has not been taken over by the Employer.

1.1.6.4 **"Force Majeure"** is defined in Clause 19 [*Force Majeure*].

1.1.6.5 **"Laws"** means all national (or state) legislation, statutes, ordinances and other laws, and regulations and by-laws of any legally constituted public authority.

20

1.1.4.11 **"保留金"** 系指雇主根据**第14.3款**[**期中付款证书的申请**]的规定扣留的累计**保留金**，根据**第14.9款**[**保留金的支付**]的规定进行支付。

1.1.4.12 **"报表"** 系指**承包商**根据**第14条**[**合同价格和付款**]的规定提交的作为付款证书申请组成部分的报表。

1.1.5
工程和货物

1.1.5.1 **"承包商设备"** 系指为实施和完成**工程**以及修补任何缺陷需要的所有仪器、机械、车辆和其他物品。但**承包商设备**不包括**临时工程**、**雇主设备**(如果有)、以及拟构成或正构成**永久工程**一部分的**生产设备**、**材料**和任何其他物品。

1.1.5.2 **"货物"** 系指**承包商设备**、**材料**、**生产设备**和**临时工程**，或视情况指其中任何一种。

1.1.5.3 **"材料"** 系指拟构成或正构成**永久工程**一部分的各类物品(**生产设备**除外)，包括根据**合同**要由**承包商**供应的只供材料(如果有)。

1.1.5.4 **"永久工程"** 系指按照**合同**规定要由**承包商**实施的永久性工程。

1.1.5.5 **"生产设备"** 系指拟构成或正构成**永久工程**一部分的仪器、机械和车辆。

1.1.5.6 **"单位工程"**[⊖]系指在**投标书附录**中确定为**单位工程**(如果有)的工程组成部分。

1.1.5.7 **"临时工程"** 系指为实施和完成**永久工程**及修补任何缺陷，在现场所需的所有各类(**承包商设备**除外)临时性工程。

1.1.5.8 **"工程"** 系指**永久工程**和**临时工程**，或视情况指二者之一。

1.1.6
其他定义

1.1.6.1 **"承包商文件"** 系指由**承包商**根据**合同**提交的所有计算书、计算机程序和其他软件、图纸、手册、模型和其他技术性文件(如果有)。

1.1.6.2 **"工程所在国"** 系指实施**永久工程**的**现场**(或其大部分)所在的国家。

1.1.6.3 **"雇主设备"** 系指**规范要求**中列明由**雇主**提供的，供**承包商**在实施工程中使用的仪器、机械和车辆(如果有)；但不包括**雇主**尚未接收的**生产设备**。

1.1.6.4 **"不可抗力"** 见**第19条**[**不可抗力**]的定义。

1.1.6.5 **"法律"** 系指所有全国性(或州)的法律、条例、法令和其他法律，以及任何合法建立的公共当局制定的规则和细则等。

⊖ 此译文系指菲迪克(FIDIC)合同专用条件或投标书附录中专门定义的、能够单独接收使用的部分工程。与我国建设项目统计中的"单位工程"大体相当,但含义不尽相同。

1.1.6.6 **"Performance Security"** means the security (or securities, if any) under Sub-Clause 4.2 [*Performance Security*].

1.1.6.7 **"Site"** means the places where the Permanent Works are to be executed and to which Plant and Materials are to be delivered, and any other places as may be specified in the Contract as forming part of the Site.

1.1.6.8 **"Unforeseeable"** means not reasonably foreseeable by an experienced contractor by the date for submission of the Tender.

1.1.6.9 **"Variation"** means any change to the Works, which is instructed or approved as a variation under Clause 13 [*Variations and Adjustments*].

1.2

Interpretation

In the Contract, except where the context requires otherwise:

(a) words indicating one gender include all genders;
(b) words indicating the singular also include the plural and words indicating the plural also include the singular;
(c) provisions including the word "agree", "agreed" or "agreement" require the agreement to be recorded in writing, and
(d) "written" or "in writing" means hand-written, type-written, printed or electronically made, and resulting in a permanent record.

The marginal words and other headings shall not be taken into consideration in the interpretation of these Conditions.

1.3

Communications

Wherever these Conditions provide for the giving or issuing of approvals, certificates, consents, determinations, notices and requests, these communications shall be:

(a) in writing and delivered by hand (against receipt), sent by mail or courier, or transmitted using any of the agreed systems of electronic transmission as stated in the Appendix to Tender; and
(b) delivered, sent or transmitted to the address for the recipient's communications as stated in the Appendix to Tender. However:

(i)   if the recipient gives notice of another address, communications shall thereafter be delivered accordingly; and
(ii)   if the recipient has not stated otherwise when requesting an approval or consent, it may be sent to the address from which the request was issued.

Approvals, certificates, consents and determinations shall not be unreasonably withheld or delayed. When a certificate is issued to a Party, the certifier shall send a copy to the other Party. When a notice is issued to a Party, by the other Party or the Engineer, a copy shall be sent to the Engineer or the other Party, as the case may be.

1.4

Law and Language

The Contract shall be governed by the law of the country (or other jurisdiction) stated in the Appendix to Tender.

If there are versions of any part of the Contract which are written in more than one language, the version which is in the ruling language stated in the Appendix to Tender shall prevail.

1.1.6.6 **"履约担保"** 系指根据第 **4.2** 款[**履约担保**]规定的担保(或各项担保,如果有)。

1.1.6.7 **"现场"** 系指将实施**永久工程**和运送**生产设备**与**材料**到达的地点,以及**合同**中可能指定为**现场**组成部分的任何其他场所。

1.1.6.8 **"不可预见"** 系指一个有经验的承包商在提交**投标书**日期前不能合理预见。

1.1.6.9 **"变更"** 系指根据第 **13** 条[**变更和调整**]的规定,经指示或批准作为变更的,对**工程**所做的任何更改。

1.2

解释

在**合同**中,除上下文中另有需要外:

(a)　表示某一性别的词,包括所有性别;

(b)　单数形式的词,也包括复数含义,反之亦然;

(c)　包括"同意(商定)"、"达成(取得)一致"、或"协议"等词的各项规定都要求用书面记载;以及

(d)　"书面"或"用书面"系指手写、打字、印刷或电子制作,并形成永久性记录。

旁注和其他标题在本**条件**的解释中不应考虑。

1.3

通信交流

本**条件**不论在何种场合规定给予或颁发批准书、证明、同意函、确定、通知和请求,这些通信信息都应:

(a)　采用书面形式,由人面交(取得对方收据),通过邮寄或信差传送,或用**投标书附录**中提出的任何商定的电子传输方式发送;以及

(b)　交付、传送或传输至**投标书附录**中规定的接收人的地址。但:

(i) 如接收人通知了另外地址时,随后通信信息应按新地址发送;以及

(ii) 如接收人在请求批准书、同意函时没有另外说明,可按请求书发出的地址发送。

批准书、证明、同意函和确定不得无故被扣压或拖延。当向**一方**发证书时,发证人应将一份复印件发送给另一方。当另一方或**工程师**给一方发通知时,亦应根据情况抄送**工程师**或另一方。

1.4

法律和语言

合同应受**投标书附录**中所述国家(或其他司法管辖区)的法律管辖。

当**合同**任何部分的文本采用一种以上语言编写时,应以**投标书附录**指定的主导语言文本为准。

The language for communications shall be that stated in the Appendix to Tender. If no language is stated there, the language for communications shall be the language in which the Contract (or most of it) is written.

1.5

Priority of Documents

The documents forming the Contract are to be taken as mutually explanatory of one another. For the purposes of interpretation, the priority of the documents shall be in accordance with the following sequence:

(a)   the Contract Agreement (if any),
(b)   the Letter of Acceptance,
(c)   the Letter of Tender,
(d)   the Particular Conditions,
(e)   these General Conditions,
(f)   the Specification,
(g)   the Drawings, and
(h)   the Schedules and any other documents forming part of the Contract.

If an ambiguity or discrepancy is found in the documents, the Engineer shall issue any necessary clarification or instruction.

1.6

Contract Agreement

The Parties shall enter into a Contract Agreement within 28 days after the Contractor receives the Letter of Acceptance, unless they agree otherwise. The Contract Agreement shall be based upon the form annexed to the Particular Conditions. The costs of stamp duties and similar charges (if any) imposed by law in connection with entry into the Contract Agreement shall be borne by the Employer.

1.7

Assignment

Neither Party shall assign the whole or any part of the Contract or any benefit or interest in or under the Contract. However, either Party:

(a)   may assign the whole or any part with the prior agreement of the other Party, at the sole discretion of such other Party, and
(b)   may, as security in favour of a bank or financial institution, assign its right to any moneys due, or to become due, under the Contract.

1.8

Care and Supply of Documents

The Specification and Drawings shall be in the custody and care of the Employer. Unless otherwise stated in the Contract, two copies of the Contract and of each subsequent Drawing shall be supplied to the Contractor, who may make or request further copies at the cost of the Contractor.

Each of the Contractor's Documents shall be in the custody and care of the Contractor, unless and until taken over by the Employer. Unless otherwise stated in the Contract, the Contractor shall supply to the Engineer six copies of each of the Contractor's Documents.

The Contractor shall keep, on the Site, a copy of the Contract, publications named in the Specification, the Contractor's Documents (if any), the Drawings and Variations and other communications given under the Contract. The Employer's Personnel shall have the right of access to all these documents at all reasonable times.

If a Party becomes aware of an error or defect of a technical nature in a document which was prepared for use in executing the Works, the Party shall promptly give notice to the other Party of such error or defect.

通信交流应使用**投标书附录**中指定的语言。如未指定，应使用**合同**(或其大部分)编写用的语言。

1.5

文件优先次序

构成合同的文件要认为是互作说明的。为了解释的目的，文件的优先次序如下：

(a) **合同协议书**(如果有)，
(b) **中标函**，
(c) **投标函**，
(d) **专用条件**，
(e) 本**通用条件**，
(f) **规范要求**，
(g) **图纸**，以及
(h) **资料表**和构成**合同**组成部分的任何其他文件。

如文件中发现有歧义或不一致，**工程师**应发出必要的澄清或指示。

1.6

合同协议书

除非另有协议，双方应在**承包商**收到**中标函**后 28 天内签定**合同协议书**。**合同协议书**应以**专用条件**所附格式为依据。为签订**合同协议书**，依法征收的印花税和类似费用(如果有)应由**雇主**承担。

1.7

权益转让

任一方都不应将**合同**的全部或任何部分，或**合同**中或根据**合同**所具有的任何利益或权益转让他人。但任一方：

(a) 在另一方完全自主决定的情况下，事先征得其同意后，可以将全部或部分转让；以及
(b) 可以作为以银行或金融机构为受款人的担保，转让其根据**合同**规定的任何到期或将到期应得款项的权利。

1.8

文件的照管和提供

规范要求和**图纸**应由**雇主**保存和照管。除非**合同**中另有规定，应给**承包商**一式两份**合同**文本和后续**图纸**，**承包商**可以自费复制或要求提供更多份数。

每份**承包商文件**都应由**承包商**保存和照管，除非并直到被**雇主**接收为止，除非**合同**中另有规定，**承包商**应向**工程师**提供**承包商文件**一式六份。

承包商应在**现场**保存一份**合同**、**规范要求**中指名的出版物、**承包商文件**(如果有)、**图纸**、**变更**，以及根据**合同**发出的其他往来文书。**雇主人员**有权在所有合理的时间使用所有这些文件。

如果一方发现为实施**工程**准备的文件中有技术性错误或缺陷，应迅速将该错误或缺陷通知另一方。

**1.9
Delayed Drawings or
Instructions**

The Contractor shall give notice to the Engineer whenever the Works are likely to be delayed or disrupted if any necessary drawing or instruction is not issued to the Contractor within a particular time, which shall be reasonable. The notice shall include details of the necessary drawing or instruction, details of why and by when it should be issued, and details of the nature and amount of the delay or disruption likely to be suffered if it is late.

If the Contractor suffers delay and/or incurs Cost as a result of a failure of the Engineer to issue the notified drawing or instruction within a time which is reasonable and is specified in the notice with supporting details, the Contractor shall give a further notice to the Engineer and shall be entitled subject to Sub-Clause 20.1 [*Contractor's Claims*] to:

(a)   an extension of time for any such delay, if completion is or will be delayed, under Sub-Clause 8.4 [*Extension of Time for Completion*], and

(b)   payment of any such Cost plus reasonable profit, which shall be included in the Contract Price.

After receiving this further notice, the Engineer shall proceed in accordance with Sub-Clause 3.5 [*Determinations*] to agree or determine these matters.

However, if and to the extent that the Engineer's failure was caused by any error or delay by the Contractor, including an error in, or delay in the submission of, any of the Contractor's Documents, the Contractor shall not be entitled to such extension of time, Cost or profit.

1.10

**Employer's Use of
Contractor's Documents**

As between the Parties, the Contractor shall retain the copyright and other intellectual property rights in the Contractor's Documents and other design documents made by (or on behalf of) the Contractor.

The Contractor shall be deemed (by signing the Contract) to give to the Employer a non-terminable transferable non-exclusive royalty-free licence to copy, use and communicate the Contractor's Documents, including making and using modifications of them. This licence shall:

(a)   apply throughout the actual or intended working life (whichever is longer) of the relevant parts of the Works,

(b)   entitle any person in proper possession of the relevant part of the Works to copy, use and communicate the Contractor's Documents for the purposes of completing, operating, maintaining, altering, adjusting, repairing and demolishing the Works, and

(c)   in the case of Contractor's Documents which are in the form of computer programs and other software, permit their use on any computer on the Site and other places as envisaged by the Contract, including replacements of any computers supplied by the Contractor.

The Contractor's Documents and other design documents made by (or on behalf of) the Contractor shall not, without the Contractor's consent, be used, copied or communicated to a third party by (or on behalf of) the Employer for purposes other than those permitted under this Sub-Clause.

1.11

**Contractor's Use of
Employer's Documents**

As between the Parties, the Employer shall retain the copyright and other intellectual property rights in the Specification, the Drawings and other documents made by (or on behalf of) the Employer. The Contractor may, at his cost, copy, use, and obtain communication of these documents for the purposes of the Contract. They shall not,

1.9 **延误的图纸或指示**	如果任何必需的图纸或指示未能在合理的特定时间内发至**承包商**，以致**工程**可能拖延或中断时，**承包商**应通知**工程师**。通知应包括必需的图纸或指示的细节，为何和何时前必须发出的详细理由，以及如果晚发出可能遭受的延误或中断的性质和程度的详情。

如果由于**工程师**未能在合理的、并在**承包商**附有支持细节的通知中规定的时间内发出图纸或指示，使**承包商**遭受延误和(或)招致增加**费用**，**承包商**应再次通知**工程师**，并根据**第 20.1 款**[**承包商的索赔**]的规定，有权要求：

(a)　根据**第 8.4 款**[**竣工时间的延长**]的规定，如果竣工已或将受到延误，对任何此类延误给予延长期；

(b)　任何此类**费用**和合理利润应计入**合同价格**，给予支付。

工程师收到此再次通知后，应按照**第 3.5 款**[**确定**]的规定，就这些事项作出商定或确定。

但是，如果**工程师**未能发出是由于**承包商**的错误或拖延，包括**承包商文件**中的错误或提交拖延造成的，**承包商**无权要求此类延长期、**费用**或利润的增加。

1.10 **雇主使用承包商文件**	就各当事方间而言，由**承包商**(或以其名义)编制的**承包商文件**及其他设计文件，其版权和其他知识产权应归**承包商**所有。

承包商(通过签署**合同**)应被认为已给予**雇主**无限期的、可转让的、不排他的、免版税的，复制、使用和传送**承包商文件**的许可，包括对它们作出的修改和使用修改后的文件的许可。这项许可应：

(a)　适用于**工程**相关部分的实际或预期寿命期(取较长的)；

(b)　允许具有**工程**相关部分正当占有权的任何人，为了完成、运行、维护、更改、调整、修复和拆除**工程**的目的，复制、使用和传送**承包商文件**；以及

(c)　在**承包商文件**是以计算机程序和其他软件形式的情况下，允许它们在**现场**和**合同**中设想的其他场所的任何计算机上使用，包括对**承包商**提供的任何计算机进行替换。

未经**承包商**同意，**雇主**(或以其名义)不得在**本款**允许以外，为其他目的使用、复制由**承包商**(或以其名义)编制的**承包商文件**和其他设计文件，或将其传送给第三方。

1.11 **承包商使用雇主文件**	就各当事**方**间而言，由**雇主**(或以其名义)编制的**规范要求**、**图纸**和其他文件，其版权和其他知识产权应归**雇主**所有。**承包商**因合同的目的，可自费复制、使用和传送上述文件。除**合同**需要外，未经**雇主**同意，**承包商**不得复

without the Employer's consent, be copied, used or communicated to a third party by the Contractor, except as necessary for the purposes of the Contract.

1.12

Confidential Details

The Contractor shall disclose all such confidential and other information as the Engineer may reasonably require in order to verify the Contractor's compliance with the Contract.

1.13

Compliance with Laws

The Contractor shall, in performing the Contract, comply with applicable Laws. Unless otherwise stated in the Particular Conditions:

(a) the Employer shall have obtained (or shall obtain) the planning, zoning or similar permission for the Permanent Works, and any other permissions described in the Specification as having been (or being) obtained by the Employer; and the Employer shall indemnify and hold the Contractor harmless against and from the consequences of any failure to do so; and

(b) the Contractor shall give all notices, pay all taxes, duties and fees, and obtain all permits, licences and approvals, as required by the Laws in relation to the execution and completion of the Works and the remedying of any defects; and the Contractor shall indemnify and hold the Employer harmless against and from the consequences of any failure to do so.

1.14

Joint and Several Liability

If the Contractor constitutes (under applicable Laws) a joint venture, consortium or other unincorporated grouping of two or more persons:

(a) these persons shall be deemed to be jointly and severally liable to the Employer for the performance of the Contract;

(b) these persons shall notify the Employer of their leader who shall have authority to bind the Contractor and each of these persons; and

(c) the Contractor shall not alter its composition or legal status without the prior consent of the Employer.

The 2 Employer

2.1

Right of Access to the Site

The Employer shall give the Contractor right of access to, and possession of, all parts of the Site within the time (or times) stated in the Appendix to Tender. The right and possession may not be exclusive to the Contractor. If, under the Contract, the Employer is required to give (to the Contractor) possession of any foundation, structure, plant or means of access, the Employer shall do so in the time and manner stated in the Specification. However, the Employer may withhold any such right or possession until the Performance Security has been received.

If no such time is stated in the Appendix to Tender, the Employer shall give the Contractor right of access to, and possession of, the Site within such times as may be required to enable the Contractor to proceed in accordance with the programme submitted under Sub-Clause 8.3 [*Programme*].

If the Contractor suffers delay and/or incurs Cost as a result of a failure by the Employer to give any such right or possession within such time, the Contractor shall give notice to the Engineer and shall be entitled subject to Sub-Clause 20.1 [*Contractor's Claims*] to:

制、使用这些文件，或将其传送给第三方。

1.12

保密事项　　　　　　　　对**工程师**为了证实**承包商**遵守**合同**的情况，合理需要的所有秘密和其他信息，**承包商**应当透露。

1.13

遵守法律　　　　　　　　**承包商**在履行**合同**期间，应遵守适用**法律**。除非**专用条件**中另有规定：

　　　　　　　　　　　　(a)　**雇主**应已(或将)为**永久工程**取得规划、区域划定、或类似的许可，以及**规范要求**中所述的**雇主**已(或将)取得的任何其他许可；**雇主**应保障和保持**承包商**免受未能完成上述工作带来的损害；以及

　　　　　　　　　　　　(b)　**承包商**应发出所有通知，缴纳各项税费，按照**法律**关于**工程**设计、实施和竣工以及**修补**任何缺陷等方面的要求，办理并领取所需要的全部许可、执照或批准；**承包商**应保障和保持**雇主**免受因未能完成上述工作带来的损害。

1.14

共同的和各自的责任　　　如果**承包商**是由两个或两个以上的当事人(依照适用**法律**)组成的联营体、联合体或其他未立案的组合：

　　　　　　　　　　　　(a)　这些当事人应被认为在履行**合同**上对**雇主**负有共同的和各自的责任；

　　　　　　　　　　　　(b)　这些当事人应将有权约束**承包商**及其每个当事人的负责人通知**雇主**；以及

　　　　　　　　　　　　(c)　未经**雇主**事先同意，**承包商**不得改变其组成或法律地位。

2　雇主

2.1

现场进入权　　　　　　　**雇主**应在**投标书附录**中规定的时间（或几个时间）内，给**承包商**进入和占用**现场**各部分的权利。此项进入和占用权可不为**承包商**独享。如果根据**合同**，要求**雇主**(向**承包商**)提供任何基础、结构、生产设备或进入手段的占用权，**雇主**应按**规范要求**规定的时间和方式提供。但是，**雇主**在收到**履约担保**前，可保留上述任何进入或占用权，暂不给予。

　　　　　　　　　　　　如果在**投标书附录**中没有规定上述时间，**雇主**应在**承包商**按**第8.3款**[**进度计划**]的规定进行施工所需要的时间内，给予**承包商**进入和占用**现场**的权利。

　　　　　　　　　　　　如果**雇主**未能及时给予**承包商**上述进入和占用的权利，使**承包商**遭受延误和(或)招致增加**费用**，**承包商**应向**工程师**发出通知，并根据**第20.1款**[**承包商的索赔**]的规定有权要求：

29

(a)   an extension of time for any such delay, if completion is or will be delayed, under Sub-Clause 8.4 [*Extension of Time for Completion*], and

(b)   payment of any such Cost plus reasonable profit, which shall be included in the Contract Price.

After receiving this notice, the Engineer shall proceed in accordance with Sub-Clause 3.5 [*Determinations*] to agree or determine these matters.

However, if and to the extent that the Employer's failure was caused by any error or delay by the Contractor, including an error in, or delay in the submission of, any of the Contractor's Documents, the Contractor shall not be entitled to such extension of time, Cost or profit.

2.2

Permits, Licences or Approvals

The Employer shall (where he is in a position to do so) provide reasonable assistance to the Contractor at the request of the Contractor:

(a)   by obtaining copies of the Laws of the Country which are relevant to the Contract but are not readily available, and

(b)   for the Contractor's applications for any permits, licences or approvals required by the Laws of the Country:

    (i)   which the Contractor is required to obtain under Sub-Clause 1.13 [*Compliance with Laws*],

    (ii)   for the delivery of Goods, including clearance through customs, and

    (iii)   for the export of Contractor's Equipment when it is removed from the Site.

2.3

Employer's Personnel

The Employer shall be responsible for ensuring that the Employer's Personnel and the Employer's other contractors on the Site:

(a)   co-operate with the Contractor's efforts under Sub-Clause 4.6 [*Co-operation*], and

(b)   take actions similar to those which the Contractor is required to take under sub-paragraphs (a), (b) and (c) of Sub-Clause 4.8 [*Safety Procedures*] and under Sub-Clause 4.18 [*Protection of the Environment*].

2.4

Employer's Financial Arrangements

The Employer shall submit, within 28 days after receiving any request from the Contractor, reasonable evidence that financial arrangements have been made and are being maintained which will enable the Employer to pay the Contract Price (as estimated at that time) in accordance with Clause 14 [*Contract Price and Payment*]. If the Employer intends to make any material change to his financial arrangements, the Employer shall give notice to the Contractor with detailed particulars.

2.5

Employer's Claims

If the Employer considers himself to be entitled to any payment under any Clause of these Conditions or otherwise in connection with the Contract, and/or to any extension of the Defects Notification Period, the Employer or the Engineer shall give notice and particulars to the Contractor. However, notice is not required for payments due under Sub-Clause 4.19 [*Electricity, Water and Gas*], under Sub-Clause 4.20 [*Employer's Equipment and Free-Issue Material*], or for other services requested by the Contractor.

The notice shall be given as soon as practicable after the Employer became aware of the event or circumstances giving rise to the claim. A notice relating to any extension of the Defects Notification Period shall be given before the expiry of such period.

(a)　根据第 **8.4 款**[**竣工时间的延长**]的规定，如竣工已或将受到延误，对任何此类延误给予延长期；以及

(b)　任何此类**费用**和合理利润应计入**合同价格**，给予支付。

在收到此通知后，**工程师**应按照**第 3.5 款**[**确定**]的规定，就这些事项进行商定或确定。

但是，如果出现**雇主**的违约是由于**承包商**的任何错误或延误，包括在任何**承包商文件**中的错误或提交延误造成的情况，**承包商**应无权得到此类延长期、**费用**或利润。

2.2

许可、执照或批准

雇主应(按其所能)根据**承包商**的请求，对其提供以下合理的协助：

(a)　取得与**合同**有关，但不易得到的**工程所在国**的**法律**文本；以及

(b)　协助**承包商**申办工程所在国法律要求的以下许可、执照或批准：

(i)　根据**第 1.13 款**[**遵守法律**]的规定，**承包商**需要得到的；

(ii)　为运送货物，包括结关需要的；和

(iii)　当**承包商**设备运离**现场**出口时需要的。

2.3

雇主人员

雇主应负责保证在**现场**的**雇主人员**和其他承包商做到：

(a)　根据**第 4.6 款**[**合作**]的规定，与**承包商**的各项努力进行合作；以及

(b)　采取与根据**第 4.8 款**[**安全程序**](a)、(b)和(c)项和**第 4.18 款**[**环境保护**]要求**承包商**采取的类似行动。

2.4

雇主的资金安排

雇主应在收到**承包商**的任何要求后 28 天内，提出其已做并将维持的资金安排的合理证据，说明**雇主**能够按照**第 14 条**[**合同价格和付款**]的规定，支付**合同价格**(按当时估算)。如果**雇主**拟对其资金安排做任何重要变更，应将其变更的详细情况通知**承包商**。

2.5

雇主的索赔

如果**雇主**认为，根据本条件任何条款，或合同有关的另外事项，他有权得到任何付款，和(或)对**缺陷通知期限**的任何延长，**雇主**或**工程师**应向**承包商**发出通知，说明细节。但对**承包商**根据**第 4.19 款**[**电、水和燃气**]或**第 4.20 款**[**雇主设备和免费供应的材料**]规定的到期应付款，或**承包商**要求的其他服务的应付款，不需发出通知。

通知应在**雇主**了解引起索赔的事件或情况后尽快发出。关于**缺陷通知期限**任何延长的通知，应在该期限到期前发出。

The particulars shall specify the Clause or other basis of the claim, and shall include substantiation of the amount and/or extension to which the Employer considers himself to be entitled in connection with the Contract. The Engineer shall then proceed in accordance with Sub-Clause 3.5 [*Determinations*] to agree or determine (i) the amount (if any) which the Employer is entitled to be paid by the Contractor, and/or (ii) the extension (if any) of the Defects Notification Period in accordance with Sub-Clause 11.3 [*Extension of Defects Notification Period*].

This amount may be included as a deduction in the Contract Price and Payment Certificates. The Employer shall only be entitled to set off against or make any deduction from an amount certified in a Payment Certificate, or to otherwise claim against the Contractor, in accordance with this Sub-Clause.

The 3 Engineer

3.1
Engineer's Duties and Authority

The Employer shall appoint the Engineer who shall carry out the duties assigned to him in the Contract. The Engineer's staff shall include suitably qualified engineers and other professionals who are competent to carry out these duties.

The Engineer shall have no authority to amend the Contract.

The Engineer may exercise the authority attributable to the Engineer as specified in or necessarily to be implied from the Contract. If the Engineer is required to obtain the approval of the Employer before exercising a specified authority, the requirements shall be as stated in the Particular Conditions. The Employer undertakes not to impose further constraints on the Engineer's authority, except as agreed with the Contractor.

However, whenever the Engineer exercises a specified authority for which the Employer's approval is required, then (for the purposes of the Contract) the Employer shall be deemed to have given approval.

Except as otherwise stated in these Conditions:

(a)   whenever carrying out duties or exercising authority, specified in or implied by the Contract, the Engineer shall be deemed to act for the Employer;

(b)   the Engineer has no authority to relieve either Party of any duties, obligations or responsibilities under the Contract; and

(c)   any approval, check, certificate, consent, examination, inspection, instruction, notice, proposal, request, test, or similar act by the Engineer (including absence of disapproval) shall not relieve the Contractor from any responsibility he has under the Contract, including responsibility for errors, omissions, discrepancies and non-compliances.

3.2
Delegation by the Engineer

The Engineer may from time to time assign duties and delegate authority to assistants, and may also revoke such assignment or delegation. These assistants may include a resident engineer, and/or independent inspectors appointed to inspect and/or test items of Plant and/or Materials. The assignment, delegation or revocation shall be in writing and shall not take effect until copies have been received by both Parties. However, unless otherwise agreed by both Parties, the Engineer shall not delegate the authority to determine any matter in accordance with Sub-Clause 3.5 [*Determinations*].

Assistants shall be suitably qualified persons, who are competent to carry out these

通知的细节应说明提出索赔根据的条款或其他依据，还应包括**雇主**认为根据**合同**他有权得到的索赔金额和（或）延长期的事实根据。然后，**工程师**应按照**第3.5款**[**确定**]的要求，商定或确定：（i）**雇主**有权得到**承包商**支付的金额（如果有），和（或）（ii）按照**第11.3款**[**缺陷通知期限的延长**]的规定，得到**缺陷通知期限**的延长期（如果有）。

上述金额可在**合同价格**和**付款证书**中列为扣减额。**雇主**应仅有权按照本**款**从**付款证书**确认的金额中冲销或做任何扣减，或另外对**承包商**提出索赔。

---

3 工程师

3.1
工程师的任务和权力

雇主应任命**工程师**，**工程师**应履行**合同**中指派给他的任务。**工程师**的职员应包括具有适当资质的工程师和能承担这些任务的其他专业人员。

工程师无权修改**合同**。

工程师可行使**合同**中规定或必然隐含的应属于**工程师**的权力。如果要求**工程师**在行使规定权力前须取得**雇主**批准，这些要求应在**专用条件**中写明。除得到**承包商**同意外，**雇主**承诺不对**工程师**的权力作进一步的限制。

但是，每当**工程师**行使需由**雇主**批准的规定权力时，则（为了合同的目的）应视为**雇主**已予批准。

除本**条件**中另有说明外：

(a) 每当**工程师**履行或行使**合同**规定或隐含的任务或权力时，应视为代表**雇主**执行；

(b) **工程师**无权解除任一方根据**合同**规定的任何任务、义务或职责；以及

(c) **工程师**的任何批准、校核、证明、同意、检查、检验、指示、通知、建议、要求、试验或类似行动（包括未表示不批准），不应解除**承包商**根据**合同**规定应承担的任何职责，包括对错误、遗漏、误差和未遵办的职责。

3.2
由工程师付托

工程师有时可向其助手指派任务和付托权力，也可撤销这种指派或付托。这些助手可包括驻地工程师，和（或）被任命为检验和（或）试验各项**工程设备**和（或）**材料**的独立检查员。以上指派、付托或撤销应用书面形式，在**双方**收到抄件后才生效。但是，除非另经**双方**同意，**工程师**不应将按照**第3.5款**[**确定**]的规定确定任何事项的权力付托他人。

助手应为具有适当资质的人员，能履行这些任务，行使此项权力，并能流利

duties and exercise this authority, and who are fluent in the language for communications defined in Sub-Clause 1.4 [*Law and Language*].

Each assistant, to whom duties have been assigned or authority has been delegated, shall only be authorised to issue instructions to the Contractor to the extent defined by the delegation. Any approval, check, certificate, consent, examination, inspection, instruction, notice, proposal, request, test, or similar act by an assistant, in accordance with the delegation, shall have the same effect as though the act had been an act of the Engineer. However:

(a)   any failure to disapprove any work, Plant or Materials shall not constitute approval, and shall therefore not prejudice the right of the Engineer to reject the work, Plant or Materials;

(b)   if the Contractor questions any determination or instruction of an assistant, the Contractor may refer the matter to the Engineer, who shall promptly confirm, reverse or vary the determination or instruction.

3.3

Instructions of the Engineer

The Engineer may issue to the Contractor (at any time) instructions and additional or modified Drawings which may be necessary for the execution of the Works and the remedying of any defects, all in accordance with the Contract. The Contractor shall only take instructions from the Engineer, or from an assistant to whom the appropriate authority has been delegated under this Clause. If an instruction constitutes a Variation, Clause 13 [*Variations and Adjustments*] shall apply.

The Contractor shall comply with the instructions given by the Engineer or delegated assistant, on any matter related to the Contract. Whenever practicable, their instructions shall be given in writing. If the Engineer or a delegated assistant:

(a)   gives an oral instruction,

(b)   receives a written confirmation of the instruction, from (or on behalf of) the Contractor, within two working days after giving the instruction, and

(c)   does not reply by issuing a written rejection and/or instruction within two working days after receiving the confirmation,

then the confirmation shall constitute the written instruction of the Engineer or delegated assistant (as the case may be).

3.4

Replacement of the Engineer

If the Employer intends to replace the Engineer, the Employer shall, not less than 42 days before the intended date of replacement, give notice to the Contractor of the name, address and relevant experience of the intended replacement Engineer. The Employer shall not replace the Engineer with a person against whom the Contractor raises reasonable objection by notice to the Employer, with supporting particulars.

3.5

Determinations

Whenever these Conditions provide that the Engineer shall proceed in accordance with this Sub-Clause 3.5 to agree or determine any matter, the Engineer shall consult with each Party in an endeavour to reach agreement. If agreement is not achieved, the Engineer shall make a fair determination in accordance with the Contract, taking due regard of all relevant circumstances.

The Engineer shall give notice to both Parties of each agreement or determination, with supporting particulars. Each Party shall give effect to each agreement or determination unless and until revised under Clause 20 [*Claims, Disputes and Arbitration*].

地使用**第 1.4 款**[*法律和语言*]规定的交流语言。

已被指派任务或付托权力的每个助手，应只被授权在付托规定的范围内向**承包商**发出指示。由助手按照付托做出的任何批准、校核、证明、同意、检查、检验、指示、通知、建议、要求、试验或类似行动，应与**工程师**做出的行动具有同样的效力。但是：

(a) 未对任何工作、**生产设备**或**材料**提出否定意见不应构成批准，因而不应影响**工程师**拒收该工作、**生产设备**或**材料**的权利；

(b) 如**承包商**对助手的确定或指示提出质疑，**承包商**可将此事项提交**工程师**，**工程师**应迅速对该确定或指示进行确认、取消或变更。

3.3

工程师的指示

工程师可(在任何时候)按照**合同**规定向**承包商**发出指示和实施工程和修补缺陷可能需要的附加或修正图纸。**承包商**仅应接受**工程师**或根据本条受托适当权力的助手的指示。如指示构成一项**变更**，应按照**第 13 条**[*变更和调整*]的规定办理。

承包商应遵循**工程师**或付托助手对**合同**有关的任何事项发出的指示。只要实际可行，他们的指示应采用书面形式。如**工程师**或付托助手：

(a) 给出口头指示，
(b) 在给出指示后两个工作日内收到**承包商**(或其代表)发来的对指示的书面确认，以及
(c) 在收到书面确认后两个工作日内，未通过发出书面拒绝和(或)指示进行答复，

这时该确认应成为**工程师**或付托助手(视情况而定)的书面指示。

3.4

工程师的替换

如果**雇主**拟替换**工程师**，**雇主**应在拟替换日期 42 天前通知**承包商**，告知拟替换**工程师**的姓名、地址和相关经验。如果**承包商**通知**雇主**，对某人提出合理的反对意见，并附有详细依据，**雇主**就不应用该人替换**工程师**。

3.5

确定

每当本**条件**规定**工程师**应按照**第 3.5 款**对任何事项进行商定或确定时，**工程师**应与每一方协商，尽量达成协议。如果达不成协议，**工程师**应对所有有关情况给予应有的考虑，按照**合同**作出公正的确定。

工程师应将每项商定意见或确定向**双方**发出通知，并附详细依据。除非并直到根据**第 20 条**[*索赔、争端和仲裁*]的规定作出修改，**各方**均应履行每项商定或确定事项。

The 4 Contractor

4.1
Contractor's General Obligations

The Contractor shall design (to the extent specified in the Contract), execute and complete the Works in accordance with the Contract and with the Engineer's instructions, and shall remedy any defects in the Works.

The Contractor shall provide the Plant and Contractor's Documents specified in the Contract, and all Contractor's Personnel, Goods, consumables and other things and services, whether of a temporary or permanent nature, required in and for this design, execution, completion and remedying of defects.

The Contractor shall be responsible for the adequacy, stability and safety of all Site operations and of all methods of construction. Except to the extent specified in the Contract, the Contractor (i) shall be responsible for all Contractor's Documents, Temporary Works, and such design of each item of Plant and Materials as is required for the item to be in accordance with the Contract, and (ii) shall not otherwise be responsible for the design or specification of the Permanent Works.

The Contractor shall, whenever required by the Engineer, submit details of the arrangements and methods which the Contractor proposes to adopt for the execution of the Works. No significant alteration to these arrangements and methods shall be made without this having previously been notified to the Engineer.

If the Contract specifies that the Contractor shall design any part of the Permanent Works, then unless otherwise stated in the Particular Conditions:

(a) the Contractor shall submit to the Engineer the Contractor's Documents for this part in accordance with the procedures specified in the Contract;

(b) these Contractor's Documents shall be in accordance with the Specification and Drawings, shall be written in the language for communications defined in Sub-Clause 1.4 [*Law and Language*], and shall include additional information required by the Engineer to add to the Drawings for co-ordination of each Party's designs;

(c) the Contractor shall be responsible for this part and it shall, when the Works are completed, be fit for such purposes for which the part is intended as are specified in the Contract; and

(d) prior to the commencement of the Tests on Completion, the Contractor shall submit to the Engineer the "as-built" documents and operation and maintenance manuals in accordance with the Specification and in sufficient detail for the Employer to operate, maintain, dismantle, reassemble, adjust and repair this part of the Works. Such part shall not be considered to be completed for the purposes of taking-over under Sub-Clause 10.1 [*Taking Over of the Works and Sections*] until these documents and manuals have been submitted to the Engineer.

4.2
Performance Security

The Contractor shall obtain (at his cost) a Performance Security for proper performance, in the amount and currencies stated in the Appendix to Tender. If an amount is not stated in the Appendix to Tender, this Sub-Clause shall not apply.

The Contractor shall deliver the Performance Security to the Employer within 28 days after receiving the Letter of Acceptance, and shall send a copy to the Engineer. The Performance Security shall be issued by an entity and from within a country (or other

4 承包商

4.1
承包商的一般义务

承包商应按照**合同**及**工程师**的指示，设计(在**合同**规定的范围内)、实施和完成**工程**，并修补**工程**中的任何缺陷。

承包商应提供**合同**规定的**生产设备**和**承包商**文件，以及此项设计、施工、竣工和修补缺陷所需的所有临时性或永久性的**承包商人员**、**货物**、消耗品及其他物品和服务。

承包商应对所有**现场**作业、所有施工方法和全部**工程**的完备性、稳定性和安全性承担责任。除非**合同**另有规定，**承包商**(i)对所有**承包商文件**、**临时工程**、及按照**合同**要求的每项**生产设备**和**材料**的设计承担责任，(ii)不应对其他**永久工程**的设计或**规范要求**负责。

当**工程师**提出要求时，**承包商**应提交其建议采用的**工程**施工安排和方法的细节。事先未通知**工程师**，对这些安排和方法不得做重要改变。

如果**合同**规定**承包商**设计**永久工程**的任何部分，则除非在**专用条件**中另有规定：

(a) **承包商**应按照**合同**规定的程序，向**工程师**提交有关该部分的**承包商文件**；

(b) 这些**承包商文件**应按照**规范要求**和**图纸**，并用**第1.4款**[**法律和语言**]规定的交流语言编写，应包括**工程师**要求的对**图纸**的附加资料，以便协调每方的设计；

(c) **工程**竣工时，**承包商**应对该部分负责，应使该部分符合**合同**规定要达到的目标；以及

(d) **竣工试验**开始前，**承包商**应按照**规范要求**向**工程师**提交竣工文件及操作和维护手册，它们应足够详细，使**雇主**能操作、维护、拆卸、再组装、调整和修复该部分**工程**。直到这些文件和手册已提交给**工程师**前，该部分不应被认为已按**第10.1款**[**工程和单位工程的接收**]规定的接收要求竣工。

4.2
履约担保

承包商应对严格履约(自费)取得**履约担保**，保证金额和币种应符合**投标书附录**中的规定。如**投标书附录**中没有提出保证金额，**本款**应不适用。

承包商应在收到**中标函**后28天内向**雇主**提交**履约担保**，并向**工程师**送一份副本。**履约担保**应由**雇主**批准的国家(或其他司法管辖区)内的实体提

jurisdiction) approved by the Employer, and shall be in the form annexed to the Particular Conditions or in another form approved by the Employer.

The Contractor shall ensure that the Performance Security is valid and enforceable until the Contractor has executed and completed the Works and remedied any defects. If the terms of the Performance Security specify its expiry date, and the Contractor has not become entitled to receive the Performance Certificate by the date 28 days prior to the expiry date, the Contractor shall extend the validity of the Performance Security until the Works have been completed and any defects have been remedied.

The Employer shall not make a claim under the Performance Security, except for amounts to which the Employer is entitled under the Contract in the event of:

(a)   failure by the Contractor to extend the validity of the Performance Security as described in the preceding paragraph, in which event the Employer may claim the full amount of the Performance Security,

(b)   failure by the Contractor to pay the Employer an amount due, as either agreed by the Contractor or determined under Sub-Clause 2.5 [*Employer's Claims*] or Clause 20 [*Claims, Disputes and Arbitration*], within 42 days after this agreement or determination,

(c)   failure by the Contractor to remedy a default within 42 days after receiving the Employer's notice requiring the default to be remedied, or

(d)   circumstances which entitle the Employer to termination under Sub-Clause 15.2 [*Termination by Employer*], irrespective of whether notice of termination has been given.

The Employer shall indemnify and hold the Contractor harmless against and from all damages, losses and expenses (including legal fees and expenses) resulting from a claim under the Performance Security to the extent to which the Employer was not entitled to make the claim.

The Employer shall return the Performance Security to the Contractor within 21 days after receiving a copy of the Performance Certificate.

4.3

Contractor's Representative

The Contractor shall appoint the Contractor's Representative and shall give him all authority necessary to act on the Contractor's behalf under the Contract.

Unless the Contractor's Representative is named in the Contract, the Contractor shall, prior to the Commencement Date, submit to the Engineer for consent the name and particulars of the person the Contractor proposes to appoint as Contractor's Representative. If consent is withheld or subsequently revoked, or if the appointed person fails to act as Contractor's Representative, the Contractor shall similarly submit the name and particulars of another suitable person for such appointment.

The Contractor shall not, without the prior consent of the Engineer, revoke the appointment of the Contractor's Representative or appoint a replacement.

The whole time of the Contractor's Representative shall be given to directing the Contractor's performance of the Contract. If the Contractor's Representative is to be temporarily absent from the Site during the execution of the Works, a suitable replacement person shall be appointed, subject to the Engineer's prior consent, and the Engineer shall be notified accordingly.

The Contractor's Representative shall, on behalf of the Contractor, receive instructions under Sub-Clause 3.3 [*Instructions of the Engineer*].

供，并采用**专用条件**所附格式或**雇主**批准的其他格式。

承包商应确保**履约担保**直到其完成**工程**的施工、竣工及修补完任何缺陷前持续有效和可执行。如果在**履约担保**的条款中规定了其期满日期，而**承包商**在该期满日期前 28 天尚无权拿到**履约证书**，**承包商**应将**履约担保**的有效期延长至**工程**竣工和修补完任何缺陷时为止。

除出现以下情况**雇主**根据**合同**规定有权获得的金额外，**雇主**不应根据**履约担保**提出索赔：

(a) **承包商**未能按前一段所述的要求延长**履约担保**的有效期，这时**雇主**可以索赔**履约担保**的全部金额；

(b) **承包商**未能在商定或确定后 42 天内，将**承包商**同意的，或按照第 2.5 款 [**雇主的索赔**] 或第 20 条 [**索赔、争端和仲裁**] 的规定确定的**承包商**应付金额付给**雇主**；

(c) **承包商**未能在收到**雇主**要求纠正违约的通知后 42 天内进行纠正；或

(d) **雇主**根据第 15.2 款 [**由雇主终止**] 的规定有权终止**合同**的情况，不管是否已发出终止通知。

雇主应保障和保持使**承包商**免受因**雇主**根据**履约担保**提出其本无权索赔范围的索赔引起的所有损害赔偿费、损失和开支 (包括法律费用和开支) 的损害。

雇主应在收到**履约证书**副本后 21 天内，将**履约担保**退还**承包商**。

4.3

承包商代表

承包商应任命**承包商代表**，并授予他代表**承包商**根据**合同**采取行动所需的全部权力。

除非**合同**中已写明了**承包商代表**的姓名，**承包商**应在开工日期前，将其拟任命为**承包商代表**的人员姓名和详细资料提交**工程师**取得同意。如未获同意，或随后撤销了同意，或任命的人不能担任**承包商代表**，**承包商**应同样地提交另外适合人选的姓名、详细资料，以取得该项任命。

未经**工程师**事先同意，**承包商**不应撤销**承包商代表**的任命，或任命替代人员。

承包商代表应将其全部时间用于指导**承包商**履行**合同**。如果**承包商代表**在**工程**施工期间要暂时离开**现场**，应事先征得**工程师**的同意，任命合适的替代人员，并相应通知**工程师**。

承包商代表应代表**承包商**接受根据第 3.3 款 [**工程师的指示**] 规定的指示。

The Contractor's Representative may delegate any powers, functions and authority to any competent person, and may at any time revoke the delegation. Any delegation or revocation shall not take effect until the Engineer has received prior notice signed by the Contractor's Representative, naming the person and specifying the powers, functions and authority being delegated or revoked.

The Contractor's Representative and all these persons shall be fluent in the language for communications defined in Sub-Clause 1.4 [*Law and Language*].

4.4
Subcontractors

The Contractor shall not subcontract the whole of the Works.

The Contractor shall be responsible for the acts or defaults of any Subcontractor, his agents or employees, as if they were the acts or defaults of the Contractor. Unless otherwise stated in the Particular Conditions:

(a)   the Contractor shall not be required to obtain consent to suppliers of Materials, or to a subcontract for which the Subcontractor is named in the Contract;

(b)   the prior consent of the Engineer shall be obtained to other proposed Subcontractors;

(c)   the Contractor shall give the Engineer not less than 28 days' notice of the intended date of the commencement of each Subcontractor's work, and of the commencement of such work on the Site; and

(d)   each subcontract shall include provisions which would entitle the Employer to require the subcontract to be assigned to the Employer under Sub-Clause 4.5 [*Assignment of Benefit of Subcontract*] (if or when applicable) or in the event of termination under Sub-Clause 15.2 [*Termination by Employer*].

4.5
Assignment of Benefit of Subcontract

If a Subcontractor's obligations extend beyond the expiry date of the relevant Defects Notification Period and the Engineer, prior to this date, instructs the Contractor to assign the benefit of such obligations to the Employer, then the Contractor shall do so. Unless otherwise stated in the assignment, the Contractor shall have no liability to the Employer for the work carried out by the Subcontractor after the assignment takes effect.

4.6
Co-operation

The Contractor shall, as specified in the Contract or as instructed by the Engineer, allow appropriate opportunities for carrying out work to:

(a)   the Employer's Personnel,

(b)   any other contractors employed by the Employer, and

(c)   the personnel of any legally constituted public authorities,

who may be employed in the execution on or near the Site of any work not included in the Contract.

Any such instruction shall constitute a Variation if and to the extent that it causes the Contractor to incur Unforeseeable Cost. Services for these personnel and other contractors may include the use of Contractor's Equipment, Temporary Works or access arrangements which are the responsibility of the Contractor.

If, under the Contract, the Employer is required to give to the Contractor possession of any foundation, structure, plant or means of access in accordance with Contractor's Documents, the Contractor shall submit such documents to the Engineer in the time and manner stated in the Specification.

承包商代表可向任何胜任的人员付托任何职权、任务和权力，并可随时撤销付托。任何付托或撤销应在**工程师**收到**承包商代表**签发的指明人员姓名，并说明付托或撤销的职权、任务和权力的事先通知后生效。

承包商代表和所有这些人员应能流利地使用**第 1.4 款**[*法律和语言*]规定的交流语言。

4.4

分包商

承包商不得将整个工程分包出去。

承包商应对任何**分包商**、其代理人或雇员的行为或违约，如同**承包商**自己的行为或违约一样地负责。除非**专用条件**中另有规定：

(a) **承包商**在选择**材料**供应商或向**合同**中已指名的**分包商**进行分包时，无需取得同意；

(b) 对其他建议的**分包商**应取得**工程师**的事先同意；

(c) **承包商**应至少提前 28 天将各**分包商**承担工作的拟定开工日期和该工作在**现场**的拟定开工日期通知**工程师**；以及

(d) 每个分包合同应包括，**雇主**有权要求根据**第 4.5 款**[*分包合同权益的转让*]（如有或适用时）的规定，或根据**第 15.2 款**[*由雇主终止*]的规定终止时，将分包合同转让给**雇主**的规定。

4.5

分包合同权益的转让

如果**分包商**的义务延伸到有关**缺陷通知期限**的期满日期以后，**工程师**在该日期前，指示**承包商**将此类义务的权益，转让给**雇主**时，**承包商**应照办。除非在转让中另有规定，在转让生效后，**承包商**对**分包商**实施的工作，不应再对**雇主**负责。

4.6

合作

承包商应依据**合同**的规定、或**工程师**的指示，为可能被雇用在**现场**或其附近从事本**合同**未包括的任何工作的下列人员进行工作提供适当的条件：

(a) **雇主人员**，
(b) **雇主**雇用的任何其他**承包商**，和
(c) 任何合法建立的公共当局的人员。

如果任何此类指示达到导致**承包商**增加**不可预见**的**费用**时，该指示应构成一项**变更**。为这些人员和其他承包商的服务，可包括使用**承包商设备**、以及由**承包商**负责的**临时工程**或进入的安排。

如果根据**合同**，要求**雇主**按照**承包商文件**向**承包商**提供任何基础、结构、生产设备、或进入手段的占用权，**承包商**应按照**规范要求**中规定的时间和方式，向**工程师**提交此类文件。

4.7	
Setting Out	

The Contractor shall set out the Works in relation to original points, lines and levels of reference specified in the Contract or notified by the Engineer. The Contractor shall be responsible for the correct positioning of all parts of the Works, and shall rectify any error in the positions, levels, dimensions or alignment of the Works.

The Employer shall be responsible for any errors in these specified or notified items of reference, but the Contractor shall use reasonable efforts to verify their accuracy before they are used.

If the Contractor suffers delay and/or incurs Cost from executing work which was necessitated by an error in these items of reference, and an experienced contractor could not reasonably have discovered such error and avoided this delay and/or Cost, the Contractor shall give notice to the Engineer and shall be entitled subject to Sub-Clause 20.1 [*Contractor's Claims*] to:

(a) an extension of time for any such delay, if completion is or will be delayed, under Sub-Clause 8.4 [*Extension of Time for Completion*], and

(b) payment of any such Cost plus reasonable profit, which shall be included in the Contract Price.

After receiving this notice, the Engineer shall proceed in accordance with Sub-Clause 3.5 [*Determinations*] to agree or determine (i) whether and (if so) to what extent the error could not reasonably have been discovered, and (ii) the matters described in sub-paragraphs (a) and (b) above related to this extent.

4.8

Safety Procedures

The Contractor shall:

(a) comply with all applicable safety regulations,

(b) take care for the safety of all persons entitled to be on the Site,

(c) use reasonable efforts to keep the Site and Works clear of unnecessary obstruction so as to avoid danger to these persons,

(d) provide fencing, lighting, guarding and watching of the Works until completion and taking over under Clause 10 [*Employer's Taking Over*], and

(e) provide any Temporary Works (including roadways, footways, guards and fences) which may be necessary, because of the execution of the Works, for the use and protection of the public and of owners and occupiers of adjacent land.

4.9

Quality Assurance

The Contractor shall institute a quality assurance system to demonstrate compliance with the requirements of the Contract. The system shall be in accordance with the details stated in the Contract. The Engineer shall be entitled to audit any aspect of the system.

Details of all procedures and compliance documents shall be submitted to the Engineer for information before each design and execution stage is commenced. When any document of a technical nature is issued to the Engineer, evidence of the prior approval by the Contractor himself shall be apparent on the document itself.

Compliance with the quality assurance system shall not relieve the Contractor of any of his duties, obligations or responsibilities under the Contract.

4.10

Site Data

The Employer shall have made available to the Contractor for his information, prior to the Base Date, all relevant data in the Employer's possession on sub-surface and hydrological conditions at the Site, including environmental aspects. The Employer

4.7 放线	承包商应按照合同规定的或工程师通知的原始基准点、基准线和基准标高对工程放线。承包商应负责对工程的所有部分正确定位，并应纠正在工程的位置、标高、尺寸或定线中的任何错误。

雇主应对规定的或通知的这几项基准的任何错误负责，但承包商应在使用前，作出合理的努力对其准确性进行核实。

如果承包商在实施工程中由于这几项基准中的某项错误必然遭受延误和(或)招致增加费用，而有经验的承包商不能合理发现此类错误，并避免此延误和(或)增加费用，承包商应通知工程师，根据第20.1款[承包商的索赔]的规定，有权要求：

(a) 根据第8.4款[竣工时间的延长]的规定，如竣工已或将受到延误，对任何此类延误给予延长期；以及
(b) 任何此类费用和合理利润应计入合同价格，给予支付。

工程师收到此通知后，应按照第3.5款[确定]的规定，商定或确定：(i)错误是否不能合理发现，(如果是)不能合理发现的程度，(ii)与该程度相关的上述(a)和(b)项所述事项。

4.8 安全程序	承包商应：

(a) 遵守所有适用的安全规则；
(b) 照料有权在现场的所有人员的安全；
(c) 尽合理的努力保持现场和工程清除不需要的障碍物，以避免对这些人员造成危险；
(d) 在工程竣工和按照第10条[雇主的接收]的规定移交前，提供围栏、照明、保卫和看守；以及
(e) 因实施工程，为公众和邻近土地的所有人、占用人使用和对其保护，提供可能需要的任何临时工程(包括道路、人行路、防护物和围栏等)。

4.9 质量保证	承包商应建立质量保证体系，以论证遵照合同要求。该体系应符合合同的详细规定。工程师有权对体系的任何方面进行审查。

承包商应在每一设计和实施阶段开始前，向工程师提交所有程序和如何贯彻要求的文件的细节，供其参考。当任何技术性文件发给工程师时，文件本身应有经承包商本人事先批准的明显证据。

遵守质量保证体系，不应解除合同规定的承包商的任何任务、义务或职责。

4.10 现场数据	雇主应在基准日期前，将其取得的现场地下、水文条件及环境方面的所有

shall similarly make available to the Contractor all such data which come into the Employer's possession after the Base Date. The Contractor shall be responsible for interpreting all such data.

To the extent which was practicable (taking account of cost and time), the Contractor shall be deemed to have obtained all necessary information as to risks, contingencies and other circumstances which may influence or affect the Tender or Works. To the same extent, the Contractor shall be deemed to have inspected and examined the Site, its surroundings, the above data and other available information, and to have been satisfied before submitting the Tender as to all relevant matters, including (without limitation):

(a)   the form and nature of the Site, including sub-surface conditions,

(b)   the hydrological and climatic conditions,

(c)   the extent and nature of the work and Goods necessary for the execution and completion of the Works and the remedying of any defects,

(d)   the Laws, procedures and labour practices of the Country, and

(e)   the Contractor's requirements for access, accommodation, facilities, personnel, power, transport, water and other services.

4.11

Sufficiency of the Accepted Contract Amount

The Contractor shall be deemed to:

(a)   have satisfied himself as to the correctness and sufficiency of the Accepted Contract Amount, and

(b)   have based the Accepted Contract Amount on the data, interpretations, necessary information, inspections, examinations and satisfaction as to all relevant matters referred to in Sub-Clause 4.10 [Site Data].

Unless otherwise stated in the Contract, the Accepted Contract Amount covers all the Contractor's obligations under the Contract (including those under Provisional Sums, if any) and all things necessary for the proper execution and completion of the Works and the remedying of any defects.

4.12

Unforeseeable Physical Conditions

In this Sub-Clause, "physical conditions" means natural physical conditions and man-made and other physical obstructions and pollutants, which the Contractor encounters at the Site when executing the Works, including sub-surface and hydro-logical conditions but excluding climatic conditions.

If the Contractor encounters adverse physical conditions which he considers to have been Unforeseeable, the Contractor shall give notice to the Engineer as soon as practicable.

This notice shall describe the physical conditions, so that they can be inspected by the Engineer, and shall set out the reasons why the Contractor considers them to be Unforeseeable. The Contractor shall continue executing the Works, using such proper and reasonable measures as are appropriate for the physical conditions, and shall comply with any instructions which the Engineer may give. If an instruction constitutes a Variation, Clause 13 [Variations and Adjustments] shall apply.

If and to the extent that the Contractor encounters physical conditions which are Unfore-seeable, gives such a notice, and suffers delay and/or incurs Cost due to these conditions, the Contractor shall be entitled subject to Sub-Clause 20.1 [Contractor's Claims] to:

(a)   an extension of time for any such delay, if completion is or will be delayed, under Sub-Clause 8.4 [Extension of Time for Completion], and

(b)   payment of any such Cost, which shall be included in the Contract Price.

44

有关数据，提供给**承包商**。同样地，**雇主**在**基准日期**后得到的所有此类资料，也应提供给**承包商**。**承包商**应负责解释所有此类资料。

在实际可行(考虑到费用和时间)的范围内，**承包商**应被认为已取得可能对**投标书**或**工程**产生影响或作用的有关风险、偶发事件和其他情况的所有必要资料。同样地，**承包商**应被认为在提交**投标书**前，已视察和检查了**现场**、周围环境、上述数据和其他得到的资料，并对所有相关事项已感到满足要求，包括(但不限于)：

(a)　**现场**的状况和性质，包括地下条件；
(b)　水文和气候条件；
(c)　为实施、完成**工程**和修补任何缺陷所需的工作和**货物**的范围和性质；

(d)　**工程所在国**的**法律**、程序和劳务惯例；以及
(e)　**承包商**对进入、食宿、设施、人员、电力、运输、水和其他服务的要求。

4.11

中标合同金额的充分性　　**承包商**应被认为：

(a)　已确信**中标合同金额**的正确性和充分性；以及

(b)　已将**中标合同金额**建立在关于**第 4.10 款**[**现场数据**]中提到的所有有关事项的数据、解释、必要的资料、视察、检查和满意的基础上。

除非**合同**中另有规定，**中标合同金额**包括**承包商**根据**合同**应承担的全部义务(包括根据**暂列金额**应承担的义务，如果有)，以及为正确地实施和完成**工程**并修补任何缺陷所需的全部有关事项的费用。

4.12

不可预见的物质条件　　**本款**中的"物质条件"系指**承包商**在**现场**施工时遇到的自然物质条件、人为的及其他物质障碍和污染物，包括地下和水文条件，但不包括气候条件。

如果**承包商**遇到他认为**不可预见**的不利物质条件，应尽快通知**工程师**。

此通知应说明物质条件，以便**工程师**进行检验，并应提出**承包商**为何认为**不可预见**的理由。**承包商**应采取适应物质条件的合理措施继续施工，并应遵循**工程师**可能给出的任何指示。如某项指示构成**变更**时，应按**第 13 条**[**变更和调整**]的规定办理。

如果**承包商**遇到**不可预见**的物质条件并发出此项通知，且因这些条件达到遭受延误和(或)增加**费用**的程度，**承包商**应有权根据**第 20.1 款**[**承包商的索赔**]的规定，要求：

(a)　根据**第 8.4 款**[**竣工时间的延长**]的规定，如竣工已或将受到延误，对任何此类延误给予延长期；以及
(b)　任何此类**费用**应计入**合同价格**，给予支付。

After receiving such notice and inspecting and/or investigating these physical conditions, the Engineer shall proceed in accordance with Sub-Clause 3.5 [*Determinations*] to agree or determine (i) whether and (if so) to what extent these physical conditions were Unforeseeable, and (ii) the matters described in sub-paragraphs (a) and (b) above related to this extent.

However, before additional Cost is finally agreed or determined under sub-paragraph (ii), the Engineer may also review whether other physical conditions in similar parts of the Works (if any) were more favourable than could reasonably have been foreseen when the Contractor submitted the Tender. If and to the extent that these more favourable conditions were encountered, the Engineer may proceed in accordance with Sub-Clause 3.5 [*Determinations*] to agree or determine the reductions in Cost which were due to these conditions, which may be included (as deductions) in the Contract Price and Payment Certificates. However, the net effect of all adjustments under sub-paragraph (b) and all these reductions, for all the physical conditions encountered in similar parts of the Works, shall not result in a net reduction in the Contract Price.

The Engineer may take account of any evidence of the physical conditions foreseen by the Contractor when submitting the Tender, which may be made available by the Contractor, but shall not be bound by any such evidence.

4.13

Rights of Way and Facilities

The Contractor shall bear all costs and charges for special and/or temporary rights-of-way which he may require, including those for access to the Site. The Contractor shall also obtain, at his risk and cost, any additional facilities outside the Site which he may require for the purposes of the Works.

4.14

Avoidance of Interference

The Contractor shall not interfere unnecessarily or improperly with:

(a)   the convenience of the public, or
(b)   the access to and use and occupation of all roads and footpaths, irrespective of whether they are public or in the possession of the Employer or of others.

The Contractor shall indemnify and hold the Employer harmless against and from all damages, losses and expenses (including legal fees and expenses) resulting from any such unnecessary or improper interference.

4.15

Access Route

The Contractor shall be deemed to have been satisfied as to the suitability and availability of access routes to the Site. The Contractor shall use reasonable efforts to prevent any road or bridge from being damaged by the Contractor's traffic or by the Contractor's Personnel. These efforts shall include the proper use of appropriate vehicles and routes.

Except as otherwise stated in these Conditions:

(a)   the Contractor shall (as between the Parties) be responsible for any maintenance which may be required for his use of access routes;
(b)   the Contractor shall provide all necessary signs or directions along access routes, and shall obtain any permission which may be required from the relevant authorities for his use of routes, signs and directions;
(c)   the Employer shall not be responsible for any claims which may arise from the use or otherwise of any access route,

46

工程师收到此类通知并对该物质条件进行检验和(或)研究后,应按照**第3.5款**[**确定**]的规定,进行商定或确定:(i)此类物质条件是否**不可预见**,(如果是)此类物质条件**不可预见**的程度,以及(ii)与此程度有关的上述(a)和(b)项所述的事项。

但是,根据上述(ii)中最终商定或确定给予增加**费用**前,**工程师**还可以审查工程类似部分(如果有)其他物质条件是否比**承包商**提交**投标书**时能合理预见的更为有利。如果达到遇见这些更为有利条件的程度,**工程师**可按照**第3.5款**[**确定**]的规定,商定或确定因这些条件引起的**费用**减少额,并(作为扣减额)计入**合同价格**和付款证书。但对工程类似部分遇到的所有物质条件根据(b)项做出的所有调整和所有这些减少额的净作用,不应造成**合同价格**净减少的结果。

工程师可以考虑**承包商**提交**投标书**时可能提供的预见的物质条件的任何证据,但不应受任何此类证据的约束。

4.13	
道路通行权和设施	**承包商**应为其所需要的专用和(或)临时道路包括**进场**道路的通行权,承担全部费用和开支。**承包商**还应自担风险和费用,取得为**工程**目的可能需要的**现场**以外的任何附加设施。

4.14	
避免干扰	**承包商**应避免对以下事项产生不必要或不当的干扰:

(a) 公众的方便,或
(b) 所有道路和人行道的进入、使用和占用,不论它们是公共的,或是**雇主**或其他人所有的。

承包商应保障和保持使**雇主**免受因任何此类不必要或不当的干扰造成的任何损害赔偿费、损失和开支(包括法律费用和开支)的损害。

4.15	
进场通路	**承包商**应被认为已对**现场**的进入通路的适宜性和可用性感到满意。**承包商**应尽合理的努力,防止任何道路或桥梁因**承包商**的通行或**承包商**人员受到损坏。这些努力应包括正确使用适宜的车辆和通路。

除本**条件**另有规定外:

(a) **承包商**应(就各方间而言)负责因他使用进场通路所需要的任何维护;

(b) **承包商**应提供进场通路的所有必需的标志或方向指示,还应为其使用这些通路、标志和方向指示,取得必要的有关当局的许可;

(c) **雇主**不对由于任何进场通路的使用或其他原因引起的索赔负责;

(d)   the Employer does not guarantee the suitability or availability of particular access routes, and

(e)   Costs due to non-suitability or non-availability, for the use required by the Contractor, of access routes shall be borne by the Contractor.

4.16

Transport of Goods

Unless otherwise stated in the Particular Conditions:

(a)   the Contractor shall give the Engineer not less than 21 days' notice of the date on which any Plant or a major item of other Goods will be delivered to the Site;

(b)   the Contractor shall be responsible for packing, loading, transporting, receiving, unloading, storing and protecting all Goods and other things required for the Works; and

(c)   the Contractor shall indemnify and hold the Employer harmless against and from all damages, losses and expenses (including legal fees and expenses) resulting from the transport of Goods, and shall negotiate and pay all claims arising from their transport.

4.17

Contractor's Equipment

The Contractor shall be responsible for all Contractor's Equipment. When brought on to the Site, Contractor's Equipment shall be deemed to be exclusively intended for the execution of the Works. The Contractor shall not remove from the Site any major items of Contractor's Equipment without the consent of the Engineer. However, consent shall not be required for vehicles transporting Goods or Contractor's Personnel off Site.

4.18

Protection of the Environment

The Contractor shall take all reasonable steps to protect the environment (both on and off the Site) and to limit damage and nuisance to people and property resulting from pollution, noise and other results of his operations.

The Contractor shall ensure that emissions, surface discharges and effluent from the Contractor's activities shall not exceed the values indicated in the Specification, and shall not exceed the values prescribed by applicable Laws.

4.19

Electricity, Water and Gas

The Contractor shall, except as stated below, be responsible for the provision of all power, water and other services he may require.

The Contractor shall be entitled to use for the purposes of the Works such supplies of electricity, water, gas and other services as may be available on the Site and of which details and prices are given in the Specification. The Contractor shall, at his risk and cost, provide any apparatus necessary for his use of these services and for measuring the quantities consumed.

The quantities consumed and the amounts due (at these prices) for such services shall be agreed or determined by the Engineer in accordance with Sub-Clause 2.5 [*Employer's Claims*] and Sub-Clause 3.5 [*Determinations*]. The Contractor shall pay these amounts to the Employer.

4.20

Employer's Equipment and Free-Issue Material

The Employer shall make the Employer's Equipment (if any) available for the use of the Contractor in the execution of the Works in accordance with the details, arrangements and prices stated in the Specification. Unless otherwise stated in the Specification:

(a)   the Employer shall be responsible for the Employer's Equipment, except that

(d) **雇主**不保证特定进场通路的适宜性和可用性；以及

(e) 因进场通路对**承包商**的使用要求不适宜、不可用而发生的**费用**应由**承包商**承担。

4.16
货物运输

除非**专用条件**中另有规定：

(a) **承包商**应在不少于 21 天前，将任何**生产设备**或每项其他主要**货物**将运到**现场**的日期，通知**工程师**；

(b) **承包商**应负责工程需要的所有**货物**和其他物品的包装、装货、运输、接收、卸货、存储和保护；以及

(c) **承包商**应保障并保持**雇主**免受因**货物**运输引起的所有损害赔偿费、损失和开支(包括法律费用和开支)的损害，并应协商和支付由于**货物**运输引起的所有索赔。

4.17
承包商设备

承包商应负责所有**承包商设备**。**承包商设备**运到**现场**后，应视作准备为工程施工专用。未经**工程师**同意，**承包商**不得从**现场**运走任何主要**承包商设备**。但运送**货物**或承包商人员离开**现场**的车辆，无需经过同意。

4.18
环境保护

承包商应采取一切适当措施，保护(**现场**内外)环境，限制由其施工作业引起的污染、噪音和其他后果对公众和财产造成的损害和妨害。

承包商应确保因其活动产生的气体排放、地面排水及排污等，不超过**规范要求**规定的数值，也不超过适用**法律**规定的数值。

4.19
电、水和燃气

除下述情况外，**承包商**应负责供应其所需的所有电、水和其他服务。

承包商应有权因工程的需要使用**现场**可供的电、水、燃气和其他服务，其详细规定和价格见**规范要求**。**承包商**应自担风险和费用，提供他使用这些服务及计量所需要的任何仪器。

这些服务的耗用数量和应付金额(按其价格)，应由**工程师**根据第 2.5 款[*雇主的索赔*]和第 3.5 款[*确定*]的要求商定或确定。**承包商**应向**雇主**支付此金额。

4.20
雇主设备和免费供应的材料

雇主应准备**雇主设备**(如果有)，供**承包商**按照**规范要求**中规定的细节、安排和价格，在工程实施中使用。除非**规范要求**中另有说明：

(a) 除下列(b)项所列情况外，**雇主**应对**雇主设备**负责；

(b)   the Contractor shall be responsible for each item of Employer's Equipment whilst any of the Contractor's Personnel is operating it, driving it, directing it or in possession or control of it.

The appropriate quantities and the amounts due (at such stated prices) for the use of Employer's Equipment shall be agreed or determined by the Engineer in accordance with Sub-Clause 2.5 [*Employer's Claims*] and Sub-Clause 3.5 [*Determinations*]. The Contractor shall pay these amounts to the Employer.

The Employer shall supply, free of charge, the "free-issue materials" (if any) in accordance with the details stated in the Specification. The Employer shall, at his risk and cost, provide these materials at the time and place specified in the Contract. The Contractor shall then visually inspect them, and shall promptly give notice to the Engineer of any shortage, defect or default in these materials. Unless otherwise agreed by both Parties, the Employer shall immediately rectify the notified shortage, defect or default.

After this visual inspection, the free-issue materials shall come under the care, custody and control of the Contractor. The Contractor's obligations of inspection, care, custody and control shall not relieve the Employer of liability for any shortage, defect or default not apparent from a visual inspection.

4.21

Progress Reports

Unless otherwise stated in the Particular Conditions, monthly progress reports shall be prepared by the Contractor and submitted to the Engineer in six copies. The first report shall cover the period up to the end of the first calendar month following the Commencement Date. Reports shall be submitted monthly thereafter, each within 7 days after the last day of the period to which it relates.

Reporting shall continue until the Contractor has completed all work which is known to be outstanding at the completion date stated in the Taking-Over Certificate for the Works.

Each report shall include:

(a)   charts and detailed descriptions of progress, including each stage of design (if any), Contractor's Documents, procurement, manufacture, delivery to Site, construction, erection and testing; and including these stages for work by each nominated Subcontractor (as defined in Clause 5 [*Nominated Subcontractors*]),

(b)   photographs showing the status of manufacture and of progress on the Site;

(c)   for the manufacture of each main item of Plant and Materials, the name of the manufacturer, manufacture location, percentage progress, and the actual or expected dates of:

   (i)   commencement of manufacture,
   (ii)   Contractor's inspections,
   (iii)   tests, and
   (iv)   shipment and arrival at the Site;

(d)   the details described in Sub-Clause 6.10 [*Records of Contractor's Personnel and Equipment*];

(e)   copies of quality assurance documents, test results and certificates of Materials;

(f)   list of notices given under Sub-Clause 2.5 [*Employer's Claims*] and notices given under Sub-Clause 20.1 [*Contractor's Claims*];

(g)   safety statistics, including details of any hazardous incidents and activities relating to environmental aspects and public relations; and

(b) 当任何**承包商人员**操作、驾驶、指挥、或占用或控制某项**雇主设备**时，**承包商**应对每项**设备**负责。

使用**雇主设备**的适当数量和应付金额（按规定价格）应由**工程师**按**第 2.5 款**[*雇主的索赔*]和**第 3.5 款**[*确定*]的要求商定或确定。**承包商**应向**雇主**支付此金额。

雇主应按照**规范要求**中规定的细节，免费提供"免费供应的材料"（如果有）。**雇主**应自行承担风险和费用，按照**合同**规定的时间和地点供应这些材料。随后，**承包商**应对其进行目视检查，并将这些材料的短少、缺陷或缺项迅速通知**工程师**。除非**双方**另有协议，**雇主**应立即改正通知指出的短少、缺陷或缺项。

目视检查后，这些免费供应的材料应由**承包商**照管、监护和控制。**承包商**的检查、照管、监护和控制的义务，不应解除**雇主**对目视检查难发现的任何短少、缺陷或缺项所负的责任。

4.21

进度报告

除非**专用条件**中另有规定，**承包商**应编制月进度报告，一式六份提交给**工程师**。第一次报告所包含的期间，应自**开工日期**起至当月的月底止。以后应每月报告一次，在每次报告期最后一天后 7 日内报出。

报告应持续到**承包商**完成**工程接收证书**注明的竣工日期时所有未完扫尾工作为止。

每次报告应包括：

(a) 设计的每个阶段（如果有）、**承包商文件**、采购、制造、货物送达**现场**、施工、安装、试验等每一阶段进展情况的图表和详细说明；包括各指定的**分包商**（按照**第 5 条**[*指定的分包商*]中的规定）所承担工作的这些阶段；

(b) 反映制造和**现场**进展情况的照片；

(c) 关于每项主要**生产设备**和**材料**的生产、制造商名称、制造地点、进度百分比，以及下列事项的实际或预计日期：

    (i) 开始制造，
    (ii) **承包商**检验，
    (iii) 试验，和
    (iv) 发货和运抵**现场**；

(d) **第 6.10 款**[*承包商人员和设备的记录*]中所述的细节；

(e) **材料**的质量保证文件、试验结果及合格证的副本；

(f) 根据**第 2.5 款**[*雇主的索赔*]的规定发出的通知和根据**第 20.1 款**[*承包商的索赔*]的规定发出的通知的清单；

(g) 安全统计，包括对环境和公共关系有危害的任何事件和活动的详细情况；以及

(h)   comparisons of actual and planned progress, with details of any events or circumstances which may jeopardise the completion in accordance with the Contract, and the measures being (or to be) adopted to overcome delays.

4.22

Security of the Site

Unless otherwise stated in the Particular Conditions:

(a)   the Contractor shall be responsible for keeping unauthorised persons off the Site, and

(b)   authorised persons shall be limited to the Contractor's Personnel and the Employer's Personnel; and to any other personnel notified to the Contractor, by the Employer or the Engineer, as authorised personnel of the Employer's other contractors on the Site.

4.23

Contractor's Operations on Site

The Contractor shall confine his operations to the Site, and to any additional areas which may be obtained by the Contractor and agreed by the Engineer as working areas. The Contractor shall take all necessary precautions to keep Contractor's Equipment and Contractor's Personnel within the Site and these additional areas, and to keep them off adjacent land.

During the execution of the Works, the Contractor shall keep the Site free from all unnecessary obstruction, and shall store or dispose of any Contractor's Equipment or surplus materials. The Contractor shall clear away and remove from the Site any wreckage, rubbish and Temporary Works which are no longer required.

Upon the issue of a Taking-Over Certificate, the Contractor shall clear away and remove, from that part of the Site and Works to which the Taking-Over Certificate refers, all Contractor's Equipment, surplus material, wreckage, rubbish and Temporary Works. The Contractor shall leave that part of the Site and the Works in a clean and safe condition. However, the Contractor may retain on Site, during the Defects Notification Period, such Goods as are required for the Contractor to fulfil obligations under the Contract.

4.24

Fossils

All fossils, coins, articles of value or antiquity, and structures and other remains or items of geological or archaeological interest found on the Site shall be placed under the care and authority of the Employer. The Contractor shall take reasonable precautions to prevent Contractor's Personnel or other persons from removing or damaging any of these findings.

The Contractor shall, upon discovery of any such finding, promptly give notice to the Engineer, who shall issue instructions for dealing with it. If the Contractor suffers delay and/or incurs Cost from complying with the instructions, the Contractor shall give a further notice to the Engineer and shall be entitled subject to Sub-Clause 20.1 [*Contractor's Claims*] to:

(a)   an extension of time for any such delay, if completion is or will be delayed, under Sub-Clause 8.4 [*Extension of Time for Completion*], and

(b)   payment of any such Cost, which shall be included in the Contract Price.

After receiving this further notice, the Engineer shall proceed in accordance with Sub-Clause 3.5 [*Determinations*] to agree or determine these matters.

(h) 实际进度与计划进度的对比，包括可能影响按合同竣工的任何事件或情况的详情，以及为消除延误正在(或准备)采取的措施。

4.22

现场保安

除非**专用条件**中另有规定：

(a) **承包商**应负责阻止未经授权的人员进入**现场**；以及

(b) 授权人员应仅限于**承包商人员**和**雇主人员**，以及由**雇主**或**工程师**通知**承包商**作为**雇主**在**现场**的其他承包商的授权人员的任何其他人员。

4.23

承包商的现场作业

承包商应将其作业限制在**现场**、以及**承包商**可得到并经**工程师**同意作为工作场地的任何附加区域内。**承包商**应采取一切必要的预防措施，以保持**承包商设备**和**承包商人员**处在**现场**和此类附加区域内，避免他们进入邻近地区。

在工程施工期间，**承包商**应保持**现场**没有一切不必要的障碍物，并应妥善存放和处置**承包商设备**或剩余的材料。**承包商**应从**现场**清除并运走任何残物、垃圾和不再需要的**临时工程**。

在颁发一项**接收证书**后，**承包商**应从**接收证书**涉及的**现场**和工程部分，清除并运走所有**承包商设备**、剩余材料、残物、垃圾和**临时工程**。**承包商**应使该部分**现场**和工程处于清洁和安全的状况。但在**缺陷通知期限**内，**承包商**可在**现场**保留其按照**合同**完成规定义务所需要的此类**货物**。

4.24

化石

在**现场**发现的所有化石、硬币、有价值的物品或古物，以及具有地质或考古意义的结构物和其他遗迹或物品，应置于**雇主**的照管和权限下。**承包商**应采取合理预防措施，防止**承包商**人员或其他人员移动或损坏任何此类发现物。

一旦发现任何上述物品，**承包商**应迅速通知**工程师**，**工程师**应就处理上述物品发出指示。如**承包商**因执行这些指示遭受延误和(或)增加**费用**，**承包商**应向**工程师**再次发出通知，应有权根据**第20.1款[承包商的索赔]**的规定要求：

(a) 根据**第8.4款[竣工时间的延长]**的规定，如竣工已或将受到延误，对任何此类延误给予延长期；以及
(b) 任何此类**费用**应计入合同价格，给予支付。

工程师收到上述再次通知后，应按照**第3.5款[确定]**的要求，商定或确定这些事项。

5 Nominated Subcontractors

5.1

Definition of "nominated Subcontractor"

In the Contract, "nominated Subcontractor" means a Subcontractor:

(a) who is stated in the Contract as being a nominated Subcontractor, or

(b) whom the Engineer, under Clause 13 [*Variations and Adjustments*], instructs the Contractor to employ as a Subcontractor.

5.2

Objection to Nomination

The Contractor shall not be under any obligation to employ a nominated Subcontractor against whom the Contractor raises reasonable objection by notice to the Engineer as soon as practicable, with supporting particulars. An objection shall be deemed reasonable if it arises from (among other things) any of the following matters, unless the Employer agrees to indemnify the Contractor against and from the consequences of the matter:

(a) there are reasons to believe that the Subcontractor does not have sufficient competence, resources or financial strength;

(b) the subcontract does not specify that the nominated Subcontractor shall indemnify the Contractor against and from any negligence or misuse of Goods by the nominated Subcontractor, his agents and employees; or

(c) the subcontract does not specify that, for the subcontracted work (including design, if any), the nominated Subcontractor shall:

  (i) undertake to the Contractor such obligations and liabilities as will enable the Contractor to discharge his obligations and liabilities under the Contract, and

  (ii) indemnify the Contractor against and from all obligations and liabilities arising under or in connection with the Contract and from the consequences of any failure by the Subcontractor to perform these obligations or to fulfil these liabilities.

5.3

Payments to nominated Subcontractors

The Contractor shall pay to the nominated Subcontractor the amounts which the Engineer certifies to be due in accordance with the subcontract. These amounts plus other charges shall be included in the Contract Price in accordance with sub-paragraph (b) of Sub-Clause 13.5 [*Provisional Sums*], except as stated in Sub-Clause 5.4 [*Evidence of Payments*].

5.4

Evidence of Payments

Before issuing a Payment Certificate which includes an amount payable to a nominated Subcontractor, the Engineer may request the Contractor to supply reasonable evidence that the nominated Subcontractor has received all amounts due in accordance with previous Payment Certificates, less applicable deductions for retention or otherwise. Unless the Contractor:

(a) submits this reasonable evidence to the Engineer, or

(b) (i) satisfies the Engineer in writing that the Contractor is reasonably entitled to withhold or refuse to pay these amounts, and

  (ii) submits to the Engineer reasonable evidence that the nominated Subcontractor has been notified of the Contractor's entitlement,

then the Employer may (at his sole discretion) pay, direct to the nominated Subcontractor, part or all of such amounts previously certified (less applicable

5 指定的分包商

5.1
"指定的分包商"的定义　　合同中"指定的**分包商**"系指以下**分包商**：

(a)　**合同**中提出的指定的**分包商**，或
(b)　**工程师**根据第 13 条[**变更和调整**]的规定指示**承包商**雇用的**分包商**。

5.2
反对指定　　对于**承包商**尽快向**工程师**发出通知，提出有依据的、合理异议的指定的**分包商**，**承包商**不应有任何雇用的义务。(其中)任何以下事项引起的反对，应被认为是合理的，除非**雇主**同意保障**承包商**免受这些事项的影响：

(a)　有理由相信，该**分包商**没有足够的能力、资源或财力；

(b)　分包合同没有明确规定，指定的**分包商**应保障**承包商**不承担指定的**分包商**及其代理人和雇员疏忽或误用货物的责任；或

(c)　分包合同没有明确规定，对分包的工作(包括设计，如果有)，指定的**分包商**应：

　　(i)　为**承包商**承担此项义务和责任，能使**承包商**履行其根据**合同**规定的义务和责任，和

　　(ii)　保障**承包商**免除根据**合同**规定或与其有关产生的所有义务和责任，以及因**分包商**任何未能完成这些义务或履行这些责任的影响产生的义务和责任。

5.3
对指定的分包商付款　　**承包商**应按**工程师**按照分包合同证明的应付金额支付指定的**分包商**。除了第 5.4 款[**付款证据**]中提出的情况外，这些金额加上其他费用，应按照第 13.5 款[**暂列金额**]的规定，计入**合同价格**。

5.4
付款证据　　**工程师**在发出包含应付指定的**分包商**金额的**付款证书**前，可要求**承包商**提供合理的证据，证明指定的**分包商**已收到按照此前**付款证书**应付的、减去合理的保留金或其他扣除后的所有金额。除非**承包商**：

(a)　向**工程师**提交此项合理证据；或
(b)　(i)提出使**工程师**满意的，承包商合理有权暂扣或拒付这些金额的书面说明；和
　　(ii)向**工程师**提交已将上述**承包商**权利通知了指定的**分包商**的合理证据。

这时，**雇主**可(自行决定)直接向指定的**分包商**支付以前已证明应付的(减

deductions) as are due to the nominated Subcontractor and for which the Contractor has failed to submit the evidence described in sub-paragraphs (a) or (b) above. The Contractor shall then repay, to the Employer, the amount which the nominated Sub-contractor was directly paid by the Employer.

6 Staff and Labour

6.1

Engagement of Staff and Labour

Except as otherwise stated in the Specification, the Contractor shall make arrangements for the engagement of all staff and labour, local or otherwise, and for their payment, housing, feeding and transport.

6.2

Rates of Wages and Conditions of Labour

The Contractor shall pay rates of wages, and observe conditions of labour, which are not lower than those established for the trade or industry where the work is carried out. If no established rates or conditions are applicable, the Contractor shall pay rates of wages and observe conditions which are not lower than the general level of wages and conditions observed locally by employers whose trade or industry is similar to that of the Contractor.

6.3

Persons in the Service of Employer

The Contractor shall not recruit, or attempt to recruit, staff and labour from amongst the Employer's Personnel.

6.4

Labour Laws

The Contractor shall comply with all the relevant labour Laws applicable to the Contractor's Personnel, including Laws relating to their employment, health, safety, welfare, immigration and emigration, and shall allow them all their legal rights.

The Contractor shall require his employees to obey all applicable Laws, including those concerning safety at work.

6.5

Working Hours

No work shall be carried out on the Site on locally recognised days of rest, or outside the normal working hours stated in the Appendix to Tender, unless:

(a)   otherwise stated in the Contract,
(b)   the Engineer gives consent, or
(c)   the work is unavoidable, or necessary for the protection of life or property or for the safety of the Works, in which case the Contractor shall immediately advise the Engineer.

6.6

Facilities for Staff and Labour

Except as otherwise stated in the Specification, the Contractor shall provide and maintain all necessary accommodation and welfare facilities for the Contractor's Personnel. The Contractor shall also provide facilities for the Employer's Personnel as stated in the Specification.

The Contractor shall not permit any of the Contractor's Personnel to maintain any temporary or permanent living quarters within the structures forming part of the Permanent Works.

6.7

Health and Safety

The Contractor shall at all times take all reasonable precautions to maintain the health and safety of the Contractor's Personnel. In collaboration with local health authorities,

去合理的扣减额），而**承包商**又没有提交以上(a)或(b)项所述证据的部分或全部金额。随后**承包商**应将**雇主**直接付给指定的**分包商**的金额付还**雇主**。

---

6 员工

6.1 员工的雇用	除**规范要求**中另有说明外，**承包商**应安排从当地或其他地方雇用所有的员工，并负责他们的报酬、住宿、膳食和交通。

6.2
工资标准和劳动条件

承包商所付工资标准及遵守的劳动条件，应不低于从事工作的地区该工种或行业制订的标准和条件。如果没有现成的标准和条件可以引用，**承包商**所付的工资标准及遵守的劳动条件，应不低于当地与**承包商**类似的工种或行业雇主所付的一般工资标准和遵守的劳动条件。

6.3
为雇主服务的人员

承包商不应从雇主人员中招收或试图招收员工。

6.4
劳动法

承包商应遵守所有适用于**承包商人员**的相关劳动法，包括有关他们的雇用、健康、安全、福利、入境和出境等**法律**，并应允许他们享有所有合法权利。

承包商应要求其雇员遵守所有适用的**法律**，包括有关工作安全的**法律**。

6.5
工作时间

除非出现下列情况，在当地公认的休息日，或**投标书附录**中规定的正常工作时间以外，不应在**现场**进行工作：

(a) **合同**中另有规定；
(b) **工程师**同意；或
(c) 为保护生命或财产、或为**工程**的安全不可避免或必需的工作，在此情况下，**承包商**应立即通知**工程师**。

6.6
为员工提供设施

除**规范要求**中另有说明外，**承包商**应为**承包商人员**提供和保持一切必要的食宿和福利设施。**承包商**还应按规范要求中的规定为**雇主人员**提供设施。

承包商不应允许**承包商人员**中的任何人，在构成**永久工程**一部分的构筑物内，保留任何临时或永久的居住场所。

6.7
健康和安全

承包商应始终采取合理的预防措施，维护**承包商人员**的健康和安全。承包

the Contractor shall ensure that medical staff, first aid facilities, sick bay and ambulance service are available at all times at the Site and at any accommodation for Contractor's and Employer's Personnel, and that suitable arrangements are made for all necessary welfare and hygiene requirements and for the prevention of epidemics.

The Contractor shall appoint an accident prevention officer at the Site, responsible for maintaining safety and protection against accidents. This person shall be qualified for this responsibility, and shall have the authority to issue instructions and take protective measures to prevent accidents. Throughout the execution of the Works, the Contractor shall provide whatever is required by this person to exercise this responsibility and authority.

The Contractor shall send, to the Engineer, details of any accident as soon as practicable after its occurrence. The Contractor shall maintain records and make reports concerning health, safety and welfare of persons, and damage to property, as the Engineer may reasonably require.

6.8
Contractor's Superintendence

Throughout the execution of the Works, and as long thereafter as is necessary to fulfil the Contractor's obligations, the Contractor shall provide all necessary superintendence to plan, arrange, direct, manage, inspect and test the work.

Superintendence shall be given by a sufficient number of persons having adequate knowledge of the language for communications (defined in Sub-Clause 1.4 [*Law and Language*]) and of the operations to be carried out (including the methods and techniques required, the hazards likely to be encountered and methods of preventing accidents), for the satisfactory and safe execution of the Works.

6.9
Contractor's Personnel

The Contractor's Personnel shall be appropriately qualified, skilled and experienced in their respective trades or occupations. The Engineer may require the Contractor to remove (or cause to be removed) any person employed on the Site or Works, including the Contractor's Representative if applicable, who:

(a)   persists in any misconduct or lack of care,
(b)   carries out duties incompetently or negligently,
(c)   fails to conform with any provisions of the Contract, or
(d)   persists in any conduct which is prejudicial to safety, health, or the protection of the environment.

If appropriate, the Contractor shall then appoint (or cause to be appointed) a suitable replacement person.

6.10
Records of Contractor's Personnel and Equipment

The Contractor shall submit, to the Engineer, details showing the number of each class of Contractor's Personnel and of each type of Contractor's Equipment on the Site. Details shall be submitted each calendar month, in a form approved by the Engineer, until the Contractor has completed all work which is known to be outstanding at the completion date stated in the Taking-Over Certificate for the Works.

6.11
Disorderly Conduct

The Contractor shall at all times take all reasonable precautions to prevent any unlawful, riotous or disorderly conduct by or amongst the Contractor's Personnel, and to preserve peace and protection of persons and property on and near the Site.

商应与当地卫生部门合作，始终确保在**现场**，以及**承包商人员**和**雇主人员**的任何住地，配备医务人员、急救设施、病房及救护车服务，并应对所有必要的福利和卫生要求，以及预防传染病作出适当安排。

承包商应指派一名事故预防员，负责**现场**的人身安全和安全事故预防工作。该人员应能胜任此项工作，并有权发布指示，及采取防止事故的保护措施。在**工程**实施过程中，**承包商**应提供该人员履行其职责和权力所需的任何事项。

任何事故发生后，**承包商**应立即将事故详情通报**工程师**。**承包商**应按**工程师**可能提出的合理要求，保持记录，并写出有关人员健康、安全和福利，以及财产损害等情况的报告。

6.8 **承包商的监督**	在**工程**实施过程中，以及其后为了完成**承包商**义务所需要的期间内，**承包商**应对工作的规划、安排、指导、管理、检验和试验，提供一切必要的监督。 此类监督应由足够的人员执行，他们应具有交流所用语言（**第1.4款**[**法律和语言**]所规定的）、以及合乎要求地、安全地实施**工程**各项作业所需的足够的知识（包括所需要的方法和技术、可能遇到的危险和预防事故的方法）。
6.9 **承包商人员**	**承包商人员**都应是在他们各自工种或职业内，具有相应资质、技能和经验的人员。**工程师**可要求**承包商**撤换（或促使撤换）受雇于**现场**或**工程**的，有下列行为的任何人员，适当时也包括**承包商代表**： (a) 经常行为不当，或工作漫不经心； (b) 无能力履行义务或玩忽职守； (c) 不遵守**合同**的任何规定；或 (d) 坚持有损安全、健康、或有损环境保护的行为。 如果适宜，**承包商**随后应指派（或促使指派）合适的替代人员。
6.10 **承包商人员和设备的记录**	**承包商**应向**工程师**提交说明**现场**各级**承包商人员**的人数和各类**承包商设备**数量的详细资料。应按**工程师**批准的格式，每月填报，直到**承包商**完成了**工程接收证书**上写明的竣工日期时的全部扫尾工作为止。
6.11 **无序行为**	**承包商**应始终采取各种合理的预防措施，防止**承包商人员**或其内部发生任何非法的、骚动的，或无序的行为，以保持安定，保护**现场**及邻近人员和财产的安全。

7 Plant Materials and Workmanship

7.1

Manner of Execution

The Contractor shall carry out the manufacture of Plant, the production and manufacture of Materials, and all other execution of the Works:

(a) in the manner (if any) specified in the Contract,

(b) in a proper workmanlike and careful manner, in accordance with recognised good practice, and

(c) with properly equipped facilities and non-hazardous Materials, except as otherwise specified in the Contract.

7.2

Samples

The Contractor shall submit the following samples of Materials, and relevant information, to the Engineer for consent prior to using the Materials in or for the Works:

(a) manufacturer's standard samples of Materials and samples specified in the Contract, all at the Contractor's cost, and

(b) additional samples instructed by the Engineer as a Variation.

Each sample shall be labelled as to origin and intended use in the Works.

7.3

Inspection

The Employer's Personnel shall at all reasonable times:

(a) have full access to all parts of the Site and to all places from which natural Materials are being obtained, and

(b) during production, manufacture and construction (at the Site and elsewhere), be entitled to examine, inspect, measure and test the materials and workmanship, and to check the progress of manufacture of Plant and production and manufacture of Materials.

The Contractor shall give the Employer's Personnel full opportunity to carry out these activities, including providing access, facilities, permissions and safety equipment. No such activity shall relieve the Contractor from any obligation or responsibility.

The Contractor shall give notice to the Engineer whenever any work is ready and before it is covered up, put out of sight, or packaged for storage or transport. The Engineer shall then either carry out the examination, inspection, measurement or testing without unreasonable delay, or promptly give notice to the Contractor that the Engineer does not require to do so. If the Contractor fails to give the notice, he shall, if and when required by the Engineer, uncover the work and thereafter reinstate and make good, all at the Contractor's cost.

7.4

Testing

This Sub-Clause shall apply to all tests specified in the Contract, other than the Tests after Completion (if any).

The Contractor shall provide all apparatus, assistance, documents and other information, electricity, equipment, fuel, consumables, instruments, labour, materials, and suitably qualified and experienced staff, as are necessary to carry out the specified tests efficiently. The Contractor shall agree, with the Engineer, the time and place for the specified testing of any Plant, Materials and other parts of the Works.

7 生产设备、材料和工艺

7.1
实施方法

承包商应按以下方法进行**生产设备**的制造，**材料**的生产加工，以及**工程**的所有其他实施作业：

(a) 按照**合同**规定的方法(如果有)；

(b) 按照公认的良好惯例，使用恰当、精巧和仔细的方法；以及

(c) 除**合同**另有规定外，使用适当配备的设施和无危险的材料。

7.2
样品

承包商应在**工程**中或为**工程**使用**材料**前，向**工程师**提交以下**材料**样品和有关资料，以取得其同意：

(a) 制造商的**材料**标准样品和**合同**规定的样品，均由**承包商**自费提供；以及

(b) **工程师**指示的作为**变更**的附加样品。

每种样品均应标明其原产地和在**工程**中的拟定用途。

7.3
检验

雇主人员应在所有合理的时间内：

(a) 有充分机会进入**现场**的所有部分、以及获得天然材料的所有地点；

(b) 有权在生产、加工和施工期间(在**现场**和其他地方)，检查、检验、测量和试验所用材料和工艺，检查**生产设备**的制造和**材料**的生产加工的进度。

承包商应为**雇主人员**进行上述活动提供一切机会，包括提供进入条件、设施、许可和安全装备。此类活动不应解除**承包商**的任何义务或职责。

每当任何工作已经做好，在覆盖、掩蔽、包装以便储存或运输前，**承包商**应通知**工程师**。这时，**工程师**应及时进行检查、检验、测量或试验，不得无故拖延，或立即通知**承包商**无需进行这些工作。如果**承包商**没有发出此类通知，而当**工程师**提出要求时，**承包商**应除去物件上的覆盖，并在随后恢复完好，全部费用由**承包商**承担。

7.4
试验

本款适用于**竣工后试验**(如果有)以外的合同规定的所有试验。

为有效进行规定的试验，**承包商**应提供所需的所有仪器、帮助、文件和其他资料、电力、装备、燃料、消耗品、工具、劳力、材料，以及具有适当资质和经验的工作人员。对任何**生产设备**、**材料**和**工程**其他部分进行规定的试验，其时间和地点，应由**承包商**与**工程师**商定。

The Engineer may, under Clause 13 [*Variations and Adjustments*], vary the location or details of specified tests, or instruct the Contractor to carry out additional tests. If these varied or additional tests show that the tested Plant, Materials or workmanship is not in accordance with the Contract, the cost of carrying out this Variation shall be borne by the Contractor, notwithstanding other provisions of the Contract.

The Engineer shall give the Contractor not less than 24 hours' notice of the Engineer's intention to attend the tests. If the Engineer does not attend at the time and place agreed, the Contractor may proceed with the tests, unless otherwise instructed by the Engineer, and the tests shall then be deemed to have been made in the Engineer's presence.

If the Contractor suffers delay and/or incurs Cost from complying with these instructions or as a result of a delay for which the Employer is responsible, the Contractor shall give notice to the Engineer and shall be entitled subject to Sub-Clause 20.1 [*Contractor's Claims*] to:

(a)   an extension of time for any such delay, if completion is or will be delayed, under Sub-Clause 8.4 [*Extension of Time for Completion*], and

(b)   payment of any such Cost plus reasonable profit, which shall be included in the Contract Price.

After receiving this notice, the Engineer shall proceed in accordance with Sub-Clause 3.5 [*Determinations*] to agree or determine these matters.

The Contractor shall promptly forward to the Engineer duly certified reports of the tests. When the specified tests have been passed, the Engineer shall endorse the Contractor's test certificate, or issue a certificate to him, to that effect. If the Engineer has not attended the tests, he shall be deemed to have accepted the readings as accurate.

7.5

Rejection

If, as a result of an examination, inspection, measurement or testing, any Plant, Materials or workmanship is found to be defective or otherwise not in accordance with the Contract, the Engineer may reject the Plant, Materials or workmanship by giving notice to the Contractor, with reasons. The Contractor shall then promptly make good the defect and ensure that the rejected item complies with the Contract.

If the Engineer requires this Plant, Materials or workmanship to be retested, the tests shall be repeated under the same terms and conditions. If the rejection and retesting cause the Employer to incur additional costs, the Contractor shall subject to Sub-Clause 2.5 [*Employer's Claims*] pay these costs to the Employer.

7.6

Remedial Work

Notwithstanding any previous test or certification, the Engineer may instruct the Contractor to:

(a)   remove from the Site and replace any Plant or Materials which is not in accordance with the Contract,

(b)   remove and re-execute any other work which is not in accordance with the Contract, and

(c)   execute any work which is urgently required for the safety of the Works, whether because of an accident, unforeseeable event or otherwise.

The Contractor shall comply with the instruction within a reasonable time, which shall be the time (if any) specified in the instruction, or immediately if urgency is specified under sub-paragraph (c).

根据第13条[变更和调整]的规定，工程师可以改变进行规定试验的位置或细节，或指示承包商进行附加的试验。如果这些改变的或附加的试验表明，经过试验的生产设备、材料或工艺不符合合同要求，不管合同有何其他规定，承包商应负担进行本项变更的费用。

工程师应至少提前24小时将参加试验的意图通知承包商。如果工程师没有在商定的时间和地点参加试验，除非工程师另有指示，承包商可自行进行试验，这些试验应被视为是在工程师在场情况下进行的。

如果由于服从这些指示或因雇主应负责的延误的结果，使承包商遭受延误和(或)招致增加费用，承包商应向工程师发出通知，并有权根据第20.1款[承包商的索赔]的规定要求：

(a) 根据第8.4款[竣工时间的延长]的规定，如果竣工已或将受到延误，对任何此类延误给予延长期；以及

(b) 任何此类费用加合理利润应计入合同价格，给予支付。

工程师收到此通知后，应按照第3.5款[确定]的规定，对这些事项进行商定或确定。

承包商应迅速向工程师提交充分证实的试验报告。当规定的试验通过时，工程师应在承包商的试验证书上签字，或向承包商颁发等效的证书。如果工程师未参加试验，他应被视为已经认可试验示数是准确的。

7.5
拒收

如果检查、检验、测量或试验结果，发现任何生产设备、材料或工艺有缺陷，或不符合合同要求，工程师可向承包商发出通知，并说明理由，拒收该生产设备、材料或工艺。承包商应迅速修复缺陷，并保证上述被拒收的项目符合合同规定。

如果工程师要求对上述生产设备、材料或工艺再次进行试验，这些试验应按相同的条款和条件重新进行。如果此项拒收和再次试验使雇主增加了费用，承包商应按照第2.5款[雇主的索赔]的规定，向雇主支付这笔费用。

7.6
修补工作

尽管已有先前的任何试验或证书，工程师仍可指示承包商进行以下工作：

(a) 将不符合合同要求的任何生产设备或材料移出现场，并进行更换；

(b) 去除不符合合同的任何其他工作，并重新实施；以及

(c) 实施因意外、不可预见的事件或其他原因引起的、为工程的安全迫切需要的任何工作。

承包商应在指示规定的合理时间(如果有)内执行该指示，或在上述(c)项规定的紧急情况下立即实施。

If the Contractor fails to comply with the instruction, the Employer shall be entitled to employ and pay other persons to carry out the work. Except to the extent that the Contractor would have been entitled to payment for the work, the Contractor shall subject to Sub-Clause 2.5 [*Employer's Claims*] pay to the Employer all costs arising from this failure.

7.7

Ownership of Plant and Materials

Each item of Plant and Materials shall, to the extent consistent with the Laws of the Country, become the property of the Employer at whichever is the earlier of the following times, free from liens and other encumbrances:

(a)   when it is delivered to the Site;
(b)   when the Contractor is entitled to payment of the value of the Plant and Materials under Sub-Clause 8.10 [*Payment for Plant and Materials in Event of Suspension*].

7.8

Royalties

Unless otherwise stated in the Specification, the Contractor shall pay all royalties, rents and other payments for:

(a)   natural Materials obtained from outside the Site, and
(b)   the disposal of material from demolitions and excavations and of other surplus material (whether natural or man-made), except to the extent that disposal areas within the Site are specified in the Contract.

8 Commencement, Delays and Suspension

8.1

Commencement of Works   The Engineer shall give the Contractor not less than 7 days' notice of the Commencement Date. Unless otherwise stated in the Particular Conditions, the Commencement Date shall be within 42 days after the Contractor receives the Letter of Acceptance.

The Contractor shall commence the execution of the Works as soon as is reasonably practicable after the Commencement Date, and shall then proceed with the Works with due expedition and without delay.

8.2

Time for Completion

The Contractor shall complete the whole of the Works, and each Section (if any), within the Time for Completion for the Works or Section (as the case may be), including:

(a)   achieving the passing of the Tests on Completion, and
(b)   completing all work which is stated in the Contract as being required for the Works or Section to be considered to be completed for the purposes of taking-over under Sub-Clause 10.1 [*Taking Over of the Works and Sections*].

8.3

Programme

The Contractor shall submit a detailed time programme to the Engineer within 28 days after receiving the notice under Sub-Clause 8.1 [*Commencement of Works*]. The Contractor shall also submit a revised programme whenever the previous programme is inconsistent with actual progress or with the Contractor's obligations. Each programme shall include:

如果**承包商**未能遵从指示，**雇主**有权雇用并付款给他人从事该工作。除**承包商**原有权从该工作所得付款的范围外，**承包商**应按照**第2.5款[雇主的索赔]**的规定，向**雇主****支付**因其未履行指示而使**雇主**支付的所有费用。

7.7

生产设备和材料的所有权

从下列二者中较早的时间起，在符合**工程所在国法律**规定的范围内，每项**生产设备**和**材料**都应无抵押权和其他阻碍地成为**雇主**的财产：

（a）当上述**生产设备**和**材料**运至**现场**时；
（b）当根据**第8.10款[暂停时对生产设备和材料的付款]**的规定，**承包商**有权得到按生产设备和材料价值的付款时。

7.8

土地(矿区)使用费

除非**规范要求**中另有说明，**承包商**应为以下事项支付所有的土地(矿区)使用费、租金和其他款项：

（a）从**现场**以外地区得到的天然**材料**；以及
（b）在**合同**规定的**现场**范围内的弃置地区以外，弃置拆除、开挖的材料和其他剩余材料(不论是天然的或人工的)。

---

8 开工、延误和暂停

8.1

工程的开工

工程师应在不少于7天前向**承包商**发出开工日期的通知。除非**专用条件**中另有说明，开工日期应在**承包商**收到**中标函**后42天内。

承包商应在开工日期后，在合理可能的情况下尽早开始工程的实施，随后应以正当速度，不拖延地进行工程。

8.2

竣工时间

承包商应在工程或单位工程(如果有)的**竣工时间**内，完成整个工程和每个单位工程(视情况而定)，包括：

（a）**竣工试验**获得通过；以及
（b）完成**合同**提出的，工程或单位工程按照**第10.1款[工程和单位工程的接收]**规定的接收要求竣工所需要的全部工作。

8.3

进度计划

承包商应在收到根据**第8.1款[工程的开工]**规定发出的通知后28天内，向**工程师**提交一份详细的进度计划。当原定进度计划与实际进度或**承包商**义务不相符时，**承包商**还应提交一份修订的进度计划。每份进度计划应包括：

(a) the order in which the Contractor intends to carry out the Works, including the anticipated timing of each stage of design (if any), Contractor's Documents, procurement, manufacture of Plant, delivery to Site, construction, erection and testing,

(b) each of these stages for work by each nominated Subcontractor (as defined in Clause 5 [*Nominated Subcontractors*]),

(c) the sequence and timing of inspections and tests specified in the Contract, and

(d) a supporting report which includes:

  (i) a general description of the methods which the Contractor intends to adopt, and of the major stages, in the execution of the Works, and

  (ii) details showing the Contractor's reasonable estimate of the number of each class of Contractor's Personnel and of each type of Contractor's Equipment, required on the Site for each major stage.

Unless the Engineer, within 21 days after receiving a programme, gives notice to the Contractor stating the extent to which it does not comply with the Contract, the Contractor shall proceed in accordance with the programme, subject to his other obligations under the Contract. The Employer's Personnel shall be entitled to rely upon the programme when planning their activities.

The Contractor shall promptly give notice to the Engineer of specific probable future events or circumstances which may adversely affect the work, increase the Contract Price or delay the execution of the Works. The Engineer may require the Contractor to submit an estimate of the anticipated effect of the future event or circumstances, and/or a proposal under Sub-Clause 13.3 [*Variation Procedure*].

If, at any time, the Engineer gives notice to the Contractor that a programme fails (to the extent stated) to comply with the Contract or to be consistent with actual progress and the Contractor's stated intentions, the Contractor shall submit a revised programme to the Engineer in accordance with this Sub-Clause.

8.4

Extension of Time for Completion

The Contractor shall be entitled subject to Sub-Clause 20.1 [*Contractor's Claims*] to an extension of the Time for Completion if and to the extent that completion for the purposes of Sub-Clause 10.1 [*Taking Over of the Works and Sections*] is or will be delayed by any of the following causes:

(a) a Variation (unless an adjustment to the Time for Completion has been agreed under Sub-Clause 13.3 [*Variation Procedure*]) or other substantial change in the quantity of an item of work included in the Contract,

(b) a cause of delay giving an entitlement to extension of time under a Sub-Clause of these Conditions,

(c) exceptionally adverse climatic conditions,

(d) Unforeseeable shortages in the availability of personnel or Goods caused by epidemic or governmental actions, or

(e) any delay, impediment or prevention caused by or attributable to the Employer, the Employer's Personnel, or the Employer's other contractors on the Site.

If the Contractor considers himself to be entitled to an extension of the Time for Completion, the Contractor shall give notice to the Engineer in accordance with Sub-Clause 20.1 [*Contractor's Claims*]. When determining each extension of time under Sub-Clause 20.1, the Engineer shall review previous determinations and may increase, but shall not decrease, the total extension of time.

(a) **承包商**计划实施**工程**的工作顺序,包括设计(如果有)、**承包商文件**、采购、**生产设备**的制造、运到**现场**、施工、安装和试验各个阶段的预期时间安排;

(b) 由各指定的**分包商**(按**第 5 条**[**指定的分包商**]定义)从事的以上各个阶段;

(c) **合同**中规定的各项检验和试验的顺序和时间安排;以及

(d) 一份支持报告,内容包括:

    (i) 在**工程**实施中各主要阶段和**承包商**拟采用的方法和各主要阶段一般描述;以及

    (ii) **承包商**对**工程**各主要阶段**现场**所需各级**承包商人员**和各类**承包商设备**合理估计数量的详细情况。

除非**工程师**在收到进度计划后 21 天内向**承包商**发出通知,指出其中不符合**合同**要求的部分,**承包商**即应按照该进度计划,并遵守**合同**规定的其他义务,进行工作。**雇主人员**应有权依照该进度计划安排他们的活动。

承包商应及时将未来可能对工作造成不利影响、增加**合同价格**、或延误**工程**施工的事件或情况,向**工程师**发出通知。**工程师**可要求**承包商**提交此类未来事件或情况预期影响的估计,和(或)根据**第 13.3 款**[**变更程序**]的规定提出建议。

如果任何时候**工程师**向**承包商**发出通知,指出进度计划(在指明的范围)不符合**合同**要求,或与实际进度和**承包商**提出的意向不一致时,**承包商**应按照**本款**向**工程师**提交一份修订进度计划。

8.4

竣工时间的延长

如果由于下列任何原因,致使达到**第 10.1 款**[**工程和单位工程的接收**]要求的竣工受到或将受到延误的程度,**承包商**应有权按照**第 20.1 款**[**承包商的索赔**]的规定提出延长竣工时间:

(a) **变更**(除非已根据**第 13.3 款**[**变更程序**]的规定,商定调整了**竣工时间**)或**合同**中某项工作量的显著变化;

(b) 根据本**条件**某款,有权获得延长期的原因;

(c) 异常不利的气候条件;

(d) 由于流行病或政府行为造成可用的人员或**货物**的**不可预见**的短缺;或

(e) 由**雇主**、**雇主人员**、或在**现场**的**雇主**的其他承包商造成或引起的任何延误、妨碍或阻碍。

如果**承包商**认为他有权提出延长竣工时间,应按照**第 20.1 款**[**承包商的索赔**]的规定,向**工程师**发出通知。**工程师**每次按照**第 20.1 款**确定延长时间时,应对以前所作的确定进行审查,可以增加,但不得减少总的延长时间。

8.5

Delays Caused by Authorities

If the following conditions apply, namely:

(a)   the Contractor has diligently followed the procedures laid down by the relevant legally constituted public authorities in the Country,

(b)   these authorities delay or disrupt the Contractor's work, and

(c)   the delay or disruption was Unforeseeable,

then this delay or disruption will be considered as a cause of delay under sub-paragraph (b) of Sub-Clause 8.4 [*Extension of Time for Completion*].

8.6

Rate of Progress

If, at any time:

(a)   actual progress is too slow to complete within the Time for Completion, and/or

(b)   progress has fallen (or will fall) behind the current programme under Sub-Clause 8.3 [*Programme*],

other than as a result of a cause listed in Sub-Clause 8.4 [*Extension of Time for Completion*], then the Engineer may instruct the Contractor to submit, under Sub-Clause 8.3 [*Programme*], a revised programme and supporting report describing the revised methods which the Contractor proposes to adopt in order to expedite progress and complete within the Time for Completion.

Unless the Engineer notifies otherwise, the Contractor shall adopt these revised methods, which may require increases in the working hours and/or in the numbers of Contractor's Personnel and/or Goods, at the risk and cost of the Contractor. If these revised methods cause the Employer to incur additional costs, the Contractor shall subject to Sub-Clause 2.5 [*Employer's Claims*] pay these costs to the Employer, in addition to delay damages (if any) under Sub-Clause 8.7 below.

8.7

Delay Damages

If the Contractor fails to comply with Sub-Clause 8.2 [*Time for Completion*], the Contractor shall subject to Sub-Clause 2.5 [*Employer's Claims*] pay delay damages to the Employer for this default. These delay damages shall be the sum stated in the Appendix to Tender, which shall be paid for every day which shall elapse between the relevant Time for Completion and the date stated in the Taking-Over Certificate. However, the total amount due under this Sub-Clause shall not exceed the maximum amount of delay damages (if any) stated in the Appendix to Tender.

These delay damages shall be the only damages due from the Contractor for such default, other than in the event of termination under Sub-Clause 15.2 [*Termination by Employer*] prior to completion of the Works. These damages shall not relieve the Contractor from his obligation to complete the Works, or from any other duties, obligations or responsibilities which he may have under the Contract.

8.8

Suspension of Work

The Engineer may at any time instruct the Contractor to suspend progress of part or all of the Works. During such suspension, the Contractor shall protect, store and secure such part or the Works against any deterioration, loss or damage.

The Engineer may also notify the cause for the suspension. If and to the extent that the cause is notified and is the responsibility of the Contractor, the following Sub-Clauses 8.9, 8.10 and 8.11 shall not apply.

| 8.5 | 如果符合下列条件，即： |
| 当局造成的延误 | |

(a) 承包商已努力遵守了工程所在国依法成立的有关公共当局所制定的程序；
(b) 这些当局延误或打乱了承包商的工作；以及
(c) 延误或中断是不可预见的；

则上述延误或中断可视为根据第8.4款[竣工时间的延长](b)项规定的延误原因。

8.6

工程进度

如果在任何时候：

(a) 实际工程进度对于在竣工时间内完工过于迟缓；和(或)
(b) 进度已(或将)落后于根据第8.3款[进度计划]的规定制订的现行进度计划；

除由于第8.4款[竣工时间的延长]中列举的某项原因造成的结果外，工程师可指示承包商根据第8.3款[进度计划]的规定提交一份修订的进度计划，以及说明承包商为加快进度在竣工时间内竣工，建议采用的修订方法的补充报告。

除非工程师另有通知，承包商应采取这些修订方法，对可能需要增加工时、和(或)承包商人员和(或)货物的数量，承包商应自行承担风险和费用。如果这些修订方法使雇主招致附加费用，承包商应按照第2.5款[雇主的索赔]的要求，连同下述第8.7款中提出的误期损害赔偿费(如果有)，向雇主支付这些费用。

8.7

误期损害赔偿费

如果承包商未能遵守第8.2款[竣工时间]的要求，承包商应当为其违约行为根据第2.5款[雇主的索赔]的要求，向雇主支付误期损害赔偿费。这些误期损害赔偿费应按投标书附录中规定的每天应付的金额，以接收证书注明的日期超过相应竣工时间的天数计算。但按本款计算的赔偿总额不得超过投标书附录中规定的误期损害赔偿费的最高限额(如果有)。

除在工程竣工前根据第15.2款[由雇主终止]的规定终止的情况外，这些误期损害赔偿费应是承包商为此类违约应付的唯一损害赔偿费。这些损害赔偿费不应解除承包商完成工程的义务，或合同规定的其可能承担的其他责任、义务或职责。

8.8

暂时停工

工程师可以随时指示承包商暂停工程某一部分或全部的施工。在暂停期间，承包商应保护、保管、并保证该部分或全部工程不致产生任何变质、损失或损害。

工程师还可通知暂停的原因。如果是已通知了原因，而且是由于承包商的职责造成的情况，则下列第8.9、8.10和8.11款应不适用。

**8.9
Consequences of
Suspension**

If the Contractor suffers delay and/or incurs Cost from complying with the Engineer's instructions under Sub-Clause 8.8 [*Suspension of Work*] and/or from resuming the work, the Contractor shall give notice to the Engineer and shall be entitled subject to Sub-Clause 20.1 [*Contractor's Claims*] to:

(a)   an extension of time for any such delay, if completion is or will be delayed, under Sub-Clause 8.4 [*Extension of Time for Completion*], and

(b)   payment of any such Cost, which shall be included in the Contract Price.

After receiving this notice, the Engineer shall proceed in accordance with Sub-Clause 3.5 [*Determinations*] to agree or determine these matters.

The Contractor shall not be entitled to an extension of time for, or to payment of the Cost incurred in, making good the consequences of the Contractor's faulty design, workmanship or materials, or of the Contractor's failure to protect, store or secure in accordance with Sub-Clause 8.8 [*Suspension of Work*].

**8.10

Payment for Plant and
Materials in Event of
Suspension**

The Contractor shall be entitled to payment of the value (as at the date of suspension) of Plant and/or Materials which have not been delivered to Site, if:

(a)   the work on Plant or delivery of Plant and/or Materials has been suspended for more than 28 days, and

(b)   the Contractor has marked the Plant and/or Materials as the Employer's property in accordance with the Engineer's instructions.

**8.11

Prolonged Suspension**

If the suspension under Sub-Clause 8.8 [*Suspension of Work*] has continued for more than 84 days, the Contractor may request the Engineer's permission to proceed. If the Engineer does not give permission within 28 days after being requested to do so, the Contractor may, by giving notice to the Engineer, treat the suspension as an omission under Clause 13 [*Variations and Adjustments*] of the affected part of the Works. If the suspension affects the whole of the Works, the Contractor may give notice of termination under Sub-Clause 16.2 [*Termination by Contractor*].

**8.12

Resumption of Work**

After the permission or instruction to proceed is given, the Contractor and the Engineer shall jointly examine the Works and the Plant and Materials affected by the suspension. The Contractor shall make good any deterioration or defect in or loss of the Works or Plant or Materials, which has occurred during the suspension.

9 Tests on Completion

**9.1
Contractor's Obligations**

The Contractor shall carry out the Tests on Completion in accordance with this Clause and Sub-Clause 7.4 [*Testing*], after providing the documents in accordance with sub-paragraph (d) of Sub-Clause 4.1 [*Contractor's General Obligations*].

The Contractor shall give to the Engineer not less than 21 days' notice of the date after which the Contractor will be ready to carry out each of the Tests on Completion. Unless otherwise agreed, Tests on Completion shall be carried out within 14 days after this date, on such day or days as the Engineer shall instruct.

In considering the results of the Tests on Completion, the Engineer shall make

8.9 暂停的后果	如果**承包商**因执行**工程师**根据**第8.8款**[**暂时停工**]的规定发出的指示，和(或)因为复工而遭受延误和(或)招致增加**费用**，**承包商**应向**工程师**发出通知，有权根据**第20.1款**[**承包商的索赔**]的规定要求：

(a) 根据**第8.4款**[**竣工时间的延长**]的规定，如竣工已或将受到延误，对任何此类延误给予延长期；以及

(b) 任何此类**费用**应计入**合同价格**，给予支付。

工程师收到此通知后，应按照**第3.5款**[**确定**]的要求，对这些事项进行商定或确定。

为弥补因**承包商**有缺陷的设计、工艺或材料，或因**承包商**未能按照**第8.8款**[**暂时停工**]的规定保护、保管或保证安全而带来的后果，**承包商**无权得到由其带来的延长期或招致**费用**的支付。

8.10 暂停时对生产设备和材料的付款	在下列条件下，**承包商**有权得到尚未运到**现场**的**生产设备**和(或)**材料**(按暂停开始的日期时)的价值的付款：

(a) **生产设备**的生产或**生产设备**和(或)**材料**的交付被暂停达28天以上；以及

(b) **承包商**已按**工程师**的指示，标明上述**生产设备**和(或)**材料**为**雇主**的财产。

8.11 拖长的暂停	如果**第8.8款**[**暂时停工**]所述的暂停已持续84天以上，**承包商**可以要求**工程师**允许继续施工。如在提出这一要求后28天内**工程师**没有给出许可，**承包商**可以通知**工程师**，将**工程**受暂停影响的部分视为根据**第13条**[**变更和调整**]规定的删减项目。如果暂停影响到整个**工程**，**承包商**可以根据**第16.2款**[**由承包商终止**]的规定发出终止的通知。

8.12 复工	在发出继续施工的许可或指示后，**承包商**和**工程师**应共同对受暂停影响的**工程**、**生产设备**和**材料**进行检查。**承包商**应负责修复在暂停期间发生的**工程**、**生产设备**或**材料**中的任何变质、缺陷或损失。

9 竣工试验

9.1 承包商的义务	**承包商**应在按照**第4.1款**[**承包商的一般义务**](d)项的规定，提供各种文件后，按照**本条**和**第7.4款**[**试验**]的要求进行**竣工试验**。

承包商应提前21天将他可以进行每项**竣工试验**的日期通知**工程师**。除非另有商定，**竣工试验**应在此通知日期后的14天内，在**工程师**指示的某日或某几日内进行。

工程师在考虑**竣工试验**结果时，应考虑到因**雇主**对**工程**的任何使用，对**工程**

allowances for the effect of any use of the Works by the Employer on the performance or other characteristics of the Works. As soon as the Works, or a Section, have passed any Tests on Completion, the Contractor shall submit a certified report of the results of these Tests to the Engineer.

9.2

Delayed Tests

If the Tests on Completion are being unduly delayed by the Employer, Sub-Clause 7.4 [*Testing*] (fifth paragraph) and/or Sub-Clause 10.3 [*Interference with Tests on Completion*] shall be applicable.

If the Tests on Completion are being unduly delayed by the Contractor, the Engineer may by notice require the Contractor to carry out the Tests within 21 days after receiving the notice. The Contractor shall carry out the Tests on such day or days within that period as the Contractor may fix and of which he shall give notice to the Engineer.

If the Contractor fails to carry out the Tests on Completion within the period of 21 days, the Employer's Personnel may proceed with the Tests at the risk and cost of the Contractor. The Tests on Completion shall then be deemed to have been carried out in the presence of the Contractor and the results of the Tests shall be accepted as accurate.

9.3

Retesting

If the Works, or a Section, fail to pass the Tests on Completion, Sub-Clause 7.5 [*Rejection*] shall apply, and the Engineer or the Contractor may require the failed Tests, and Tests on Completion on any related work, to be repeated under the same terms and conditions.

9.4

Failure to Pass Tests on Completion

If the Works, or a Section, fail to pass the Tests on Completion repeated under Sub-Clause 9.3 [*Retesting*], the Engineer shall be entitled to:

(a) order further repetition of Tests on Completion under Sub-Clause 9.3;
(b) if the failure deprives the Employer of substantially the whole benefit of the Works or Section, reject the Works or Section (as the case may be), in which event the Employer shall have the same remedies as are provided in sub-paragraph (c) of Sub-Clause 11.4 [*Failure to Remedy Defects*]; or
(c) issue a Taking-Over Certificate, if the Employer so requests.

In the event of sub-paragraph (c), the Contractor shall proceed in accordance with all other obligations under the Contract, and the Contract Price shall be reduced by such amount as shall be appropriate to cover the reduced value to the Employer as a result of this failure. Unless the relevant reduction for this failure is stated (or its method of calculation is defined) in the Contract, the Employer may require the reduction to be (i) agreed by both Parties (in full satisfaction of this failure only) and paid before this Taking-Over Certificate is issued, or (ii) determined and paid under Sub-Clause 2.5 [*Employer's Claims*] and Sub-Clause 3.5 [*Determinations*].

10 Employer's Taking Over

10.1

Taking Over of the Works and Sections

Except as stated in Sub-Clause 9.4 [*Failure to Pass Tests on Completion*], the Works shall be taken over by the Employer when (i) the Works have been completed in accordance with the Contract, including the matters described in Sub-Clause 8.2 [*Time for Completion*] and except as allowed in sub-paragraph (a) below, and (ii) a

的性能或其他特性的影响。一旦**工程**或某**单位工程**通过了**竣工试验**，**承包商**应向**工程师**提供一份经证实的这些试验结果的报告。

9.2

延误的试验

如果**雇主**不当地延误**竣工试验**，应适用**第 7.4 款**[**试验**]（第 5 段）和（或）**第 10.3 款**[**对竣工试验的干扰**]的规定。

如果**承包商**不当地延误了**竣工试验**，**工程师**可通知**承包商**，要求在接到通知后 21 天内进行**竣工试验**。**承包商**应在上述期限内他能确定的某日或某几日内进行**竣工试验**，并将该日期通知**工程师**。

如果**承包商**未在规定的 21 天内进行**竣工试验**，**雇主人员**可自行进行这些试验，试验的风险和费用应由**承包商**承担。这些**竣工试验**应被视为是**承包商**在场时进行的，试验结果应认为准确，予以认可。

9.3

重新试验

如果**工程**或某**单位工程**未能通过**竣工试验**，应适用**第 7.5 款**[**拒收**]的规定，**工程师**或**承包商**可要求按相同的条款和条件，重新进行此项未通过的试验和相关工程的**竣工试验**。

9.4

未能通过竣工试验

如果**工程**或某**单位工程**未能通过根据**第 9.3 款**[**重新试验**]的规定重新进行的**竣工试验**，**工程师**应有权：

(a) 下令根据**第 9.3 款**[**重新试验**]再次重复**竣工试验**；

(b) 如果此项试验未通过，使**雇主**实质上丧失了**工程**或**单位工程**的整个利益时，拒收**工程**或**单位工程**（视情况而定），在此情况下，**雇主**应采取与**第 11.4 款**[**未能修补缺陷**](c)项规定的相同的补救措施；或

(c) 如果**雇主**要求，颁发**接收证书**。

在采用(c)项办法的情况下，**承包商**应继续履行**合同**规定的所有其他义务，但**合同价格**应予减少，减少的金额应足以弥补此项试验未通过的后果给**雇主**带来的价值损失。除非对此项试验未通过相应减少的**合同价格**在**合同**中另有说明（或规定了计算方法），**雇主**可以要求该减少额要(i)经双方商定（仅限于满足此项试验未通过的要求），并在此项**接收证书**颁发前支付，或(ii)根据**第 2.5 款**[**雇主的索赔**]和**第 3.5 款**[**确定**]的规定，确定并支付。

10 雇主的接收

10.1

工程和单位工程的接收

除**第9.4款**[**未能通过竣工试验**]中所述情况外，当(i)除下面(a)项允许的情况以外，**工程**已按**合同**规定，包括**第8.2款**[**竣工时间**]中提出的事项竣

Taking-Over Certificate for the Works has been issued, or is deemed to have been issued in accordance with this Sub-Clause.

The Contractor may apply by notice to the Engineer for a Taking-Over Certificate not earlier than 14 days before the Works will, in the Contractor's opinion, be complete and ready for taking over. If the Works are divided into Sections, the Contractor may similarly apply for a Taking-Over Certificate for each Section.

The Engineer shall, within 28 days after receiving the Contractor's application:

(a)   issue the Taking-Over Certificate to the Contractor, stating the date on which the Works or Section were completed in accordance with the Contract, except for any minor outstanding work and defects which will not substantially affect the use of the Works or Section for their intended purpose (either until or whilst this work is completed and these defects are remedied); or

(b)   reject the application, giving reasons and specifying the work required to be done by the Contractor to enable the Taking-Over Certificate to be issued. The Contractor shall then complete this work before issuing a further notice under this Sub-Clause.

If the Engineer fails either to issue the Taking-Over Certificate or to reject the Contractor's application within the period of 28 days, and if the Works or Section (as the case may be) are substantially in accordance with the Contract, the Taking-Over Certificate shall be deemed to have been issued on the last day of that period.

10.2

**Taking Over
of Parts of the Works**

The Engineer may, at the sole discretion of the Employer, issue a Taking-Over Certificate for any part of the Permanent Works.

The Employer shall not use any part of the Works (other than as a temporary measure which is either specified in the Contract or agreed by both Parties) unless and until the Engineer has issued a Taking-Over Certificate for this part. However, if the Employer does use any part of the Works before the Taking-Over Certificate is issued:

(a)   the part which is used shall be deemed to have been taken over as from the date on which it is used,

(b)   the Contractor shall cease to be liable for the care of such part as from this date, when responsibility shall pass to the Employer, and

(c)   if requested by the Contractor, the Engineer shall issue a Taking-Over Certificate for this part.

After the Engineer has issued a Taking-Over Certificate for a part of the Works, the Contractor shall be given the earliest opportunity to take such steps as may be necessary to carry out any outstanding Tests on Completion. The Contractor shall carry out these Tests on Completion as soon as practicable before the expiry date of the relevant Defects Notification Period.

If the Contractor incurs Cost as a result of the Employer taking over and/or using a part of the Works, other than such use as is specified in the Contract or agreed by the Contractor, the Contractor shall (i) give notice to the Engineer and (ii) be entitled subject to Sub-Clause 20.1 [*Contractor's Claims*] to payment of any such Cost plus reasonable profit, which shall be included in the Contract Price. After receiving this notice, the Engineer shall proceed in accordance with Sub-Clause 3.5 [*Determinations*] to agree or determine this Cost and profit.

工；(ii)已按照本**款**规定颁发**工程接收证书**，或被视为已颁发时，**雇主**应接收工程。

承包商可在他认为工程将竣工并做好接收准备的日期前不少于 14 天，向**工程师**发出申请**接收证书**的通知。如工程分成若干单位工程，**承包商**可类似地为每个单位工程申请**接收证书**。

工程师在收到**承包商**的申请通知后 28 天内，应：

(a)　向**承包商**颁发**接收证书**，注明**工程**或单位工程按照**合同**要求竣工的日期，任何对**工程**或单位工程预期使用目的没有实质影响的少量收尾工作和缺陷(直到或当收尾工作和缺陷修补完成时)除外；或

(b)　拒绝申请，说明理由，并指出在能颁发**接收证书**前**承包商**需做的工作。**承包商**应在再次根据本**款**发生申请通知前，完成此项工作。

如果**工程师**在 28 天期限内既未颁发**接收证书**，又未拒绝**承包商**的申请，而**工程**或单位工程(视情况而定)实质上符合**合同**规定，**接收证书**应视为已在上述规定期限的最后一日颁发。

10.2

部分工程的接收

在**雇主**完全自主决定情况下，**工程师**可颁发**永久工程**任何部分的**接收证书**。

除非并直到**工程师**已颁发任何部分工程的**接收证书**，**雇主**不得使用该部分工程(除**合同**规定或经**双方**同意作为临时措施外)。但是，如果**雇主**在颁发**接收证书**前确实使用了任何部分工程，则：

(a)　使用的部分应视为从开始使用的日期起已被接收；

(b)　**承包商**应从此日起不再承担该部分的照管责任，应转由**雇主**负责；以及

(c)　如**承包商**提出要求，**工程师**应颁发该部分的**接收证书**。

工程师颁发部分工程的**接收证书**后，应使**承包商**能尽早采取可能必要的步骤，进行任何尚未完成的**竣工试验**。**承包商**应在有关**缺陷通知期限**期满日期前，尽快进行这些**竣工试验**。

除**合同**规定或**承包商**同意使用的以外，如果由于**雇主**接收和(或)使用部分工程，导致**承包商**增加费用，**承包商**应(i)向**工程师**发出通知，并(ii)有权要求按照**第 20.1 款**[**承包商的索赔**]的规定，对任何此类**费用**和合理利润应计入**合同价格**，给予支付。**工程师**收到此通知后，应按照**第 3.5 款**[**确定**]的规定，对此项**费用**和利润，进行商定或确定。

If a Taking-Over Certificate has been issued for a part of the Works (other than a Section), the delay damages thereafter for completion of the remainder of the Works shall be reduced. Similarly, the delay damages for the remainder of the Section (if any) in which this part is included shall also be reduced. For any period of delay after the date stated in this Taking-Over Certificate, the proportional reduction in these delay damages shall be calculated as the proportion which the value of the part so certified bears to the value of the Works or Section (as the case may be) as a whole. The Engineer shall proceed in accordance with Sub-Clause 3.5 [*Determinations*] to agree or determine these proportions. The provisions of this paragraph shall only apply to the daily rate of delay damages under Sub-Clause 8.7 [*Delay Damages*], and shall not affect the maximum amount of these damages.

10.3

Interference with Tests on Completion

If the Contractor is prevented, for more than 14 days, from carrying out the Tests on Completion by a cause for which the Employer is responsible, the Employer shall be deemed to have taken over the Works or Section (as the case may be) on the date when the Tests on Completion would otherwise have been completed.

The Engineer shall then issue a Taking-Over Certificate accordingly, and the Contractor shall carry out the Tests on Completion as soon as practicable, before the expiry date of the Defects Notification Period. The Engineer shall require the Tests on Completion to be carried out by giving 14 days' notice and in accordance with the relevant provisions of the Contract.

If the Contractor suffers delay and/or incurs Cost as a result of this delay in carrying out the Tests on Completion, the Contractor shall give notice to the Engineer and shall be entitled subject to Sub-Clause 20.1 [*Contractor's Claims*] to:

(a) an extension of time for any such delay, if completion is or will be delayed, under Sub-Clause 8.4 [*Extension of Time for Completion*], and
(b) payment of any such Cost plus reasonable profit, which shall be included in the Contract Price.

After receiving this notice, the Engineer shall proceed in accordance with Sub-Clause 3.5 [*Determinations*] to agree or determine these matters.

10.4

Surfaces Requiring Reinstatement

Except as otherwise stated in a Taking-Over Certificate, a certificate for a Section or part of the Works shall not be deemed to certify completion of any ground or other surfaces requiring reinstatement.

11 Defects Liability

11.1
Completion of Outstanding Work and Remedying Defects

In order that the Works and Contractor's Documents, and each Section, shall be in the condition required by the Contract (fair wear and tear excepted) by the expiry date of the relevant Defects Notification Period or as soon as practicable thereafter, the Contractor shall:

(a) complete any work which is outstanding on the date stated in a Taking-Over Certificate, within such reasonable time as is instructed by the Engineer, and
(b) execute all work required to remedy defects or damage, as may be notified by (or on behalf of) the Employer on or before the expiry date of the Defects Notification Period for the Works or Section (as the case may be).

如果已经颁发了部分工程(不是单位工程)的**接收证书**,此后工程剩余部分的竣工误期损害赔偿费应予减少。与此类似,包括该部分的**单位工程**(如果有)的剩余部分的误期损害赔偿费也应减少。对**接收证书**注明日期以后的任何延误期,这些误期损害赔偿费的比例减少额,应按已颁发证书部分的价值,占整个工程或单位工程(视情况而定)价值的比例计算。**工程师**应按照**第3.5款**[**确定**]的规定,对这些比例进行商定或确定。本段的规定仅适用于**第8.7款**[**误期损害赔偿费**]规定的误期损害赔偿费的每日费率,不应影响该损害赔偿费的最高限额。

10.3

对竣工试验的干扰

如果由于**雇主**应负责的原因妨碍**承包商**进行**竣工试验**达14天以上,**雇主**应被视为已在**竣工试验**原应完成的日期接收了**工程**或**单位工程**(视情况而定)。

这时**工程师**应相应地颁发**接收证书**,**承包商**应在**缺陷通知期限**期满日期前,尽快进行**竣工试验**。**工程师**应要求**竣工试验**要提前14天发出通知,并按照**合同**中的有关规定进行。

如果由于进行**竣工试验**的此项延误,使**承包商**遭受延误和(或)招致增加**费用**,**承包商**应向**工程师**发出通知,并应有权根据**第20.1款**[**承包商的索赔**]的规定要求:

(a) 根据**第8.4款**[**竣工时间的延长**]的规定,如竣工已或将受到延误,对任何此类延误给予延长期;以及

(b) 任何此类**费用**加合理利润,应计入**合同价格**,给予支付。

工程师收到此通知后,应按照**第3.5款**[**确定**]的规定,对这些事项进行商定或确定。

10.4

需要复原的地面

除**接收证书**中另有说明外,**单位工程**或**部分工程**的**接收证书**,不应视为任何需要复原的场地或其他地面已经完成的证明。

---

11 缺陷责任

11.1
完成扫尾工作和修补缺陷

为了使**工程**、**承包商**文件和每个**单位工程**在相应**缺陷通知期限**期满日期或其后,尽快达到**合同**要求(合理的损耗除外),**承包商**应:

(a) 在**工程师**指示的合理时间内,完成**接收证书**注明日期时尚未完成的任何工作;以及

(b) 在**工程**或**单位工程**(视情况而定)的**缺陷通知期限**期满日期或其以前,按照**雇主**(或其代表)可能通知的要求,完成修补缺陷或损害所需的所有工作。

If a defect appears or damage occurs, the Contractor shall be notified accordingly, by (or on behalf of) the Employer.

11.2

Cost of Remedying Defects

All work referred to in sub-paragraph (b) of Sub-Clause 11.1 [*Completion of Outstanding Work and Remedying Defects*] shall be executed at the risk and cost of the Contractor, if and to the extent that the work is attributable to:

(a)   any design for which the Contractor is responsible,

(b)   Plant, Materials or workmanship not being in accordance with the Contract, or

(c)   failure by the Contractor to comply with any other obligation.

If and to the extent that such work is attributable to any other cause, the Contractor shall be notified promptly by (or on behalf of) the Employer, and Sub-Clause 13.3 [*Variation Procedure*] shall apply.

11.3

Extension of Defects Notification Period

The Employer shall be entitled subject to Sub-Clause 2.5 [*Employer's Claims*] to an extension of the Defects Notification Period for the Works or a Section if and to the extent that the Works, Section or a major item of Plant (as the case may be, and after taking over) cannot be used for the purposes for which they are intended by reason of a defect or damage. However, a Defects Notification Period shall not be extended by more than two years.

If delivery and/or erection of Plant and/or Materials was suspended under Sub-Clause 8.8 [*Suspension of Work*] or Sub-Clause 16.1 [*Contractor's Entitlement to Suspend Work*], the Contractor's obligations under this Clause shall not apply to any defects or damage occurring more than two years after the Defects Notification Period for the Plant and/or Materials would otherwise have expired.

11.4

Failure to Remedy Defects

If the Contractor fails to remedy any defect or damage within a reasonable time, a date may be fixed by (or on behalf of) the Employer, on or by which the defect or damage is to be remedied. The Contractor shall be given reasonable notice of this date.

If the Contractor fails to remedy the defect or damage by this notified date and this remedial work was to be executed at the cost of the Contractor under Sub-Clause 11.2 [*Cost of Remedying Defects*], the Employer may (at his option):

(a)   carry out the work himself or by others, in a reasonable manner and at the Contractor's cost, but the Contractor shall have no responsibility for this work; and the Contractor shall subject to Sub-Clause 2.5 [*Employer's Claims*] pay to the Employer the costs reasonably incurred by the Employer in remedying the defect or damage;

(b)   require the Engineer to agree or determine a reasonable reduction in the Contract Price in accordance with Sub-Clause 3.5 [*Determinations*]; or

(c)   if the defect or damage deprives the Employer of substantially the whole benefit of the Works or any major part of the Works, terminate the Contract as a whole, or in respect of such major part which cannot be put to the intended use. Without prejudice to any other rights, under the Contract or otherwise, the Employer shall then be entitled to recover all sums paid for the Works or for such part (as the case may be), plus financing costs and the cost of dismantling the same, clearing the Site and returning Plant and Materials to the Contractor.

如果出现缺陷或发生损害，**雇主**(或其代表)应相应地通知**承包商**。

11.2

修补缺陷的费用

第 **11.1 款**[**完成扫尾工作和修补缺陷**]的(b)项中提出的所有工作，如果在归因于以下原因的范围，其实施中的风险和费用应由**承包商**承担：

(a) **承包商**负责的设计；
(b) **生产设备**、**材料**或工艺不符合**合同**要求；或

(c) **承包商**未能遵守任何其他义务。

如果此类工作在归因于任何其他原因的范围，**雇主**(或其代表)应迅速通知**承包商**，并应适用**第 13.3 款**[**变更程序**]的规定。

11.3

缺陷通知期限的延长

如果因为某项缺陷或损害达到使**工程**、**单位工程**或某项主要**生产设备**(视情况而定,并在接收以后)不能按原定目的使用的程度，**雇主**应有权根据**第 2.5 款**[**雇主的索赔**]的规定，对**工程**或某一**单位工程**的**缺陷通知期限**提出延长期。但**缺陷通知期限**的延长不得超过两年。

当**生产设备**和(或)**材料**的交付和(或)安装，已根据**第 8.8 款**[**暂时停工**]或**第 16.1 款**[**承包商暂停工作的权利**]的规定暂停进行时，对于**生产设备**和(或)**材料**的**缺陷通知期限**原期满日期两年后发生的任何缺陷或损害，本条规定的**承包商**各项义务应不适用。

11.4

未能修补缺陷

如果**承包商**未能在合理的时间内修补任何缺陷或损害，**雇主**(或其代表)可确定一个日期，要求到或不迟于该日期修补好缺陷和损害。应将该日期向**承包商**发出合理的通知。

如果**承包商**到该通知的日期仍未修补好缺陷或损害，且此项修补工作根据**第 11.2 款**[**修补缺陷的费用**]的规定，应由**承包商**承担实施的费用，**雇主**可以(自行选择)：

(a) 以合理的方式由他自己或他人进行此项工作，由**承包商**承担费用，但**承包商**对此项工作将不再负责任；**承包商**应按照**第 2.5 款**[**雇主的索赔**]的规定向**雇主**支付由**雇主**修补缺陷或损害而发生的合理费用；

(b) 要求**工程师**按照**第 3.5 款**[**确定**]的规定，商定或确定**合同价格**的合理减少额；或

(c) 如果缺陷或损害使**雇主**实质上丧失了**工程**或工程的任何主要部分的整个利益时，终止整个**合同**、或其有关不能按原定意图使用的该主要部分。**雇主**还应有权在不损害根据**合同**或其他规定所具有的任何其他权利的情况下，收回对**工程**或该部分工程(视情况而定)的全部支出总额，加上融资费用和拆除**工程**、清理**现场**、以及将**生产设备和材料**退还给**承包商**所支付的费用。

11.5

Removal of Defective Work

If the defect or damage cannot be remedied expeditiously on the Site and the Employer gives consent, the Contractor may remove from the Site for the purposes of repair such items of Plant as are defective or damaged. This consent may require the Contractor to increase the amount of the Performance Security by the full replacement cost of these items, or to provide other appropriate security.

11.6

Further Tests

If the work of remedying of any defect or damage may affect the performance of the Works, the Engineer may require the repetition of any of the tests described in the Contract. The requirement shall be made by notice within 28 days after the defect or damage is remedied.

These tests shall be carried out in accordance with the terms applicable to the previous tests, except that they shall be carried out at the risk and cost of the Party liable, under Sub-Clause 11.2 [*Cost of Remedying Defects*], for the cost of the remedial work.

11.7

Right of Access

Until the Performance Certificate has been issued, the Contractor shall have such right of access to the Works as is reasonably required in order to comply with this Clause, except as may be inconsistent with the Employer's reasonable security restrictions.

11.8

Contractor to Search

The Contractor shall, if required by the Engineer, search for the cause of any defect, under the direction of the Engineer. Unless the defect is to be remedied at the cost of the Contractor under Sub-Clause 11.2 [*Cost of Remedying Defects*], the Cost of the search plus reasonable profit shall be agreed or determined by the Engineer in accordance with Sub-Clause 3.5 [*Determinations*] and shall be included in the Contract Price.

11.9

Performance Certificate

Performance of the Contractor's obligations shall not be considered to have been completed until the Engineer has issued the Performance Certificate to the Contractor, stating the date on which the Contractor completed his obligations under the Contract.

The Engineer shall issue the Performance Certificate within 28 days after the latest of the expiry dates of the Defects Notification Periods, or as soon thereafter as the Contractor has supplied all the Contractor's Documents and completed and tested all the Works, including remedying any defects. A copy of the Performance Certificate shall be issued to the Employer.

Only the Performance Certificate shall be deemed to constitute acceptance of the Works.

11.10

Unfulfilled Obligations

After the Performance Certificate has been issued, each Party shall remain liable for the fulfilment of any obligation which remains unperformed at that time. For the purposes of determining the nature and extent of unperformed obligations, the Contract shall be deemed to remain in force.

11.11

Clearance of Site

Upon receiving the Performance Certificate, the Contractor shall remove any remaining Contractor's Equipment, surplus material, wreckage, rubbish and Temporary Works from the Site.

If all these items have not been removed within 28 days after the Employer receives a copy of the Performance Certificate, the Employer may sell or

11.5 **移出有缺陷的工程**	如果缺陷或损害在**现场**无法迅速修复，**承包商**可经**雇主**同意，将此类有缺陷或损害的各项**生产设备**移出**现场**进行修复。**雇主**此项同意可要求**承包商**按该项设备的全部重置成本，增加**履约担保**的金额，或提供其他适宜的担保。
11.6 **进一步试验**	如果任何缺陷或损害的修补可能对**工程**的性能产生影响，**工程师**可要求重新进行**合同**提出的任何试验。此要求应在该缺陷或损害修补后 28 天内发出通知提出。
	这些试验，除应根据**第 11.2 款**[**修补缺陷的费用**]的规定，由对修补费用负责的一方承担风险和费用外，应按适用于先前试验的条款进行。
11.7 **进入权**	在颁发**履约证书**前，**承包商**应有为遵照本条要求而合理需要的工程进入权，但不符合**雇主**的合理保安限制的情况除外。
11.8 **承包商调查**	如果工程师要求调查任何缺陷的原因，**承包商**应在工程师的指导下进行调查。除非根据**第 11.2 款**[**修补缺陷的费用**]的规定，应由**承包商**承担修补费用的情况，调查**费用**加合理利润，应由**工程师**按照**第 3.5 款**[**确定**]的要求商定或确定，并计入**合同价格**。
11.9 **履约证书**	直到工程师向**承包商**颁发**履约证书**，注明**承包商**完成**合同**规定的各项义务的日期后，才应认为**承包商**的义务已经完成。
	履约证书应由工程师在最后一个**缺陷通知期限**期满日期后 28 天内颁发，或在**承包商**提供所有**承包商文件**，完成所有**工程**的施工和试验，包括修补任何缺陷后尽快颁发。**履约证书**应抄送**雇主**。
	只有**履约证书**应被视为构成对**工程**的认可。
11.10 **未履行的义务**	颁发**履约证书**后，每一方仍应负责完成当时尚未履行的任何义务。为了确定这些未完义务的性质和范围，**合同**应被视为仍然有效。
11.11 **现场清理**	在收到**履约证书**时，**承包商**应从**现场**撤走任何剩余的**承包商设备**、多余材料、残余物、垃圾和临时工程等。
	如果所有这些物品，在**雇主**收到**履约证书**副本后 28 天内，尚未被运走，**雇**

otherwise dispose of any remaining items. The Employer shall be entitled to be paid the costs incurred in connection with, or attributable to, such sale or disposal and restoring the Site.

Any balance of the moneys from the sale shall be paid to the Contractor. If these moneys are less than the Employer's costs, the Contractor shall pay the outstanding balance to the Employer.

12 Measurement and Evaluation

12.1

Works to be Measured

The Works shall be measured, and valued for payment, in accordance with this Clause.

Whenever the Engineer requires any part of the Works to be measured, reasonable notice shall be given to the Contractor's Representative, who shall:

(a) promptly either attend or send another qualified representative to assist the Engineer in making the measurement, and

(b) supply any particulars requested by the Engineer.

If the Contractor fails to attend or send a representative, the measurement made by (or on behalf of) the Engineer shall be accepted as accurate.

Except as otherwise stated in the Contract, wherever any Permanent Works are to be measured from records, these shall be prepared by the Engineer. The Contractor shall, as and when requested, attend to examine and agree the records with the Engineer, and shall sign the same when agreed. If the Contractor does not attend, the records shall be accepted as accurate.

If the Contractor examines and disagrees the records, and/or does not sign them as agreed, then the Contractor shall give notice to the Engineer of the respects in which the records are asserted to be inaccurate. After receiving this notice, the Engineer shall review the records and either confirm or vary them. If the Contractor does not so give notice to the Engineer within 14 days after being requested to examine the records, they shall be accepted as accurate.

12.2

Method of Measurement

Except as otherwise stated in the Contract and notwithstanding local practice:

(a) measurement shall be made of the net actual quantity of each item of the Permanent Works, and

(b) the method of measurement shall be in accordance with the Bill of Quantities or other applicable Schedules.

12.3

Evaluation

Except as otherwise stated in the Contract, the Engineer shall proceed in accordance with Sub-Clause 3.5 [*Determinations*] to agree or determine the Contract Price by evaluating each item of work, applying the measurement agreed or determined in accordance with the above Sub-Clauses 12.1 and 12.2 and the appropriate rate or price for the item.

For each item of work, the appropriate rate or price for the item shall be the rate or price specified for such item in the Contract or, if there is no such item, specified for similar work. However, a new rate or price shall be appropriate for an item of work if:

主可以出售或另行处理任何这些剩余物品。**雇主**应有权收回有关或由于此类出售或处理、以及恢复**现场**所发生的费用。

此类出售的余款应付给**承包商**。如果出售收入少于**雇主**支出的费用，**承包商**应将差额付给**雇主**。

12 测量和估价

12.1
需测量的工程

为了付款，应按照本**条**规定对**工程**进行测量和估价。

当**工程师**要求测量**工程**任何部分时，应向**承包商代表**发出合理通知，**承包商代表**应：

(a) 及时亲自或另派合格代表，协助**工程师**进行测量；以及

(b) 提供**工程师**要求的任何具体资料。

如果**承包商**未能到场或派代表，**工程师**(或其代表)所作测量应作为准确予以认可。

除**合同**另有规定外，凡需根据记录进行测量的任何**永久工程**，此类记录应由**工程师**准备。**承包商**应按并在要求时，到场与**工程师**对记录进行检查和协商，达成一致后，应在记录上签字。如**承包商**未到场，应认为该记录准确，予以认可。

如果**承包商**检查后不同意该记录，和(或)不签字表示同意，**承包商**应向**工程师**发出通知，说明认为该记录不准确的部分。**工程师**收到通知后，应审查该记录，进行确认或更改。如果**承包商**被要求检查记录后 14 天内，没有发出此类通知，该记录应认为准确，予以认可。

12.2
测量方法

除**合同**另有规定外，无论当地有何惯例：

(a) 应测量**永久工程**各项内容的实际净数量；以及

(b) 测量的方法应按照**工程量表**或其他适用**资料表**的规定。

12.3
估价

除**合同**另有规定外，**工程师**应通过上述第 **12.1 款**和**12.2 款**商定或确定的测量方法和适宜的费率和价格，对各项工作内容进行估价，再按照第 **3.5 款**[**确定**]的规定，商定或确定**合同价格**。

各项工作内容的适宜费率或价格，应为**合同**对此类工作内容规定的费率或价格，如**合同**中无某项内容，应取类似工作的费率或价格。但在以下情况下，宜对有关工作内容采用新的费率或价格：

(a)   (i)   the measured quantity of the item is changed by more than 10% from the quantity of this item in the Bill of Quantities or other Schedule,

       (ii)   this change in quantity multiplied by such specified rate for this item exceeds 0.01% of the Accepted Contract Amount,

       (iii)   this change in quantity directly changes the Cost per unit quantity of this item by more than 1%, and

       (iv)   this item is not specified in the Contract as a "fixed rate item";

or

(b)   (i)   the work is instructed under Clause 13 [*Variations and Adjustments*],

       (ii)   no rate or price is specified in the Contract for this item, and

       (iii)   no specified rate or price is appropriate because the item of work is not of similar character, or is not executed under similar conditions, as any item in the Contract.

Each new rate or price shall be derived from any relevant rates or prices in the Contract, with reasonable adjustments to take account of the matters described in sub-paragraph (a) and/or (b), as applicable. If no rates or prices are relevant for the derivation of a new rate or price, it shall be derived from the reasonable Cost of executing the work, together with reasonable profit, taking account of any other relevant matters.

Until such time as an appropriate rate or price is agreed or determined, the Engineer shall determine a provisional rate or price for the purposes of Interim Payment Certificates.

12.4

Omissions

Whenever the omission of any work forms part (or all) of a Variation, the value of which has not been agreed, if:

(a)   the Contractor will incur (or has incurred) cost which, if the work had not been omitted, would have been deemed to be covered by a sum forming part of the Accepted Contract Amount;

(b)   the omission of the work will result (or has resulted) in this sum not forming part of the Contract Price; and

(c)   this cost is not deemed to be included in the evaluation of any substituted work;

then the Contractor shall give notice to the Engineer accordingly, with supporting particulars. Upon receiving this notice, the Engineer shall proceed in accordance with Sub-Clause 3.5 [*Determinations*] to agree or determine this cost, which shall be included in the Contract Price.

Variations and Adjustments

13.1

Right to Vary

Variations may be initiated by the Engineer at any time prior to issuing the Taking-Over Certificate for the Works, either by an instruction or by a request for the Contractor to submit a proposal.

The Contractor shall execute and be bound by each Variation, unless the Contractor promptly gives notice to the Engineer stating (with supporting particulars) that the Contractor cannot readily obtain the Goods required for the Variation. Upon receiving this notice, the Engineer shall cancel, confirm or vary the instruction.

Each Variation may include:

(a) (i) 该项工作测出的数量变化超过**工程量表**或其他**资料表**中所列数量的 10% 以上；

    (ii) 此数量变化与该项工作上述规定的费率的乘积，超过**中标合同金额**的 0.01%；

    (iii) 此数量变化直接改变该项工作的单位成本超过 1%；以及

    (iv) **合同**中没有规定该项工作为"固定费率项目"；

或

(b) (i) 根据**第 13 条**[**变更和调整**]的规定指示的工作；

    (ii) **合同**中没有规定该项工作的费率或价格；以及

    (iii) 由于工作性质不同，或在与**合同**中任何工作不同的条件下实施，未规定适宜的费率或价格。

新的费率或价格应考虑(a)和(或)(b)项中描述的有关事项对**合同**中相关费率或价格加以合理调整后得出。如果没有相关的费率或价格可供推算新的费率或价格，应根据实施该工作的合理**成本**和合理利润，并考虑其他相关事项后得出。

工程师应在商定或确定适宜费率或价格前，确定用于**期中付款证书**的临时费率或价格。

12.4

删减

当任何工作的删减构成一项**变更**的一部分(或全部)，而对其价值尚未达成一致时，如果存在下列情况：

(a) 如该工作未被删减，**承包商**将(或已)招致的费用，本应包含在**中标合同金额**的某部分款额中；

(b) 删减该工作将(或已)导致此项款额不构成**合同价格**的一部分；以及

(c) 此项费用不被视为要包括在任何替代工作的估价中；

承包商应据此向**工程师**发出通知，并附相应的详细资料。**工程师**收到通知后，应按照**第 3.5 款**[**确定**]的规定，商定或确定此项费用，并计入**合同价格**。

13 变更和调整

13.1

变更权

在颁发**工程接收证书**前的任何时间，**工程师**可通过发布指示或要求**承包商**提交建议书的方式，提出**变更**。

承包商应遵守并执行每项**变更**，除非**承包商**迅速向**工程师**发出通知，说明(附详细根据)**承包商**难以取得**变更**所需的货物。**工程师**接到此类通知后，应取消、确认或改变原指示。

每项**变更**可包括：

(a)   changes to the quantities of any item of work included in the Contract (however, such changes do not necessarily constitute a Variation),

(b)   changes to the quality and other characteristics of any item of work,

(c)   changes to the levels, positions and/or dimensions of any part of the Works,

(d)   omission of any work unless it is to be carried out by others,

(e)   any additional work, Plant, Materials or services necessary for the Permanent Works, including any associated Tests on Completion, boreholes and other testing and exploratory work, or

(f)   changes to the sequence or timing of the execution of the Works.

The Contractor shall not make any alteration and/or modification of the Permanent Works, unless and until the Engineer instructs or approves a Variation.

13.2

Value Engineering

The Contractor may, at any time, submit to the Engineer a written proposal which (in the Contractor's opinion) will, if adopted, (i) accelerate completion, (ii) reduce the cost to the Employer of executing, maintaining or operating the Works, (iii) improve the efficiency or value to the Employer of the completed Works, or (iv) otherwise be of benefit to the Employer.

The proposal shall be prepared at the cost of the Contractor and shall include the items listed in Sub-Clause 13.3 [*Variation Procedure*].

If a proposal, which is approved by the Engineer, includes a change in the design of part of the Permanent Works, then unless otherwise agreed by both Parties:

(a)   the Contractor shall design this part,

(b)   sub-paragraphs (a) to (d) of Sub-Clause 4.1 [*Contractor's General Obligations*] shall apply, and

(c)   if this change results in a reduction in the contract value of this part, the Engineer shall proceed in accordance with Sub-Clause 3.5 [*Determinations*] to agree or determine a fee, which shall be included in the Contract Price. This fee shall be half (50%) of the difference between the following amounts:

    (i)   such reduction in contract value, resulting from the change, excluding adjustments under Sub-Clause 13.7 [*Adjustments for Changes in Legislation*] and Sub-Clause 13.8 [*Adjustments for Changes in Cost*],and

    (ii)   the reduction (if any) in the value to the Employer of the varied works, taking account of any reductions in quality, anticipated life or operational efficiencies.

However, if amount (i) is less than amount (ii), there shall not be a fee.

13.3

Variation Procedure

If the Engineer requests a proposal, prior to instructing a Variation, the Contractor shall respond in writing as soon as practicable, either by giving reasons why he cannot comply (if this is the case) or by submitting:

(a)   a description of the proposed work to be performed and a programme for its execution,

(b)   the Contractor's proposal for any necessary modifications to the programme according to Sub-Clause 8.3 [*Programme*] and to the Time for Completion, and

(c)   the Contractor's proposal for evaluation of the Variation.

The Engineer shall, as soon as practicable after receiving such proposal (under Sub-Clause 13.2 [*Value Engineering*] or otherwise), respond with approval, disapproval or comments. The Contractor shall not delay any work whilst awaiting a response.

(a) **合同**中包括的任何工作内容的数量的改变(但此类改变不一定构成**变更**);

(b) 任何工作内容的质量或其他特性的改变;

(c) 任何部分**工程**的标高、位置和(或)尺寸的改变;

(d) 任何工作的删减,但要交他人实施的工作除外;

(e) **永久工程**所需的任何附加工作、**生产设备**、**材料**或服务,包括任何有关的**竣工试验**、钻孔和其他试验和勘探工作;或

(f) 实施**工程**的顺序或时间安排的改变。

除非并直到**工程师**指示或批准了**变更**,**承包商**不得对**永久工程**作任何改变和(或)修改。

13.2

价值工程

承包商可随时向**工程师**提交书面建议,提出(他认为)采纳后将:(i)加快竣工,(ii)降低**雇主**的工程施工、维护或运行的费用,(iii)提高**雇主**的竣工**工程**的效率或价值,或(iv)给**雇主**带来其他利益的建议。

此类建议书应由**承包商**自费编制,并应包括**第 13.3 款**[**变更程序**]所列内容。

如经**工程师**批准的建议书中包括部分**永久工程**设计的改变,则除非经双方同意:

(a) **承包商**应设计这一部分;

(b) 应按照**第 4.1 款**[**承包商的一般义务**]中的(a)至(d)项办理;以及

(c) 如此项改变导致该部分的合同价值减少,**工程师**应按照**第 3.5 款**[**确定**]的规定,商定或确定应包括在**合同价格**内的费用。此项费用应为以下两项金额之差的一半(50%):

(i) 由此项改变引起的合同价值的此类减少,不包括根据**第 13.7 款**[**因法律改变的调整**]和**第 13.8 款**[**因成本改变的调整**]的规定做出的调整;和

(ii) 改变后的工程由于任何质量、预期寿命或运行效率的降低,对**雇主**的价值的减少(如果有)。

但是,如(i)中金额小于(ii)中金额,则不应有此项费用。

13.3

变更程序

如果**工程师**在发出**变更**指示前要求**承包商**提出一份建议书,**承包商**应尽快做出书面回应,或提出他不能照办的理由(如果情况如此),或提交:

(a) 对建议要完成的工作的说明,以及实施的进度计划;

(b) 根据**第 8.3 款**[**进度计划**]和**竣工时间**的要求,**承包商**对进度计划做出必要修改的建议书;以及

(c) **承包商**对**变更**估价的建议书。

工程师收到此类(根据**第 13.2 款**[**价值工程**]的规定或其他规定提出的)建议书后,应尽快给予批准、不批准、或提出意见的回复。在等待答复期间,**承包商**不应延误任何工作。

87

Each instruction to execute a Variation, with any requirements for the recording of Costs, shall be issued by the Engineer to the Contractor, who shall acknowledge receipt.

Each Variation shall be evaluated in accordance with Clause 12 [*Measurement and Evaluation*], unless the Engineer instructs or approves otherwise in accordance with this Clause.

13.4

Payment in Applicable Currencies

If the Contract provides for payment of the Contract Price in more than one currency, then whenever an adjustment is agreed, approved or determined as stated above, the amount payable in each of the applicable currencies shall be specified. For this purpose, reference shall be made to the actual or expected currency proportions of the Cost of the varied work, and to the proportions of various currencies specified for payment of the Contract Price.

13.5

Provisional Sums

Each Provisional Sum shall only be used, in whole or in part, in accordance with the Engineer's instructions, and the Contract Price shall be adjusted accordingly. The total sum paid to the Contractor shall include only such amounts, for the work, supplies or services to which the Provisional Sum relates, as the Engineer shall have instructed. For each Provisional Sum, the Engineer may instruct:

(a)   work to be executed (including Plant, Materials or services to be supplied) by the Contractor and valued under Sub-Clause 13.3 [*Variation Procedure*]; and/or

(b)   Plant, Materials or services to be purchased by the Contractor, from a nominated Subcontractor (as defined in Clause 5 [*Nominated Subcontractors*]) or otherwise; and for which there shall be included in the Contract Price:

(i)   the actual amounts paid (or due to be paid) by the Contractor, and

(ii)   a sum for overhead charges and profit, calculated as a percentage of these actual amounts by applying the relevant percentage rate (if any) stated in the appropriate Schedule. If there is no such rate, the percentage rate stated in the Appendix to Tender shall be applied.

The Contractor shall, when required by the Engineer, produce quotations, invoices, vouchers and accounts or receipts in substantiation.

13.6

Daywork

For work of a minor or incidental nature, the Engineer may instruct that a Variation shall be executed on a daywork basis. The work shall then be valued in accordance with the Daywork Schedule included in the Contract, and the following procedure shall apply. If a Daywork Schedule is not included in the Contract, this Sub-Clause shall not apply.

Before ordering Goods for the work, the Contractor shall submit quotations to the Engineer. When applying for payment, the Contractor shall submit invoices, vouchers and accounts or receipts for any Goods.

Except for any items for which the Daywork Schedule specifies that payment is not due, the Contractor shall deliver each day to the Engineer accurate statements in duplicate which shall include the following details of the resources used in executing the previous day's work:

(a)   the names, occupations and time of Contractor's Personnel,

(b)   the identification, type and time of Contractor's Equipment and Temporary Works, and

(c)   the quantities and types of Plant and Materials used.

应由**工程师**向**承包商**发出执行每项**变更**并附做好各项**费用**记录的任何要求的指示，**承包商**应确认收到该指示。

除非**工程师**按照本**条**另有指示或批准，每项**变更**应按照**第 12 条**[**测量和估价**]的规定进行估价。

13.4

以适用货币支付

如果**合同**规定**合同价格**以一种以上货币支付，在上述商定、批准或确定**变更**调整时，应规定以每种适用货币支付的款额。为此，应参考变更后工作**费用**的实际或预期的货币比例，以及规定的**合同价格**支付中的各种货币比例。

13.5

暂列金额

每笔**暂列金额**只应按照**工程师**的指示全部或部分地使用，**合同价格**应相应进行调整。付给**承包商**的总金额只应包括**工程师**已指示的，与**暂列金额**有关的工作、供货或服务的应付款项。对于每笔**暂列金额**，**工程师**可指示用于下列支付：

(a) 根据**第 13.3 款**[**变更程序**]的规定进行估价的、要由**承包商**实施的工作(包括要提供的**生产设备**、**材料**或服务)；和/或

(b) 应包括在**合同价格**中的，要由**承包商**从指定的**分包商**(按**第 5 条**[**指定的分包商**]的定义)或其他单位购买的**生产设备**、**材料**或服务，所需的下列费用：

(i) **承包商**已付(或应付)的实际金额；和

(ii) 以相应**资料表**规定的有关百分率(如果有)计算的，这些实际金额的一个百分比，作为管理费和利润的金额。如无此类百分率，应采用**投标书附录**中的百分率。

当**工程师**要求时，**承包商**应出示报价单、发票、凭证以及账单或收据等证明。

13.6

计日工作

对于一些小的或附带性的工作，**工程师**可指示按计日工作实施**变更**。这时，工作应按照包括在**合同**中的**计日工作计划表**进行估价，并应施用下述程序。如果**合同**中未包括**计日工作计划表**，则本**款**不适用。

在为工作订购**货物**前，**承包商**应向**工程师**提交报价单。当申请支付时，**承包商**应提交各种**货物**的发票、凭证，以及账单或收据。

除**计日工作计划表**中规定不应支付的任何项目外，**承包商**应向**工程师**提交每日的精确报表，一式两份，报表应包括前一日工作中使用的各项资源的详细资料：

(a) **承包商人员**的姓名、职业和使用时间；

(b) **承包商设备**和**临时工程**的标识、型号和使用时间；以及

(c) 所用的**生产设备**和**材料**的数量和型号。

One copy of each statement will, if correct, or when agreed, be signed by the Engineer and returned to the Contractor. The Contractor shall then submit priced statements of these resources to the Engineer, prior to their inclusion in the next Statement under Sub-Clause 14.3 [*Application for Interim Payment Certificates*].

13.7

Adjustments for Changes in Legislation

The Contract Price shall be adjusted to take account of any increase or decrease in Cost resulting from a change in the Laws of the Country (including the introduction of new Laws and the repeal or modification of existing Laws) or in the judicial or official governmental interpretation of such Laws, made after the Base Date, which affect the Contractor in the performance of obligations under the Contract.

If the Contractor suffers (or will suffer) delay and/or incurs (or will incur) additional Cost as a result of these changes in the Laws or in such interpretations, made after the Base Date, the Contractor shall give notice to the Engineer and shall be entitled subject to Sub-Clause 20.1 [*Contractor's Claims*] to:

(a)   an extension of time for any such delay, if completion is or will be delayed, under Sub-Clause 8.4 [*Extension of Time for Completion*], and

(b)   payment of any such Cost, which shall be included in the Contract Price.

After receiving this notice, the Engineer shall proceed in accordance with Sub-Clause 3.5 [*Determinations*] to agree or determine these matters.

13.8

Adjustments for Changes in Cost

In this Sub-Clause, "table of adjustment data" means the completed table of adjustment data included in the Appendix to Tender. If there is no such table of adjustment data, this Sub-Clause shall not apply.

If this Sub-Clause applies, the amounts payable to the Contractor shall be adjusted for rises or falls in the cost of labour, Goods and other inputs to the Works, by the addition or deduction of the amounts determined by the formulae prescribed in this Sub-Clause. To the extent that full compensation for any rise or fall in Costs is not covered by the provisions of this or other Clauses, the Accepted Contract Amount shall be deemed to have included amounts to cover the contingency of other rises and falls in costs.

The adjustment to be applied to the amount otherwise payable to the Contractor, as valued in accordance with the appropriate Schedule and certified in Payment Certificates, shall be determined from formulae for each of the currencies in which the Contract Price is payable. No adjustment is to be applied to work valued on the basis of Cost or current prices. The formulae shall be of the following general type:

$$Pn = a + b\frac{Ln}{Lo} + c\frac{En}{Eo} + d\frac{Mn}{Mo} + \ldots$$

where:

"**Pn**" is the adjustment multiplier to be applied to the estimated contract value in the relevant currency of the work carried out in period "n", this period being a month unless otherwise stated in the Appendix to Tender;

"**a**" is a fixed coefficient, stated in the relevant table of adjustment data, representing the non-adjustable portion in contractual payments;

"**b**", "**c**", "**d**", ... are coefficients representing the estimated proportion of each cost element related to the execution of the Works, as stated in the relevant

报表如果正确或经同意,将由**工程师**签署并退回**承包商**一份。**承包商**应在将它们纳入其后根据**第 14.3 款[期中付款证书的申请]**的规定提交的报表前,先向**工程师**提交关于这些资源的估价报表。

13.7

因法律改变的调整

对于**基准日期**后工程所在国的**法律**有改变(包括施用新的**法律**,废除或修改现有**法律**)或对此类**法律**的司法或政府解释有改变,影响**承包商**履行**合同**规定的义务的,**合同价格**应考虑上述改变导致的任何**费用**增减进行调整。

如果由于这些**基准日期**后做出的**法律**或此类解释的改变,使**承包商**已(或将)遭受延误和(或)已(或将)招致增加**费用**,**承包商**应向**工程师**发出通知,并应有权根据**第 20.1 款[承包商的索赔]**的规定要求:

(a)   根据**第 8.4 款[竣工时间的延长]**的规定,如竣工已或将受到延误,对任何此类延误给予延长期;以及

(b)   任何此类**费用**应计入**合同价格**,给予支付。

工程师收到此类通知后,应按照**第 3.5 款[确定]**的要求,对这些事项进行商定或确定。

13.8

因成本改变的调整

在本款中,"调整数据表"系指**投标书附录**中填好的调整数据表。如无此类调整数据表,本**款**应不适用。

如本**款**适用,可付给**承包商**的款额,应就**工程**所用的劳动力、**货物**和其他投入的成本的涨落,按本款规定的公式确定增减额进行调整。在本**条**或他**条**规定对**成本**的任何涨落不能完全补偿的情况下,**中标合同金额**应视为已包括其他成本涨落的应急费用。

按照适当的**资料表**估价,并在**付款证书**中确认的,付给**承包商**的其他应付款要做的调整,应按**合同价格**应付每种货币的公式确定。对于根据**成本**或现行价格进行估价的工作,不予调整。所用公式应采用以下一般形式:

$$Pn = a + b\frac{Ln}{Lo} + c\frac{En}{Eo} + d\frac{Mn}{Mo} + \cdots\cdots$$

式中:

"Pn"是用于在"n"期间所完成的工作以相应货币的估计合同价值的调整乘数,除非**投标书附录**中另有说明,此期间单位为一个月;

"a"是在相关调整数据表中规定的固定系数,表示合同付款中的不予调整的部分;

"b","c","d",…是代表相关调整数据表中列出的,与**工程施工**

table of adjustment data; such tabulated cost elements may be indicative of resources such as labour, equipment and materials;

"L_n", "E_n", "M_n", ... are the current cost indices or reference prices for period "n", expressed in the relevant currency of payment, each of which is applicable to the relevant tabulated cost element on the date 49 days prior to the last day of the period (to which the particular Payment Certificate relates); and

"L_o", "E_o", "M_o", ... are the base cost indices or reference prices, expressed in the relevant currency of payment, each of which is applicable to the relevant tabulated cost element on the Base Date.

The cost indices or reference prices stated in the table of adjustment data shall be used. If their source is in doubt, it shall be determined by the Engineer. For this purpose, reference shall be made to the values of the indices at stated dates (quoted in the fourth and fifth columns respectively of the table) for the purposes of clarification of the source; although these dates (and thus these values) may not correspond to the base cost indices.

In cases where the "currency of index" (stated in the table) is not the relevant currency of payment, each index shall be converted into the relevant currency of payment at the selling rate, established by the central bank of the Country, of this relevant currency on the above date for which the index is required to be applicable.

Until such time as each current cost index is available, the Engineer shall determine a provisional index for the issue of Interim Payment Certificates. When a current cost index is available, the adjustment shall be recalculated accordingly.

If the Contractor fails to complete the Works within the Time for Completion, adjustment of prices thereafter shall be made using either (i) each index or price applicable on the date 49 days prior to the expiry of the Time for Completion of the Works, or (ii) the current index or price: whichever is more favourable to the Employer.

The weightings (coefficients) for each of the factors of cost stated in the table(s) of adjustment data shall only be adjusted if they have been rendered unreasonable, unbalanced or inapplicable, as a result of Variations.

14 Contract Price and Payment

14.1
The Contract Price

Unless otherwise stated in the Particular Conditions:

(a) the Contract Price shall be agreed or determined under Sub-Clause 12.3 [*Evaluation*] and be subject to adjustments in accordance with the Contract;

(b) the Contractor shall pay all taxes, duties and fees required to be paid by him under the Contract, and the Contract Price shall not be adjusted for any of these costs except as stated in Sub-Clause 13.7 [*Adjustments for Changes in Legislation*];

(c) any quantities which may be set out in the Bill of Quantities or other Schedule are estimated quantities and are not to be taken as the actual and correct quantities:

(i) of the Works which the Contractor is required to execute, or
(ii) for the purposes of Clause 12 [*Measurement and Evaluation*]; and

有关各成本要素的估计比例系数；表列此类成本要素，可表示劳动力、设备和材料等资源；

　　"Ln"，"En"，"Mn"，…是适用于(与特定**付款证书**有关的)期间最后一天49天前的表列相关成本要素的，"n"期间现行成本指数或参考价格，用相应支付货币表示；

　　"Lo"，"Eo"，"Mo"，…是适用于**基准日期**时表列相关成本要素的基准成本指数或参考价格，用相应支付货币表示。

应使用调整数据表中列明的成本指数或参考价格。如对其来源有疑问，应由**工程师**确定。为此目的，应参考所述日期的指数值(分别在该表第4列和第5列)，以澄清来源；尽管，这些日期(因而还有这些数值)可能与基准成本指数不相对应。

当"指数对应的货币"(表中所列)不是相应支付货币时，每个指数应按**工程所在国**中央银行规定的此相应支付货币在上述要应用该指数的日期的卖出汇率，换算成该相应支付货币。

在获得每种现行成本指数前，**工程师**应确定一个临时指数，用以颁发**期中付款证书**。当得到现行成本指数时，应据此重新计算调整。

如果**承包商**未能在**竣工时间**内完成工程，其后应利用(i)适用于**工程竣工时间**期满前第49天的各指数或价格，或(ii)现行指数或价格：取两者中对**雇主**更有利的，对价格做出调整。

只有当由于**变更**使调整数据表中所列的各项成本要素的权重(系数)变得不合理、不平衡或不适用时，才应对其进行调整。

14　合同价格和付款

14.1
合同价格

除非**专用条件**中另有规定：

(a)　**合同价格**应根据**第12.3款**[估价]的规定进行商定或确定，并应按照**合同**进行调整；

(b)　**承包商**应支付根据**合同**要求应由其支付的各项税金、关税和费用。除**第13.7款**[因法律改变的调整]说明的情况外，**合同价格**不应因任何这些费用进行调整；

(c)　**工程量表**或其他**资料表**可能列出的任何数量都是估计数，不是要作为下述内容的实际和正确的数量：

　　(i)　要求**承包商**实施的工程；或
　　(ii)　用于**第12条**[测量和估价]的；以及

93

(d)   the Contractor shall submit to the Engineer, within 28 days after the Commencement Date, a proposed breakdown of each lump sum price in the Schedules. The Engineer may take account of the breakdown when preparing Payment Certificates, but shall not be bound by it.

14.2

Advance Payment

The Employer shall make an advance payment, as an interest-free loan for mobilisation, when the Contractor submits a guarantee in accordance with this Sub-Clause. The total advance payment, the number and timing of instalments (if more than one), and the applicable currencies and proportions, shall be as stated in the Appendix to Tender.

Unless and until the Employer receives this guarantee, or if the total advance payment is not stated in the Appendix to Tender, this Sub-Clause shall not apply.

The Engineer shall issue an Interim Payment Certificate for the first instalment after receiving a Statement (under Sub-Clause 14.3 [*Application for Interim Payment Certificates*]) and after the Employer receives (i) the Performance Security in accordance with Sub-Clause 4.2 [*Performance Security*] and (ii) a guarantee in amounts and currencies equal to the advance payment. This guarantee shall be issued by an entity and from within a country (or other jurisdiction) approved by the Employer, and shall be in the form annexed to the Particular Conditions or in another form approved by the Employer.

The Contractor shall ensure that the guarantee is valid and enforceable until the advance payment has been repaid, but its amount may be progressively reduced by the amount repaid by the Contractor as indicated in the Payment Certificates. If the terms of the guarantee specify its expiry date, and the advance payment has not been repaid by the date 28 days prior to the expiry date, the Contractor shall extend the validity of the guarantee until the advance payment has been repaid.

The advance payment shall be repaid through percentage deductions in Payment Certificates. Unless other percentages are stated in the Appendix to Tender:

(a)   deductions shall commence in the Payment Certificate in which the total of all certified interim payments (excluding the advance payment and deductions and repayments of retention) exceeds ten per cent (10%) of the Accepted Contract Amount less Provisional Sums; and

(b)   deductions shall be made at the amortisation rate of one quarter (25%) of the amount of each Payment Certificate (excluding the advance payment and deductions and repayments of retention) in the currencies and proportions of the advance payment, until such time as the advance payment has been repaid.

If the advance payment has not been repaid prior to the issue of the Taking-Over Certificate for the Works or prior to termination under Clause 15 [*Termination by Employer*], Clause 16 [*Suspension and Termination by Contractor*] or Clause 19 [*Force Majeure*] (as the case may be), the whole of the balance then outstanding shall immediately become due and payable by the Contractor to the Employer.

14.3

Application for Interim Payment Certificates

The Contractor shall submit a Statement in six copies to the Engineer after the end of each month, in a form approved by the Engineer, showing in detail the amounts to which the Contractor considers himself to be entitled, together with supporting documents which shall include the report on the progress during this month in accordance with Sub-Clause 4.21 [*Progress Reports*].

(d) **承包商**在开工日期后 28 天内，应向**工程师**提交**资料表**中所列每项总价的建议分类细目。**工程师**编制**付款证书**时可以考虑此类分类细目，但不受其约束。

14.2

预付款

当**承包商**按照本款提交保函后，**雇主**应支付一笔预付款，作为用于动员的无息贷款。预付款总额、分期预付的次数和时间安排(如次数多于一次)，以及适用的货币和比例，应按**投标书附录**中的规定。

除非和直到**雇主**收到此保函，或如果**投标书附录**中未列明预付款总额，本**款**应不适用。

工程师应在收到(根据**第 14.3 款**[*期中付款证书的申请*]规定的) **报表**，以及**雇主**收到(i)按照**第 4.2 款**[*履约担保*]要求提交的**履约担保**，和(ii)由**雇主**批准的国家(或其他司法管辖区)的实体，按**专用条件**所附格式或**雇主**批准的其他格式签发的，金额和货币种类与预付款一致的保函后，为首次分期付款发出**期中付款证书**。

在还清预付款前，**承包商**应确保此保函一直有效并可执行，但其总额可根据**付款证书**列明的**承包商**付还的金额逐渐减少。如果保函条款中规定了期满日期，而在期满日期前 28 天预付款尚未还清时，**承包商**应将保函有效期延至预付款还清为止。

预付款应通过**付款证书**中按百分比扣减的方式付还。除非**投标书附录**中规定了其他百分比：

(a) 扣减应从确认的期中付款(不包括预付款、扣减额和保留金的付还)累计额超过**中标合同金额**减去**暂列金额**后余额的百分之十(10%)时的**付款证书**开始；以及

(b) 扣减应按每次**付款证书**中金额(不包括预付款、扣减额和保留金的付还)的四分之一(25%)的摊还比率，并按预付款的货币和比例计算，直到预付款还清时为止。

如果在颁发工程接收证书前，或根据**第 15 条**[*由雇主终止*]、**第 16 条**[*由承包商暂停和终止*]，或**第 19 条**[*不可抗力*](视情况而定)的规定终止前，预付款尚未还清，则全部余额应立即成为**承包商**对**雇主**的到期应付款。

14.3

期中付款证书的申请

承包商应在每个月末后，按工程师批准的格式向**工程师**提交**报表**，一式六份，详细说明**承包商**自己认为有权得到的款额，同时提交包括按**第 4.21 款**[*进度报告*]的规定编制的相关进度报告在内的证明文件。

The Statement shall include the following items, as applicable, which shall be expressed in the various currencies in which the Contract Price is payable, in the sequence listed:

(a) the estimated contract value of the Works executed and the Contractor's Documents produced up to the end of the month (including Variations but excluding items described in sub-paragraphs (b) to (g) below);

(b) any amounts to be added and deducted for changes in legislation and changes in cost, in accordance with Sub-Clause 13.7 [*Adjustments for Changes in Legislation*] and Sub-Clause 13.8 [*Adjustments for Changes in Cost*];

(c) any amount to be deducted for retention, calculated by applying the percentage of retention stated in the Appendix to Tender to the total of the above amounts, until the amount so retained by the Employer reaches the limit of Retention Money (if any) stated in the Appendix to Tender;

(d) any amounts to be added and deducted for the advance payment and repayments in accordance with Sub-Clause 14.2 [*Advance Payment*];

(e) any amounts to be added and deducted for Plant and Materials in accordance with Sub-Clause 14.5 [*Plant and Materials intended for the Works*];

(f) any other additions or deductions which may have become due under the Contract or otherwise, including those under Clause 20 [*Claims, Disputes and Arbitration*]; and

(g) the deduction of amounts certified in all previous Payment Certificates.

14.4
Schedule of Payments

If the Contract includes a schedule of payments specifying the instalments in which the Contract Price will be paid, then unless otherwise stated in this schedule:

(a) the instalments quoted in this schedule of payments shall be the estimated contract values for the purposes of sub-paragraph (a) of Sub-Clause 14.3 [*Application for Interim Payment Certificates*];

(b) Sub-Clause 14.5 [*Plant and Materials intended for the Works*] shall not apply; and

(c) if these instalments are not defined by reference to the actual progress achieved in executing the Works, and if actual progress is found to be less than that on which this schedule of payments was based, then the Engineer may proceed in accordance with Sub-Clause 3.5 [*Determinations*] to agree or determine revised instalments, which shall take account of the extent to which progress is less than that on which the instalments were previously based.

If the Contract does not include a schedule of payments, the Contractor shall submit non-binding estimates of the payments which he expects to become due during each quarterly period. The first estimate shall be submitted within 42 days after the Commencement Date. Revised estimates shall be submitted at quarterly intervals, until the Taking-Over Certificate has been issued for the Works.

14.5
Plant and Materials intended for the Works

If this Sub-Clause applies, Interim Payment Certificates shall include, under sub-paragraph (e) of Sub-Clause 14.3, (i) an amount for Plant and Materials which have been sent to the Site for incorporation in the Permanent Works, and (ii) a reduction when the contract value of such Plant and Materials is included as part of the Permanent Works under sub-paragraph (a) of Sub-Clause 14.3 [*Application for Interim Payment Certificates*].

If the lists referred to in sub-paragraphs (b)(i) or (c)(i) below are not included in the Appendix to Tender, this Sub-Clause shall not apply.

The Engineer shall determine and certify each addition if the following conditions are satisfied:

适用时，该**报表**应包括下列项目，以**合同价格**应付的各种货币表示，并按下列顺序排列：

(a) 截至月末已实施的**工程**和已提出的**承包商文件**的估算合同价值（包括各项**变更**，但不包括以下(b)至(g)项所列项目）；

(b) 按照**第13.7款**[*因法律改变的调整*]和**第13.8款**[*因成本改变的调整*]的规定，由于法律改变和成本改变，应增减的任何款额；

(c) 至**雇主**提取的保留金额达到**投标书附录**中规定的保留金限额（如果有）前，用**投标书附录**中规定的保留金百分比乘以上述款项总额计算的应扣减的任何保留金额；

(d) 按照**第14.2款**[*预付款*]的规定，因预付款的支付和付还，应增加和扣减的任何款额；

(e) 按照**第14.5款**[*拟用于工程的生产设备和材料*]的规定，为生产设备和**材料**应增加和扣减的任何款额；

(f) 根据**合同**或包括**第20条**[*索赔、争端和仲裁*]规定等其他理由，应付的任何其他增加或扣减额；以及

(g) 所有以前**付款证书**中确认的扣减额。

14.4

付款计划表

如果**合同**包括对**合同价格**的支付规定了分期支付的**付款计划表**，除非该表中另有规定：

(a) 该付款计划表所列分期付款额，应是为了应对**第14.3款**[*期中付款证书的申请*]中(a)项，估算的**合同价值**；

(b) **第14.5款**[*拟用于工程的生产设备和材料*]的规定应不适用；以及

(c) 如果分期付款额不是参照工程实施达到的实际进度确定，且发现实际进度比付款计划表依据的进度落后时，**工程师**可按照**第3.5款**[*确定*]的要求进行商定或确定，修改分期付款额，这种修改应考虑实际进度落后于该分期付款额原依据的进度的程度。

如果**合同**未包括付款计划表，**承包商**应每个季度提交他预计应付的无约束性估算付款额。第一次估算应在**开工日期**后42天内提交。直到颁发**工程接收证书**前，应按季度提交修正的估算。

14.5

拟用于工程的生产设备和材料

如本款适用，则根据**第14.3款**(e)项的规定，**期中付款证书**应包括，(i)已运往**现场**为永久工程用的**生产设备和材料**的金额，以及(ii)当此类**生产设备和材料**的合同价值已根据**第14.3款**[*期中付款证书的申请*](a)项规定，作为永久工程一部分包含在内时的减少额。

如果**投标书附录**中没有下述(b)(i)或(c)(i)项提到的所列内容，本**款**应不适用。

如满足以下条件，**工程师**应确定和确认各项增加金额：

(a)   the Contractor has:

    (i)   kept satisfactory records (including the orders, receipts, Costs and use of Plant and Materials) which are available for inspection, and

    (ii)   submitted a statement of the Cost of acquiring and delivering the Plant and Materials to the Site, supported by satisfactory evidence;

and either:

(b)   the relevant Plant and Materials:

    (i)   are those listed in the Appendix to Tender for payment when shipped,

    (ii)   have been shipped to the Country, en route to the Site, in accordance with the Contract; and

    (iii)   are described in a clean shipped bill of lading or other evidence of shipment, which has been submitted to the Engineer together with evidence of payment of freight and insurance, any other documents reasonably required, and a bank guarantee in a form and issued by an entity approved by the Employer in amounts and currencies equal to the amount due under this Sub-Clause: this guarantee may be in a similar form to the form referred to in Sub-Clause 14.2 [*Advance Payment*] and shall be valid until the Plant and Materials are properly stored on Site and protected against loss, damage or deterioration;

or

(c)   the relevant Plant and Materials:

    (i)   are those listed in the Appendix to Tender for payment when delivered to the Site, and

    (ii)   have been delivered to and are properly stored on the Site, are protected against loss, damage or deterioration, and appear to be in accordance with the Contract.

The additional amount to be certified shall be the equivalent of eighty percent of the Engineer's determination of the cost of the Plant and Materials (including delivery to Site), taking account of the documents mentioned in this Sub-Clause and of the contract value of the Plant and Materials.

The currencies for this additional amount shall be the same as those in which payment will become due when the contract value is included under sub-paragraph (a) of Sub-Clause 14.3 [*Application for Interim Payment Certificates*]. At that time, the Payment Certificate shall include the applicable reduction which shall be equivalent to, and in the same currencies and proportions as, this additional amount for the relevant Plant and Materials.

14.6

Issue of Interim Payment Certificates

No amount will be certified or paid until the Employer has received and approved the Performance Security. Thereafter, the Engineer shall, within 28 days after receiving a Statement and supporting documents, issue to the Employer an Interim Payment Certificate which shall state the amount which the Engineer fairly determines to be due, with supporting particulars.

However, prior to issuing the Taking-Over Certificate for the Works, the Engineer shall not be bound to issue an Interim Payment Certificate in an amount which would (after retention and other deductions) be less than the minimum amount of Interim Payment Certificates (if any) stated in the Appendix to Tender. In this event, the Engineer shall give notice to the Contractor accordingly.

(a) 　承包商已:

　　(i) 　保存了符合要求、可供检验的(包括生产设备和材料的订单、收据、费用和使用的)记录;和

　　(ii) 　提交了购买生产设备和材料并将其运至现场的费用报表,并附有符合要求的证据;

和(或):
(b) 　有关生产设备和材料:

　　(i) 　是投标书附录中所列装运付费的物品,

　　(ii) 　按照合同已运到工程所在国,在往现场的途中;

　　(iii) 　已写入清洁装运提单或其他装运证明,此类提单和证明,已与运费和保险费的支付证据、其他合理要求的文件、以及由雇主批准的实体按雇主同意的格式出具的、与根据本款规定应付金额和货币一致的银行保函,一并提交给工程师,此保函可具有与第14.2款[预付款]中提到的格式相类似的格式,并应做到在生产设备和材料已在现场妥善储存并做好防止损失、损害或变质的保护以前,一直有效;

或
(c) 　有关生产设备和材料:

　　(i) 　是投标书附录中所列运到现场时付款的物品;和

　　(ii) 　已运到现场和妥善储存,并已做好防止损失、损害或变质的保护,看来已符合合同要求。

要确认的增加金额,应是工程师考虑本款提到的各项文件及生产设备和材料的合同价值,确定的生产设备和材料(包括运送到现场)的费用的百分之八十。

此项增加金额的货币,应与根据第14.3款[期中付款证书的申请](a)项规定包括的合同价值应付的货币相同。此时,付款证书应计入适当的减少额,该减少额应与相关生产设备和材料的增加金额相等,并采用同样的货币和比例。

14.6

期中付款证书的颁发　在雇主收到并认可履约担保前,不确认或办理付款。其后,工程师应在收到有关报表和证明文件后28天内,向雇主发出期中付款证书,说明工程师公正地确定的应付金额,并附支持资料。

但在颁发工程接收证书前,工程师无需签发金额(扣除保留金和其他应扣款项后)少于投标书附录中期中付款证书的最低额(如果有)的期中付款证书。在此情况下,工程师应相应通知承包商。

An Interim Payment Certificate shall not be withheld for any other reason, although:

(a) if any thing supplied or work done by the Contractor is not in accordance with the Contract, the cost of rectification or replacement may be withheld until rectification or replacement has been completed; and/or

(b) if the Contractor was or is failing to perform any work or obligation in accordance with the Contract, and had been so notified by the Engineer, the value of this work or obligation may be withheld until the work or obligation has been performed.

The Engineer may in any Payment Certificate make any correction or modification that should properly be made to any previous Payment Certificate. A Payment Certificate shall not be deemed to indicate the Engineer's acceptance, approval, consent or satisfaction.

14.7

Payment

The Employer shall pay to the Contractor:

(a) the first instalment of the advance payment within 42 days after issuing the Letter of Acceptance or within 21 days after receiving the documents in accordance with Sub-Clause 4.2 [*Performance Security*] and Sub-Clause 14.2 [*Advance Payment*], whichever is later;

(b) the amount certified in each Interim Payment Certificate within 56 days after the Engineer receives the Statement and supporting documents; and

(c) the amount certified in the Final Payment Certificate within 56 days after the Employer receives this Payment Certificate.

Payment of the amount due in each currency shall be made into the bank account, nominated by the Contractor, in the payment country (for this currency) specified in the Contract.

14.8

Delayed Payment

If the Contractor does not receive payment in accordance with Sub-Clause 14.7 [*Payment*], the Contractor shall be entitled to receive financing charges compounded monthly on the amount unpaid during the period of delay. This period shall be deemed to commence on the date for payment specified in Sub-Clause 14.7 [*Payment*], irrespective (in the case of its sub-paragraph (b)) of the date on which any Interim Payment Certificate is issued.

Unless otherwise stated in the Particular Conditions, these financing charges shall be calculated at the annual rate of three percentage points above the discount rate of the central bank in the country of the currency of payment, and shall be paid in such currency.

The Contractor shall be entitled to this payment without formal notice or certification, and without prejudice to any other right or remedy.

14.9

Payment of Retention Money

When the Taking-Over Certificate has been issued for the Works, the first half of the Retention Money shall be certified by the Engineer for payment to the Contractor. If a Taking-Over Certificate is issued for a Section or part of the Works, a proportion of the Retention Money shall be certified and paid. This proportion shall be two-fifths (40%) of the proportion calculated by dividing the estimated contract value of the Section or part, by the estimated final Contract Price.

Promptly after the latest of the expiry dates of the Defects Notification Periods, the outstanding balance of the Retention Money shall be certified by the Engineer for payment to the Contractor. If a Taking-Over Certificate was issued for a Section, a

虽然存在以下情况，对**期中付款证书**不应因任何其他原因予以扣发：

(a)   如果**承包商**供应的任何物品或完成的工作不符合**合同**要求，在完成修正和更换前，可以扣发该修正和更换所需费用；和(或)

(b)   如果**承包商**未能按照**合同**要求履行任何工作或义务，且**工程师**已曾为此发出通知时，可在该项工作或义务完成前，扣发该工作或义务的价值。

工程师可在任一次付款证书中，对以前任何**付款证书**作出任何正当的改正或修改。**付款证书**不应被视为表明**工程师**的接受、批准、同意或满意。

14.7
付款

雇主应向**承包商**支付：

(a)   首期预付款，支付时间在**中标函**颁发后 42 天，或在收到按照**第 4.2 款**[**履约担保**]和**第 14.2 款**[**预付款**]规定提交的文件后 21 天，二者中较晚的日期内；

(b)   各**期中付款证书**确认的金额，支付时间在**工程师**收到**报表**和证明文件后 56 天内；以及

(c)   **最终付款证书**确认的金额，支付时间在**雇主**收到该**付款证书**后 56 天内。

每种货币的应付款额应汇入**合同**(为此货币)指定的付款国境内的**承包商**指定的银行账户。

14.8
延误的付款

如果**承包商**没有在按照**第 14.7 款**[**付款**]规定的时间收到付款，**承包商**应有权就未付款额按月计算复利，收取延误期的融资费用。该延误期应视为从**第 14.7 款**[**付款**]规定的支付日期算起，而不考虑(如该款(b)项的情况)颁发任何**期中付款证书**的日期。

除非**专用条件**中另有规定，上述融资费用应以高出支付货币所在国中央银行的贴现率三个百分点的年利率进行计算，并应用同种货币支付。

承包商应有权得到上述付款，无需正式通知或证明，且不损害他的任何其他权利或补偿。

14.9
保留金的支付

当已颁发工程**接收证书**时，**工程师**应确认将**保留金**的前一半支付给**承包商**。如果某**单位工程**或部分工程颁发了**接收证书**，**保留金**应按一定比例予以确认和支付。此比例应是该**单位工程**或部分工程估算的**合同**价值，除以估算的最终**合同价格**所得比例的五分之二(40%)。

在各**缺陷通知期限**的最末一个期满日期后，**工程师**应迅速确认将**保留金**未付的余额付给**承包商**。如对某**单位工程**颁发了**接收证书**，**保留金**后一半

proportion of the second half of the Retention Money shall be certified and paid promptly after the expiry date of the Defects Notification Period for the Section. This proportion shall be two-fifths (40%) of the proportion calculated by dividing the estimated contract value of the Section by the estimated final Contract Price.

However, if any work remains to be executed under Clause 11 [*Defects Liability*], the Engineer shall be entitled to withhold certification of the estimated cost of this work until it has been executed.

When calculating these proportions, no account shall be taken of any adjustments under Sub-Clause 13.7 [*Adjustments for Changes in Legislation*] and Sub-Clause 13.8 [*Adjustments for Changes in Cost*].

14.10

Statement at Completion

Within 84 days after receiving the Taking-Over Certificate for the Works, the Contractor shall submit to the Engineer six copies of a Statement at completion with supporting documents, in accordance with Sub-Clause 14.3 [*Application for Interim Payment Certificates*], showing:

(a)   the value of all work done in accordance with the Contract up to the date stated in the Taking-Over Certificate for the Works,
(b)   any further sums which the Contractor considers to be due, and
(c)   an estimate of any other amounts which the Contractor considers will become due to him under the Contract. Estimated amounts shall be shown separately in this Statement at completion.

The Engineer shall then certify in accordance with Sub-Clause 14.6 [*Issue of Interim Payment Certificates*].

14.11

Application for Final Payment Certificate

Within 56 days after receiving the Performance Certificate, the Contractor shall submit, to the Engineer, six copies of a draft final statement with supporting documents showing in detail in a form approved by the Engineer:

(a)   the value of all work done in accordance with the Contract, and
(b)   any further sums which the Contractor considers to be due to him under the Contract or otherwise.

If the Engineer disagrees with or cannot verify any part of the draft final statement, the Contractor shall submit such further information as the Engineer may reasonably require and shall make such changes in the draft as may be agreed between them. The Contractor shall then prepare and submit to the Engineer the final statement as agreed. This agreed statement is referred to in these Conditions as the "Final Statement".

However if, following discussions between the Engineer and the Contractor and any changes to the draft final statement which are agreed, it becomes evident that a dispute exists, the Engineer shall deliver to the Employer (with a copy to the Contractor) an Interim Payment Certificate for the agreed parts of the draft final statement.   Thereafter, if the dispute is finally resolved under Sub-Clause 20.4 [*Obtaining Dispute Adjudication Board's Decision*] or Sub-Clause 20.5 [*Amicable Settlement*], the Contractor shall then prepare and submit to the Employer (with a copy to the Engineer) a Final Statement.

14.12

Discharge

When submitting the Final Statement, the Contractor shall submit a written discharge which confirms that the total of the Final Statement represents full and final settlement

的一个比例额在该单位工程的**缺陷通知期限**期满日期后，应迅速确认并支付。此比例应是该单位工程的估算合同价值，除以估算的最终**合同价格**所得比例的五分之二(40%)。

但如果根据**第11条**[**缺陷责任**]的规定，还有任何工作要做，**工程师**应有权在该项工作完成前，暂不颁发该工作估算费用的证书。

计算这些比例时，无需考虑**第13.7款**[**因法律改变的调整**]和**第13.8款**[**因成本改变的调整**]中规定的任何调整。

14.10
竣工报表

承包商在收到**工程接收证书**后84天内，应按照**第14.3款**[**期中付款证书的申请**]的要求，向**工程师**提交竣工**报表**及证明文件，一式六份，列出：

(a) 截止**工程接收证书**载明的日期，按合同要求完成的所有工作的价值；

(b) **承包商**认为应付的任何其他款额；以及

(c) **承包商**认为根据合同规定将应付给他的任何其他款项的估计款额。估计款额在竣工**报表**中应单独列出。

此时**工程师**应按照**第14.6款**[**期中付款证书的颁发**]的规定予以确认。

14.11
最终付款证书的申请

承包商应在收到**履约证书**后56天内，向**工程师**提交按照**工程师**批准的格式编制的最终报表草案，并附证明文件，一式六份，详细列出：

(a) 根据**合同**完成的所有工作的价值；以及

(b) **承包商**认为根据合同或其他规定应支付给他的任何其他款额。

如果**工程师**不同意或无法核实最终报表草案中的任何部分，**承包商**应按**工程师**可能提出的合理要求提交补充资料，并按双方可能商定的意见，对该草案进行修改。然后，**承包商**应按商定的意见编制并向**工程师**提交最终报表。这份经商定的报表在本条件中称为"**最终报表**"。

如果在**工程师**和**承包商**协商并就协商一致的意见对最终报表草案进行修改过程中，明显存在争端，**工程师**应向**雇主**报送最终报表草案中已同意部分的**期中付款证书**(给承包商一份副本)。此后，如果争端根据**第20.4款**[**取得争端裁决委员会的决定**]或**第20.5款**[**友好解决**]的规定，最终得到解决，**承包商**随后应编制并向**雇主**提交**最终报表**(给工程师一份副本)。

14.12
结清证明

承包商在提交**最终报表**时，应提交一份书面结清证明，确认**最终报表**上的总额代表了根据合同或与合同有关的事项，应付给**承包商**的所有款项的全

of all moneys due to the Contractor under or in connection with the Contract. This discharge may state that it becomes effective when the Contractor has received the Performance Security and the outstanding balance of this total, in which event the discharge shall be effective on such date.

14.13

Issue of Final Payment Certificate

Within 28 days after receiving the Final Statement and written discharge in accordance with Sub-Clause 14.11 [*Application for Final Payment Certificate*] and Sub-Clause 14.12 [*Discharge*], the Engineer shall issue, to the Employer, the Final Payment Certificate which shall state:

(a)   the amount which is finally due, and

(b)   after giving credit to the Employer for all amounts previously paid by the Employer and for all sums to which the Employer is entitled, the balance (if any) due from the Employer to the Contractor or from the Contractor to the Employer, as the case may be.

If the Contractor has not applied for a Final Payment Certificate in accordance with Sub-Clause 14.11 [*Application for Final Payment Certificate*] and Sub-Clause 14.12 [*Discharge*], the Engineer shall request the Contractor to do so. If the Contractor fails to submit an application within a period of 28 days, the Engineer shall issue the Final Payment Certificate for such amount as he fairly determines to be due.

14.14

Cessation of Employer's Liability

The Employer shall not be liable to the Contractor for any matter or thing under or in connection with the Contract or execution of the Works, except to the extent that the Contractor shall have included an amount expressly for it:

(a)   in the Final Statement and also

(b)   (except for matters or things arising after the issue of the Taking-Over Certificate for the Works) in the Statement at completion described in Sub-Clause 14.10 [*Statement at Completion*].

However, this Sub-Clause shall not limit the Employer's liability under his indemnification obligations, or the Employer's liability in any case of fraud, deliberate default or reckless misconduct by the Employer.

14.15

Currencies of Payment

The Contract Price shall be paid in the currency or currencies named in the Appendix to Tender. Unless otherwise stated in the Particular Conditions, if more than one currency is so named, payments shall be made as follows:

(a)   if the Accepted Contract Amount was expressed in Local Currency only:

(i)   the proportions or amounts of the Local and Foreign Currencies, and the fixed rates of exchange to be used for calculating the payments, shall be as stated in the Appendix to Tender, except as otherwise agreed by both Parties;

(ii)   payments and deductions under Sub-Clause 13.5 [*Provisional Sums*] and Sub-Clause 13.7 [*Adjustments for Changes in Legislation*] shall be made in the applicable currencies and proportions; and

(iii)   other payments and deductions under sub-paragraphs (a) to (d) of Sub-Clause 14.3 [*Application for Interim Payment Certificates*] shall be made in the currencies and proportions specified in sub-paragraph (a)(i) above;

(b)   payment of the damages specified in the Appendix to Tender shall be made in the currencies and proportions specified in the Appendix to Tender;

部和最终的结算总额。该结清证明可注明在**承包商**收到退回的**履约担保**和该总额中尚未付清的余额后生效，在此情况下，结清证明应在该日期生效。

14.13
最终付款证书的颁发

工程师在收到按照第 **14.11 款**[**最终付款证书的申请**]和第 **14.12 款**[**结清证明**]中规定的**最终报表**和结清证明后 28 天内，应向**雇主**发出最终**付款证书**，其中说明：

(a) 最终应支付的款额；以及
(b) 确认**雇主**先前已付的所有款额、以及**雇主**有权得到的全部款额后，**雇主**尚需付给**承包商**，或**承包商**尚需付给**雇主**（视情况而定）的余额（如果有）。

如果**承包商**未按第 **14.11 款**[**最终付款证书的申请**]和第 **14.12 款**[**结清证明**]的规定申请**最终付款证书**，**工程师**应要求**承包商**提出申请。如**承包商**在 28 天期限内未能提交申请，**工程师**应按其公正确定的应付款额颁发**最终付款证书**。

14.14
雇主责任的中止

除了**承包商**在下列文件中，为**合同**或**工程**实施引发的或与之有关的任何问题或事项，明确提出款项要求以外，**雇主**应不再为之对**承包商**承担责任：

(a) 在**最终报表**中；以及
(b) 在第 **14.10 款**[**竣工报表**]所述的竣工**报表**中（颁发**工程接收证书**后发生的问题或事项除外）。

但本**款**不应减少**雇主**因其保障义务，或因其任何欺骗、有意违约、或轻率的不当行为等情况引起的责任。

14.15
支付的货币

合同价格应按**投标书附录**中规定的货币或几种货币支付。除非**专用条件**中另有说明，如果规定了一种以上货币，应按以下办法支付：

(a) 如果**中标合同金额**只是用**当地货币**表示的：

(i)   **当地货币**和**外币**的比例或款额，以及计算付款采用的固定汇率，除**双方**另有商定外，应按**投标书附录**中的规定；

(ii) 根据第 **13.5 款**[**暂列金额**]和第 **13.7 款**[**因法律改变的调整**]规定的付款和扣减，应按适用的货币和比例；和

(iii) 根据第 **14.3 款**[**期中付款证书的申请**](a)至(d)项做出的其他支付和扣减，应按上述(a)(i)项规定的货币和比例；

(b) **投标书附录**中规定的对损害赔偿费的支付应按**投标书附录**中规定的货币和比例；

(c)   other payments to the Employer by the Contractor shall be made in the currency in which the sum was expended by the Employer, or in such currency as may be agreed by both Parties;

(d)   if any amount payable by the Contractor to the Employer in a particular currency exceeds the sum payable by the Employer to the Contractor in that currency, the Employer may recover the balance of this amount from the sums otherwise payable to the Contractor in other currencies; and

(e)   if no rates of exchange are stated in the Appendix to Tender, they shall be those prevailing on the Base Date and determined by the central bank of the Country.

15 Termination by Employer

15.1
Notice to Correct

If the Contractor fails to carry out any obligation under the Contract, the Engineer may by notice require the Contractor to make good the failure and to remedy it within a specified reasonable time.

15.2
Termination by Employer

The Employer shall be entitled to terminate the Contract if the Contractor:

(a)   fails to comply with Sub-Clause 4.2 [*Performance Security*] or with a notice under Sub-Clause 15.1 [*Notice to Correct*],

(b)   abandons the Works or otherwise plainly demonstrates the intention not to continue performance of his obligations under the Contract,

(c)   without reasonable excuse fails:

(i)   to proceed with the Works in accordance with Clause 8 [*Commencement, Delays and Suspension*], or

(ii)   to comply with a notice issued under Sub-Clause 7.5 [*Rejection*] or Sub-Clause 7.6 [*Remedial Work*], within 28 days after receiving it,

(d)   subcontracts the whole of the Works or assigns the Contract without the required agreement,

(e)   becomes bankrupt or insolvent, goes into liquidation, has a receiving or administration order made against him, compounds with his creditors, or carries on business under a receiver, trustee or manager for the benefit of his creditors, or if any act is done or event occurs which (under applicable Laws) has a similar effect to any of these acts or events, or

(f)   gives or offers to give (directly or indirectly) to any person any bribe, gift, gratuity, commission or other thing of value, as an inducement or reward:

(i)   for doing or forbearing to do any action in relation to the Contract, or

(ii)   for showing or forbearing to show favour or disfavour to any person in relation to the Contract,

or if any of the Contractor's Personnel, agents or Subcontractors gives or offers to give (directly or indirectly) to any person any such inducement or reward as is described in this sub-paragraph (f). However, lawful inducements and rewards to Contractor's Personnel shall not entitle termination.

In any of these events or circumstances, the Employer may, upon giving 14 days' notice to the Contractor, terminate the Contract and expel the Contractor from the Site. However, in the case of sub-paragraph (e) or (f), the Employer may by notice terminate the Contract immediately.

(c) 由**承包商**付给**雇主**的其他款项应以**雇主**花费该款实际用的货币，或双方可能商定的货币；

(d) 如果**承包商**应付给**雇主**的某种货币的款额，超过了**雇主**应付给**承包商**的该种货币的款额，**雇主**可从另应付给**承包商**的其他货币的款额中，收回该项差额；以及

(e) 如果**投标书附录**中未说明汇率，应采用**基准日期**当天**工程**所在国中央银行确定的汇率。

15　由雇主终止

15.1

通知改正

如果**承包商**未能根据**合同**履行任何义务，**工程师**可通知**承包商**，要求其在规定的合理时间内，纠正并补救上述未履约。

15.2

由雇主终止

如果**承包商**有下列行为，**雇主**应有权终止**合同**：

(a) 未能遵守**第 4.2 款**[**履约担保**]的规定，或根据**第 15.1 款**[**通知改正**]的规定发出通知的要求；

(b) 放弃**工程**，或明确表现出不愿继续按照**合同**履行其义务的意向；

(c) 无合理解释，未能：

　(i) 按照**第 8 条**[**开工、延误和暂停**]的规定进行**工程**；或

　(ii) 在收到按照**第 7.5 款**[**拒收**]或**第 7.6 款**[**修补工作**]的规定发出通知后 28 天内，遵守通知要求；

(d) 未经必要的许可，将整个**工程**分包出去，或将**合同**转让他人；

(e) 破产或无力偿债，停业清理，已有对其财产的接管令或管理令，与债权人达成和解，或为其债权人的利益在财产接管人、受托人或管理人的监督下营业，或采取了任何行动或发生任何事件（根据有关适用**法律**）具有与前述行动或事件相似的效果；或

(f) （直接或间接）向任何人付给或企图付给任何贿赂、礼品、赏金、回扣或其他贵重物品，以引诱或报偿他人：

　(i) 采取或不采取有关**合同**的任何行动；或
　(ii) 对与**合同**有关的任何人做出或不做有利或不利的表示；

或任何**承包商人员**、代理人或**分包商**（直接或间接）向任何人付给或企图付给本**款**(f)项所述的任何此类引诱物或报偿。但对给予**承包商人员**的合法鼓励和奖偿无权终止。

在出现任何上述事件或情况时，**雇主**可提前 14 天向**承包商**发出通知，终止**合同**，并要求其离开**现场**。但在(e)或(f)项情况下，**雇主**可发出通知立即终止**合同**。

107

The Employer's election to terminate the Contract shall not prejudice any other rights of the Employer, under the Contract or otherwise.

The Contractor shall then leave the Site and deliver any required Goods, all Contractor's Documents, and other design documents made by or for him, to the Engineer. However, the Contractor shall use his best efforts to comply immediately with any reasonable instructions included in the notice (i) for the assignment of any subcontract, and (ii) for the protection of life or property or for the safety of the Works.

After termination, the Employer may complete the Works and/or arrange for any other entities to do so. The Employer and these entities may then use any Goods, Contractor's Documents and other design documents made by or on behalf of the Contractor.

The Employer shall then give notice that the Contractor's Equipment and Temporary Works will be released to the Contractor at or near the Site. The Contractor shall promptly arrange their removal, at the risk and cost of the Contractor. However, if by this time the Contractor has failed to make a payment due to the Employer, these items may be sold by the Employer in order to recover this payment. Any balance of the proceeds shall then be paid to the Contractor.

15.3

Valuation at Date of Termination

As soon as practicable after a notice of termination under Sub-Clause 15.2 [Termination by Employer] has taken effect, the Engineer shall proceed in accordance with Sub-Clause 3.5 [Determinations] to agree or determine the value of the Works, Goods and Contractor's Documents, and any other sums due to the Contractor for work executed in accordance with the Contract.

15.4

Payment after Termination

After a notice of termination under Sub-Clause 15.2 [Termination by Employer] has taken effect, the Employer may:

(a) proceed in accordance with Sub-Clause 2.5 [Employer's Claims],

(b) withhold further payments to the Contractor until the costs of execution, completion and remedying of any defects, damages for delay in completion (if any), and all other costs incurred by the Employer, have been established, and/or

(c) recover from the Contractor any losses and damages incurred by the Employer and any extra costs of completing the Works, after allowing for any sum due to the Contractor under Sub-Clause 15.3 [Valuation at Date of Termination]. After recovering any such losses, damages and extra costs, the Employer shall pay any balance to the Contractor.

15.5

Employer's Entitlement to Termination

The Employer shall be entitled to terminate the Contract, at any time for the Employer's convenience, by giving notice of such termination to the Contractor. The termination shall take effect 28 days after the later of the dates on which the Contractor receives this notice or the Employer returns the Performance Security. The Employer shall not terminate the Contract under this Sub-Clause in order to execute the Works himself or to arrange for the Works to be executed by another contractor.

After this termination, the Contractor shall proceed in accordance with Sub-Clause 16.3 [Cessation of Work and Removal of Contractor's Equipment] and shall be paid in accordance with Sub-Clause 19.6 [Optional Termination, Payment and Release].

雇主做出终止合同的选择，不应损害其根据合同或其他规定所享有的其他任何权利。

此时，承包商应撤离现场，并将任何需要的货物、所有承包商文件，以及由(或为)他编制的其他设计文件交给工程师。但承包商应立即尽最大努力遵从包括通知中关于(i)转让任何分包合同，及(ii)保护生命或财产、或工程的安全的任何合理指示。

终止后，雇主可以继续完成工程，和(或)安排其他实体完成。这时雇主和这些实体可以使用任何货物、承包商文件和由承包商或以其名义编制的其他设计文件。

其后雇主应发出通知，将在现场或其附近把承包商设备和临时工程放还给承包商。承包商应自行承担风险和费用，迅速安排将它们运走。但如果此时承包商还有应付雇主的款项没有付清，雇主可以出售这些物品，以收回欠款。收益的任何余款应付给承包商。

15.3

终止日期时的估价

在根据第15.2款[由雇主终止]的规定发出的终止通知生效后，工程师应尽快按照第3.5款[确定]的要求商定或确定工程、货物和承包商文件的价值，以及承包商按照合同实施的工作应得的任何其他款项。

15.4

终止后的付款

在根据第15.2款[由雇主终止]的规定发出的终止通知生效后，雇主可以：

(a) 按照第2.5款[雇主的索赔]的规定进行；

(b) 在确定施工、竣工和修补任何缺陷的费用、因延误竣工(如果有)的损害赔偿费、以及由雇主负担的全部其他费用前，暂不向承包商支付进一步款项；和(或)

(c) 在根据第15.3款[终止日期时的估价]的规定答应付给承包商的任何款额后，先从承包商处收回雇主蒙受的任何损失和损害赔偿费，以及完成工程所需的任何额外费用。在收回任何此类损失、损害赔偿费和额外费用后，雇主应将任何余额付给承包商。

15.5

雇主终止的权利

雇主应有权在对他方便的任何时候，通过向承包商发出终止通知，终止合同。此项终止应在承包商收到该通知或雇主退回履约担保两者中较晚的日期后第28天生效。雇主不应为了要自己实施或安排另外的承包商实施工程，而根据本款终止合同。

在此项终止后，承包商应按照第16.3款[停止工作和承包商设备的撤离]的规定执行，并应按照第19.6款[自主选择终止、付款和解除]的规定获得付款。

16 Suspension and Termination by Contractor

16.1
Contractor's Entitlement to Suspend Work

If the Engineer fails to certify in accordance with Sub-Clause 14.6 [*Issue of Interim Payment Certificates*] or the Employer fails to comply with Sub-Clause 2.4 [*Employer's Financial Arrangements*] or Sub-Clause 14.7 [*Payment*], the Contractor may, after giving not less than 21 days' notice to the Employer, suspend work (or reduce the rate of work) unless and until the Contractor has received the Payment Certificate, reasonable evidence or payment, as the case may be and as described in the notice.

The Contractor's action shall not prejudice his entitlements to financing charges under Sub-Clause 14.8 [*Delayed Payment*] and to termination under Sub-Clause 16.2 [*Termination by Contractor*].

If the Contractor subsequently receives such Payment Certificate, evidence or payment (as described in the relevant Sub-Clause and in the above notice) before giving a notice of termination, the Contractor shall resume normal working as soon as is reasonably practicable.

If the Contractor suffers delay and/or incurs Cost as a result of suspending work (or reducing the rate of work) in accordance with this Sub-Clause, the Contractor shall give notice to the Engineer and shall be entitled subject to Sub-Clause 20.1 [*Contractor's Claims*] to:

(a)   an extension of time for any such delay, if completion is or will be delayed, under Sub-Clause 8.4 [*Extension of Time for Completion*], and

(b)   payment of any such Cost plus reasonable profit, which shall be included in the Contract Price.

After receiving this notice, the Engineer shall proceed in accordance with Sub-Clause 3.5 [*Determinations*] to agree or determine these matters.

16.2
Termination by Contractor

The Contractor shall be entitled to terminate the Contract if:

(a)   the Contractor does not receive the reasonable evidence within 42 days after giving notice under Sub-Clause 16.1 [*Contractor's Entitlement to Suspend Work*] in respect of a failure to comply with Sub-Clause 2.4 [*Employer's Financial Arrangements*],

(b)   the Engineer fails, within 56 days after receiving a Statement and supporting documents, to issue the relevant Payment Certificate,

(c)   the Contractor does not receive the amount due under an Interim Payment Certificate within 42 days after the expiry of the time stated in Sub-Clause 14.7 [*Payment*] within which payment is to be made (except for deductions in accordance with Sub-Clause 2.5 [*Employer's Claims*]),

(d)   the Employer substantially fails to perform his obligations under the Contract,

(e)   the Employer fails to comply with Sub-Clause 1.6 [*Contract Agreement*] or Sub-Clause 1.7 [*Assignment*],

(f)   a prolonged suspension affects the whole of the Works as described in Sub-Clause 8.11 [*Prolonged Suspension*], or

(g)   the Employer becomes bankrupt or insolvent, goes into liquidation, has a receiving or administration order made against him, compounds with his creditors, or carries on business under a receiver, trustee or manager for the

16 由承包商暂停和终止

16.1
承包商暂停工作的权利

如果**工程师**未能按照**第 14.6 款**[期中付款证书的颁发]的规定确认发证，或**雇主**未能遵守**第 2.4 款**[雇主的资金安排]或**第 14.7 款**[付款]的规定，**承包商**可在不少于 21 天前通知**雇主**，暂停工作（或放慢工作速度），除非并直到**承包商**根据情况和通知中所述，收到了**付款证书**、合理的证明或付款为止。

承包商的上述行动，不应影响他根据**第 14.8 款**[延误的付款]的规定获得融资费，以及用和根据**第 16.2 款**[由承包商终止]的规定提出终止的权利。

如果在发出终止通知前，**承包商**随后收到了**付款证书**、证明或付款（如有关**条款**和上述通知中所述），**承包商**应在合理可能的情况下，尽快恢复正常工作。

如果因按照**本款**暂停工作（或放慢工作速度），使**承包商**遭受延误和（或）招致增加**费用**，**承包商**应向**工程师**发出通知，有权根据**第 20.1 款**[承包商的索赔]的规定，要求：

(a)   根据**第 8.4 款**[竣工时间的延长]的规定，如竣工已或将受到延误，对任何此类延误给予延长期；以及

(b)   任何此类**费用**加合理利润应计入**合同价格**，给予支付。

工程师收到此通知后，应按照**第 3.5 款**[确定]的规定，对这些事项进行商定或确定。

16.2

由承包商终止

如出现下列情况，**承包商**应有权终止合同：

(a)   **承包商**在根据**第 16.1 款**[承包商暂停工作的权利]的规定，就未能遵循**第 2.4 款**[雇主的资金安排]规定的事项发出通知后 42 天内，仍未收到合理的证据；

(b)   **工程师**未能在收到**报表**和证明文件后 56 天内发出有关的**付款证书**；

(c)   在**第 14.7 款**[付款]规定的付款时间到期后 42 天内，**承包商**仍未收到根据期中付款证书的应付款额（按照**第 2.5 款**[雇主的索赔]规定的扣减部分除外）；

(d)   **雇主**实质上未能根据**合同**规定履行其义务；

(e)   **雇主**未遵守**第 1.6 款**[合同协议书]或**第 1.7 款**[权益转让]的规定；

(f)   **第 8.11 款**[拖长的暂停]所述的拖长的停工影响了整个工程；或

(g)   **雇主**破产或无力偿债，停业清理，已有对其财产的接管令或管理令，与债权人达成和解，或为其债权人的利益在财产接管人、受托人

benefit of his creditors, or if any act is done or event occurs which (under applicable Laws) has a similar effect to any of these acts or events.

In any of these events or circumstances, the Contractor may, upon giving 14 days' notice to the Employer, terminate the Contract. However, in the case of sub-paragraph (f) or (g), the Contractor may by notice terminate the Contract immediately.

The Contractor's election to terminate the Contract shall not prejudice any other rights of the Contractor, under the Contract or otherwise.

16.3
Cessation of Work and Removal of Contractor's Equipment

After a notice of termination under Sub-Clause 15.5 [*Employer's Entitlement to Termination*], Sub-Clause 16.2 [*Termination by Contractor*] or Sub-Clause 19.6 [*Optional Termination, Payment and Release*] has taken effect, the Contractor shall promptly:

(a)   cease all further work, except for such work as may have been instructed by the Engineer for the protection of life or property or for the safety of the Works,

(b)   hand over Contractor's Documents, Plant, Materials and other work, for which the Contractor has received payment, and

(c)   remove all other Goods from the Site, except as necessary for safety, and leave the Site.

16.4
Payment on Termination

After a notice of termination under Sub-Clause 16.2 [*Termination by Contractor*] has taken effect, the Employer shall promptly:

(a)   return the Performance Security to the Contractor,

(b)   pay the Contractor in accordance with Sub-Clause 19.6 [*Optional Termination, Payment and Release*], and

(c)   pay to the Contractor the amount of any loss of profit or other loss or damage sustained by the Contractor as a result of this termination.

17 Risk and Responsibility

17.1
Indemnities

The Contractor shall indemnify and hold harmless the Employer, the Employer's Personnel, and their respective agents, against and from all claims, damages, losses and expenses (including legal fees and expenses) in respect of:

(a)   bodily injury, sickness, disease or death, of any person whatsoever arising out of or in the course of or by reason of the Contractor's design (if any), the execution and completion of the Works and the remedying of any defects, unless attributable to any negligence, wilful act or breach of the Contract by the Employer, the Employer's Personnel, or any of their respective agents, and

(b)   damage to or loss of any property, real or personal (other than the Works), to the extent that such damage or loss:

(i)   arises out of or in the course of or by reason of the Contractor's design (if any), the execution and completion of the Works and the remedying of any defects, and

(ii)   is attributable to any negligence, wilful act or breach of the Contract by the Contractor, the Contractor's Personnel, their respective agents, or anyone directly or indirectly employed by any of them.

或管理人的监督下营业，或采取了任何行动或发生任何事件(根据有关适用**法律**)具有与前述行动或事件相似的效果。

在上述任何事件或情况下，**承包商**可通知**雇主**，14 天后终止**合同**。但在(f)或(g)项情况下，**承包商**可发出通知立即终止**合同**。

承包商做出终止**合同**的选择，不应影响其根据**合同**或其他规定所享有的其他任何权利。

16.3

停止工作和承包商设备的撤离　根据第 **15.5 款**[*雇主终止合同的权利*]、第 **16.2 款**[*由承包商终止*]或第 **19.6 款**[*自主选择终止、付款和解除*]的规定发出的终止通知生效后，**承包商**应迅速：

(a) 停止所有进一步的工作，但**工程师**为保护生命或财产或**工程**的安全可能指示的工作除外；
(b) 移交**承包商**已得到付款的**承包商文件**、**生产设备**、**材料**和其他工作；以及
(c) 从**现场**运走除为了安全需要以外的所有其他**货物**，并撤离**现场**。

16.4

终止时的付款　在根据第 **16.2 款**[*由承包商终止*]的规定发出的终止通知生效后，**雇主**应迅速：

(a) 将履约担保退还**承包商**；
(b) 按照第 **19.6 款**[*自主选择终止、付款和解除*]的规定，向**承包商**付款；以及
(c) 付给**承包商**因此项终止而蒙受的任何利润损失、或其他损失或损害的款额。

17　风险与职责

17.1

保障　**承包商**应保障和保持使**雇主**、**雇主人员**以及他们各自的代理人免受以下所有索赔、损害赔偿费、损失和开支(包括法律费用和开支)带来的损害：

(a) 任何人员的人身伤害、患病、疾病或死亡，不论是由于**承包商**设计(如果有)施工和竣工、以及修补任何缺陷引起，或在其过程中，或因其原因产生的，除非是由于**雇主**、**雇主人员**、或他们各自的任何代理人的任何疏忽、故意行为、或违反**合同**造成的；以及

(b) 由下列情况造成的对任何财产、不动产或动产(**工程**除外)的损害或损失：

(i) 由于**承包商**的设计(如果有)、施工和竣工、以及修补任何缺陷引起，或在其过程中、或因其原因产生的；和

(ii) 由**承包商**、**承包商人员**、他们各自的代理人，或由他们中任何人员直接或间接雇用的任何人员的疏忽、故意行为、或违反**合同**造成的。

The Employer shall indemnify and hold harmless the Contractor, the Contractor's Personnel, and their respective agents, against and from all claims, damages, losses and expenses (including legal fees and expenses) in respect of (1) bodily injury, sickness, disease or death, which is attributable to any negligence, wilful act or breach of the Contract by the Employer, the Employer's Personnel, or any of their respective agents, and (2) the matters for which liability may be excluded from insurance cover, as described in sub-paragraphs (d)(i), (ii) and (iii) of Sub-Clause 18.3 [*Insurance Against Injury to Persons and Damage to Property*].

17.2

Contractor's Care of the Works

The Contractor shall take full responsibility for the care of the Works and Goods from the Commencement Date until the Taking-Over Certificate is issued (or is deemed to be issued under Sub-Clause 10.1 [*Taking Over of the Works and Sections*]) for the Works, when responsibility for the care of the Works shall pass to the Employer. If a Taking-Over Certificate is issued (or is so deemed to be issued) for any Section or part of the Works, responsibility for the care of the Section or part shall then pass to the Employer.

After responsibility has accordingly passed to the Employer, the Contractor shall take responsibility for the care of any work which is outstanding on the date stated in a Taking-Over Certificate, until this outstanding work has been completed.

If any loss or damage happens to the Works, Goods or Contractor's Documents during the period when the Contractor is responsible for their care, from any cause not listed in Sub-Clause 17.3 [*Employer's Risks*], the Contractor shall rectify the loss or damage at the Contractor's risk and cost, so that the Works, Goods and Contractor's Documents conform with the Contract.

The Contractor shall be liable for any loss or damage caused by any actions performed by the Contractor after a Taking-Over Certificate has been issued. The Contractor shall also be liable for any loss or damage which occurs after a Taking-Over Certificate has been issued and which arose from a previous event for which the Contractor was liable.

17.3

Employer's Risks

The risks referred to in Sub-Clause 17.4 below are:

(a)   war, hostilities (whether war be declared or not), invasion, act of foreign enemies,

(b)   rebellion, terrorism, revolution, insurrection, military or usurped power, or civil war, within the Country,

(c)   riot, commotion or disorder within the Country by persons other than the Contractor's Personnel and other employees of the Contractor and Subcontractors,

(d)   munitions of war, explosive materials, ionising radiation or contamination by radio-activity, within the Country, except as may be attributable to the Contractor's use of such munitions, explosives, radiation or radio-activity,

(e)   pressure waves caused by aircraft or other aerial devices travelling at sonic or supersonic speeds,

(f)   use or occupation by the Employer of any part of the Permanent Works, except as may be specified in the Contract,

(g)   design of any part of the Works by the Employer's Personnel or by others for whom the Employer is responsible, and

(h)   any operation of the forces of nature which is Unforeseeable or against which an experienced contractor could not reasonably have been expected to have taken adequate preventative precautions.

雇主应保障和保持**承包商**、**承包商人员**以及他们各自的代理人，免受以下所有索赔、损害赔偿费、损失和开支(包括法律费用和开支)带来的损害：(1)由**雇主**、**雇主人员**、或他们各自的代理人的任何疏忽、故意行为、或违反**合同**造成的人身伤害、患病、疾病或死亡；以及(2)如**第18.3款[人身伤害和财产损害险]**(d)项(i)、(ii)和(iii)目中所述的其责任可以不包括在保险范围的各类事项。

17.2

承包商对工程的照管

承包商应从开工日期起承担照管**工程**及**货物**的全部职责，直到颁发**工程接收证书**(或根据**第10.1款[工程和单位工程的接收]**的规定应视为已颁发)之日止，这时**工程**照管职责应移交给**雇主**。如果对某**单位工程**或部分工程已颁发(或如上述应视为已颁发)**接收证书**，则对该**单位工程**或部分工程的照管职责届时应移交给**雇主**。

在照管职责按上述移交给**雇主**后，**承包商**仍应对在**接收证书**上注明日期时的任何扫尾工作承担照管职责，直到该扫尾工作完成为止。

如在**承包商**负责照管期间，由于**第17.3款[雇主的风险]**中所列风险以外的原因，致使**工程**、**货物**，或**承包商文件**发生任何损失或损害，**承包商**应自行承担风险和费用，修正该项损失或损害，使**工程**、**货物**或**承包商文件**符合**合同**要求。

承包商应对颁发**接收证书**后由其采取的任何行动造成的任何损失或损害负责。**承包商**还应对颁发**接收证书**后发生的，由**承包商**负责的以前的事件引起的任何损失或损害负责。

17.3

雇主的风险

在下述**第17.4款**谈到的风险是指：

(a) 战争、敌对行动(不论宣战与否)、入侵、外敌行动；

(b) **工程所在国**内的叛乱、恐怖主义、革命、暴动、军事政变或篡夺政权、或内战；

(c) **承包商人员**及**承包商**和分包商的其他雇员以外的人员，在**工程所在国**内的暴乱、骚动、喧闹或混乱；

(d) **工程所在国**内的战争军火、爆炸物资、电离辐射或放射性引起的污染，但可能由**承包商**使用此类军火、炸药、辐射或放射性引起的除外；

(e) 由音速或超音速飞行的飞机或飞行装置所产生的压力波；

(f) 除**合同**规定以外**雇主**使用或占有的**永久工程**的任何部分；

(g) 由**雇主人员**或**雇主**对其负责的其他人员所做的**工程**任何部分的设计；以及

(h) **不可预见**的、或不能合理预期一个有经验的承包商已采取适宜预防措施的任何自然力的作用。

17.4
Consequences of
Employer's Risks

If and to the extent that any of the risks listed in Sub-Clause 17.3 above results in loss or damage to the Works, Goods or Contractor's Documents, the Contractor shall promptly give notice to the Engineer and shall rectify this loss or damage to the extent required by the Engineer.

If the Contractor suffers delay and/or incurs Cost from rectifying this loss or damage, the Contractor shall give a further notice to the Engineer and shall be entitled subject to Sub-Clause 20.1 [*Contractor's Claims*] to:

(a)   an extension of time for any such delay, if completion is or will be delayed, under Sub-Clause 8.4 [*Extension of Time for Completion*], and
(b)   payment of any such Cost, which shall be included in the Contract Price. In the case of sub-paragraphs (f) and (g) of Sub-Clause 17.3 [*Employer's Risks*], reasonable profit on the Cost shall also be included.

After receiving this further notice, the Engineer shall proceed in accordance with Sub-Clause 3.5 [*Determinations*] to agree or determine these matters.

17.5

Intellectual and Industrial
Property Rights

In this Sub-Clause, "infringement" means an infringement (or alleged infringement) of any patent, registered design, copyright, trade mark, trade name, trade secret or other intellectual or industrial property right relating to the Works; and "claim" means a claim (or proceedings pursuing a claim) alleging an infringement.

Whenever a Party does not give notice to the other Party of any claim within 28 days of receiving the claim, the first Party shall be deemed to have waived any right to indemnity under this Sub-Clause.

The Employer shall indemnify and hold the Contractor harmless against and from any claim alleging an infringement which is or was:

(a)   an unavoidable result of the Contractor's compliance with the Contract, or
(b)   a result of any Works being used by the Employer:

(i)   for a purpose other than that indicated by, or reasonably to be inferred from, the Contract, or
(ii)   in conjunction with any thing not supplied by the Contractor, unless such use was disclosed to the Contractor prior to the Base Date or is stated in the Contract.

The Contractor shall indemnify and hold the Employer harmless against and from any other claim which arises out of or in relation to (i) the manufacture, use, sale or import of any Goods, or (ii) any design for which the Contractor is responsible.

If a Party is entitled to be indemnified under this Sub-Clause, the indemnifying Party may (at its cost) conduct negotiations for the settlement of the claim, and any litigation or arbitration which may arise from it. The other Party shall, at the request and cost of the indemnifying Party, assist in contesting the claim. This other Party (and its Personnel) shall not make any admission which might be prejudicial to the indemnifying Party, unless the indemnifying Party failed to take over the conduct of any negotiations, litigation or arbitration upon being requested to do so by such other Party.

17.6

Limitation of Liability

Neither Party shall be liable to the other Party for loss of use of any Works, loss of profit, loss of any contract or for any indirect or consequential loss or damage which may be suffered by the other Party in connection with the Contract, other than under

17.4
雇主风险的后果

如果上述第 **17.3** 款列举的任何风险达到对**工程**、**货物**，或**承包商**文件造成损失或损害的程度，**承包商**应立即通知**工程师**，并应按**工程师**的要求，修正此类损失或损害。

如果因修正此类损失或损害使**承包商**遭受延误和(或)招致增加**费用**，**承包商**应进一步通知**工程师**，有权根据第 **20.1** 款［**承包商的索赔**］的规定，要求：

(a) 根据第 **8.4** 款［**竣工时间的延长**］的规定，如竣工已或将受到延误，对任何此类延误给予延长期；以及

(b) 任何此类**费用**应计入**合同价格**，给予支付。如有第 **17.3** 款［**雇主的风险**］的(f)和(g)项的情况，还应计入**费用**的合理利润。

工程师收到此类进一步通知后，应按照第 **3.5** 款［*确定*］的规定，对这些事项进行商定或确定。

17.5
知识产权和工业产权

在本款中，"侵权"是指侵犯(或被指称侵犯)与**工程**有关的任何专利权、已登记的设计、版权、商标、商号商品名称、商业机密、或其他知识产权或工业产权；"索赔"是指对指称一项侵权的索赔(或为索赔进行的诉讼)。

当一方未能在收到任何索赔的 28 天内，向另一方发出关于该索赔的通知时，该方应被认为已放弃根据本款规定的任何受保障的权利。

雇主应保障并保持**承包商**免受因以下情况提出的指称侵权的任何索赔引起的损害：

(a) 因**承包商**遵从**合同**要求而造成的不可避免的结果；或

(b) 因**雇主**为以下原因使用任何**工程**的结果：

  (i) 为了**合同**中指明的、或根据**合同**可合理推断的事项以外的目的；或

  (ii) 与非**承包商**提供的任何物品联合使用，除非此项使用已在**基准日期**前向**承包商**透露，或在**合同**中有规定。

承包商应保障并保持**雇主**免受由以下事项产生或与之有关的任何其他索赔引起的损害：(i)任何**货物**的制造、使用、销售或进口，或(ii)**承包商**负责的任何设计。

如果一方根据本款规定有权受保障，保障方可(由其承担费用)组织解决索赔的谈判，以及可能由其引起的任何诉讼或仲裁。在保障方请求并承担费用的情况下，另一方应协助争辩该索赔。此另一方(及其人员)不应做出可能损害保障方的任何承认，除非保障方未能在该另一方请求下，接办组织任何谈判、诉讼或仲裁事宜。

17.6
责任限度

除根据第 **16.4** 款［**终止时的付款**］和第 **17.1** 款［**保障**］的规定外，任何一方不应对另一方使用任何**工程**中的损失、利润损失、任何**合同**的损失，或对另一方可能遭受的与**合同**有关的任何间接的或引发的损失或损害负责。

117

Sub-Clause 16.4 [*Payment on Termination*] and Sub-Clause 17.1 [*Indemnities*].

The total liability of the Contractor to the Employer, under or in connection with the Contract other than under Sub-Clause 4.19 [*Electricity, Water and Gas*], Sub-Clause 4.20 [*Employer's Equipment and Free-Issue Material*], Sub-Clause 17.1 [*Indemnities*] and Sub-Clause 17.5 [*Intellectual and Industrial Property Rights*], shall not exceed the sum stated in the Particular Conditions or (if a sum is not so stated) the Accepted Contract Amount.

This Sub-Clause shall not limit liability in any case of fraud, deliberate default or reckless misconduct by the defaulting Party.

Insurance 18

**18.1
General Requirements
for Insurances**

In this Clause, "insuring Party" means, for each type of insurance, the Party responsible for effecting and maintaining the insurance specified in the relevant Sub-Clause.

Wherever the Contractor is the insuring Party, each insurance shall be effected with insurers and in terms approved by the Employer. These terms shall be consistent with any terms agreed by both Parties before the date of the Letter of Acceptance. This agreement of terms shall take precedence over the provisions of this Clause.

Wherever the Employer is the insuring Party, each insurance shall be effected with insurers and in terms consistent with the details annexed to the Particular Conditions.

If a policy is required to indemnify joint insured, the cover shall apply separately to each insured as though a separate policy had been issued for each of the joint insured. If a policy indemnifies additional joint insured, namely in addition to the insured specified in this Clause, (i) the Contractor shall act under the policy on behalf of these additional joint insured except that the Employer shall act for Employer's Personnel, (ii) additional joint insured shall not be entitled to receive payments directly from the insurer or to have any other direct dealings with the insurer, and (iii) the insuring Party shall require all additional joint insured to comply with the conditions stipulated in the policy.

Each policy insuring against loss or damage shall provide for payments to be made in the currencies required to rectify the loss or damage. Payments received from insurers shall be used for the rectification of the loss or damage.

The relevant insuring Party shall, within the respective periods stated in the Appendix to Tender (calculated from the Commencement Date), submit to the other Party:

(a)   evidence that the insurances described in this Clause have been effected, and
(b)   copies of the policies for the insurances described in Sub-Clause 18.2 [*Insurance for Works and Contractor's Equipment*] and Sub-Clause 18.3 [*Insurance against Injury to Persons and Damage to Property*].

When each premium is paid, the insuring Party shall submit evidence of payment to the other Party. Whenever evidence or policies are submitted, the insuring Party shall also give notice to the Engineer.

Each Party shall comply with the conditions stipulated in each of the insurance policies. The insuring Party shall keep the insurers informed of any relevant changes

除根据第4.19款[电、水和燃气]、第4.20款[雇主设备和免费供应的材料]、第17.1款[保障]和第17.5款[知识产权和工业产权]的规定外，承包商根据或有关合同对雇主的全部责任不应超过专用条件中规定的总额，或（如果没有上述规定的总额）中标合同金额。

本款不应限制违约方的欺骗、有意违约、或轻率的不当行为等任何情况的责任。

18 保险

18.1
有关保险的一般要求

在本条中，对于每种类型的保险，"应投保方"是指对办理并保持相关条款中规定的保险负有责任的一方。

当承包商是应投保方时，应按照雇主批准的条件向保险人办理每项保险。这些条件应与双方在中标函颁布日期前协商同意的任何条件相一致。这一条件协议的地位应优先于本条各项规定。

当雇主是应投保方时，应按照与专用条件所附的详细内容相一致的条件，向保险人办理每项保险。

如果保险单需要对联合被保人提供保障，保险赔偿应如同已向联合被保人的每一方发出单独保险单一样，对每个被保人分别施用。如果保险单对附加联合被保人提供保障，即在本条规定的被保人之外附加，则(i)除雇主应代表雇主人员行动外，承包商应代表这些附加联合被保人根据保险单行动；(ii)附加联合被保人无权从保险人处直接获得付款，或与保险人有其他直接往来；以及(iii)应投保方应要求所有附加联合被保人遵守保险单规定的条件。

每份承保损失或损害的保险单应以修正损失或损害所需要的货币进行赔偿。从保险人处收到的付款应用于修正损失或损害。

有关应投保方应在投标书附录中规定的各自期限内（从开工日期算起）向另一方提交：

(a) 本条中所述保险已经生效的证据；以及
(b) 第18.2款[工程和承包商设备的保险]和第18.3款[人身伤害和财产损害险]所述保险的保险单副本。

当每笔保险费已付时，应投保方应向另一方提交支付证据。每次提交证据或保险单时，应投保方还应通知工程师。

每方应遵守每份保险单规定的条件。应投保方应保持使保险人随时了解工

to the execution of the Works and ensure that insurance is maintained in accordance with this Clause.

Neither Party shall make any material alteration to the terms of any insurance without the prior approval of the other Party. If an insurer makes (or attempts to make) any alteration, the Party first notified by the insurer shall promptly give notice to the other Party.

If the insuring Party fails to effect and keep in force any of the insurances it is required to effect and maintain under the Contract, or fails to provide satisfactory evidence and copies of policies in accordance with this Sub-Clause, the other Party may (at its option and without prejudice to any other right or remedy) effect insurance for the relevant coverage and pay the premiums due. The insuring Party shall pay the amount of these premiums to the other Party, and the Contract Price shall be adjusted accordingly.

Nothing in this Clause limits the obligations, liabilities or responsibilities of the Contractor or the Employer, under the other terms of the Contract or otherwise. Any amounts not insured or not recovered from the insurers shall be borne by the Contractor and/or the Employer in accordance with these obligations, liabilities or responsibilities. However, if the insuring Party fails to effect and keep in force an insurance which is available and which it is required to effect and maintain under the Contract, and the other Party neither approves the omission nor effects insurance for the coverage relevant to this default, any moneys which should have been recoverable under this insurance shall be paid by the insuring Party.

Payments by one Party to the other Party shall be subject to Sub-Clause 2.5 [*Employer's Claims*] or Sub-Clause 20.1 [*Contractor's Claims*], as applicable.

18.2

Insurance for Works and Contractor's Equipment

The insuring Party shall insure the Works, Plant, Materials and Contractor's Documents for not less than the full reinstatement cost including the costs of demolition, removal of debris and professional fees and profit. This insurance shall be effective from the date by which the evidence is to be submitted under sub-paragraph (a) of Sub-Clause 18.1 [*General Requirements for Insurances*], until the date of issue of the Taking-Over Certificate for the Works.

The insuring Party shall maintain this insurance to provide cover until the date of issue of the Performance Certificate, for loss or damage for which the Contractor is liable arising from a cause occurring prior to the issue of the Taking-Over Certificate, and for loss or damage caused by the Contractor in the course of any other operations (including those under Clause 11 [*Defects Liability*]).

The insuring Party shall insure the Contractor's Equipment for not less than the full replacement value, including delivery to Site. For each item of Contractor's Equipment, the insurance shall be effective while it is being transported to the Site and until it is no longer required as Contractor's Equipment.

Unless otherwise stated in the Particular Conditions, insurances under this Sub-Clause:

(a)   shall be effected and maintained by the Contractor as insuring Party,
(b)   shall be in the joint names of the Parties, who shall be jointly entitled to receive payments from the insurers, payments being held or allocated between the Parties for the sole purpose of rectifying the loss or damage,
(c)   shall cover all loss and damage from any cause not listed in Sub-Clause 17.3 [*Employer's Risks*],

程实施中的任何相关变化，并确保按照本条要求维持保险。

没有得到另一方的事先批准，任一方都不应对任何保险的条件做出实质性变动。如果保险人做出（或要做出）任何变动，首先收到保险人通知的一方应迅速通知另一方。

如果应投保方对合同要求办理并维持的任何保险未能按要求办好并保持有效，或未能按本款要求提供满意的证据和保险单副本，另一方可以（由其选择，并在不影响任何其他权利或补偿的情况下）办理该保险范围的保险，并支付应交的保险费。应投保方应向另一方支付这些保险费，并相应调整合同价格。

本条规定不限制合同其余条款或其他文件所规定的承包商或雇主的义务、责任、或职责。任何未保险或未能从保险人收回的款项，应由承包商和（或）雇主按照这些义务、责任、或职责的规定承担。但是，如果应投保方对于能做到的并在合同中规定要办理并保持的某项保险，未能按要求办好并保持有效，而另一方既没有认可这项省略，又没有办理与此项违约有关的保险范围的保险，则根据此项保险应能收回的任何款额应由应投保方支付。

一方向另一方的支付，应按适用情况，根据第 2.5 款[雇主的索赔]或第 20.1 款[承包商的索赔]的规定办理。

18.2

工程和承包商设备的保险

应投保方应为工程、生产设备、材料和承包商文件投保，保险额不低于全部复原费用，包括拆除、运走废弃物的费用、以及专业费用和利润。该保险应从第 18.1 款[有关保险的一般要求](a)项规定的提交证据的日期起，至颁发工程接收证书的日期止保持有效。

应投保方应维持该保险在直到颁发履约证书的日期为止的期间继续有效，以便对承包商应负责的，由颁发接收证书前发生的某项原因引起的损失或损害，以及由承包商在任何其他作业（包括第 11 条[缺陷责任]规定的作业）过程中造成的损失或损害，提供保险。

应投保方应对承包商设备投保，保险额不低于全部重置价值，包括运至现场的费用。对每项承包商设备，该保险都应从该设备运往现场的过程起，直到其不需再作为承包商设备为止的期间保持有效。

除非在专用条件中另有规定，本款规定的各项保险：

(a) 应由承包商作为应投保方办理和维持；
(b) 应由共同有权从保险人处得到赔偿的各方联名投保，保险赔偿金在各方间保有或分配，唯一用于修正损失或损害；
(c) 应对未列入第 17.3 款[雇主的风险]列举的任何原因造成的所有损失和损害提供保险；

(d)   shall also cover loss or damage to a part of the Works which is attributable to the use or occupation by the Employer of another part of the Works, and loss or damage from the risks listed in sub-paragraphs (c), (g) and (h) of Sub-Clause 17.3 [*Employer's Risks*], excluding (in each case) risks which are not insurable at commercially reasonable terms, with deductibles per occurrence of not more than the amount stated in the Appendix to Tender (if an amount is not so stated, this sub-paragraph (d) shall not apply), and

(e)   may however exclude loss of, damage to, and reinstatement of:

(i)   a part of the Works which is in a defective condition due to a defect in its design, materials or workmanship (but cover shall include any other parts which are lost or damaged as a direct result of this defective condition and not as described in sub-paragraph (ii) below),

(ii)   a part of the Works which is lost or damaged in order to reinstate any other part of the Works if this other part is in a defective condition due to a defect in its design, materials or workmanship,

(iii)   a part of the Works which has been taken over by the Employer, except to the extent that the Contractor is liable for the loss or damage, and

(iv)   Goods while they are not in the Country, subject to Sub-Clause 14.5 [*Plant and Materials intended for the Works*].

If, more than one year after the Base Date, the cover described in sub-paragraph (d) above ceases to be available at commercially reasonable terms, the Contractor shall (as insuring Party) give notice to the Employer, with supporting particulars. The Employer shall then (i) be entitled subject to Sub-Clause 2.5 [*Employer's Claims*] to payment of an amount equivalent to such commercially reasonable terms as the Contractor should have expected to have paid for such cover, and (ii) be deemed, unless he obtains the cover at commercially reasonable terms, to have approved the omission under Sub-Clause 18.1 [*General Requirements for Insurances*].

18.3

Insurance against Injury to Persons and Damage to Property

The insuring Party shall insure against each Party's liability for any loss, damage, death or bodily injury which may occur to any physical property (except things insured under Sub-Clause 18.2 [*Insurance for Works and Contractor's Equipment*]) or to any person (except persons insured under Sub-Clause 18.4 [*Insurance for Contractor's Personnel*]), which may arise out of the Contractor's performance of the Contract and occurring before the issue of the Performance Certificate.

This insurance shall be for a limit per occurrence of not less than the amount stated in the Appendix to Tender, with no limit on the number of occurrences. If an amount is not stated in the Appendix to Tender, this Sub-Clause shall not apply.

Unless otherwise stated in the Particular Conditions, the insurances specified in this Sub-Clause:

(a)   shall be effected and maintained by the Contractor as insuring Party,

(b)   shall be in the joint names of the Parties,

(c)   shall be extended to cover liability for all loss and damage to the Employer's property (except things insured under Sub-Clause 18.2) arising out of the Contractor's performance of the Contract, and

(d)   may however exclude liability to the extent that it arises from:

(i)   the Employer's right to have the Permanent Works executed on, over, under, in or through any land, and to occupy this land for the Permanent Works,

(ii)   damage which is an unavoidable result of the Contractor's obligations to execute the Works and remedy any defects, and

(d) 还应对由于**雇主**使用或占用**工程**另一部分而造成的**工程**某一部分的损失或损害，以及**第 17.3 款**[**雇主的风险**](c)、(g)和(h)项所列的风险造成的损失或损害提供保险，（每种情况）都不包括不能按商务合理条件投保的风险，每次事件的免赔额不应超过**投标书附录**中规定的数额（如果没有规定**此数额**,本(d)项应不适用）；以及

(e) 但可以不包括下列部分的损失、损害及复原：

(i) 由于其本身的设计、材料或工艺缺陷造成的处于有缺陷状况的**工程**部分(但保险应包括不属于下面第(ii)项所述情况的，由上述有缺陷状况直接造成损失或损害的任何其他部分)；

(ii) 为复原因设计、材料、或工艺缺陷造成的其他处于有缺陷状况的**工程**部分，而遭受损失或损害的某一**工程**部分；

(iii) **雇主**已经接收的工程部分，但**承包商**对其损失或损害应负责的除外；和

(iv) 根据**第 14.5 款**[**拟用于工程的生产设备和材料**]的规定，不在**工程所在国**的**货物**。

如果在**基准日期**后一年以上，上述(d)项所述保险不能在合理的商务条件下继续投保，**承包商**（作为应投保方）应通知**雇主**，并附详细说明。这时，**雇主**应(i)有权根据**第 2.5 款**[**雇主的索赔**]的规定，获得等同于在该合理商务条件下，**承包商**为该类保险预期要支付的款额；及(ii)除非他在商务合理条件下获得该保险，被认为已根据**第 18.1 款**[**有关保险的一般要求**]的规定，批准了此项省略。

18.3

人身伤害和财产损害险

应投保方应为可能由**承包商**履行**合同**引起、并在**履约证书**颁发前发生的，任何物质财产（根据**第 18.2 款**[**工程和承包商设备的保险**]规定被保险的物品除外）的任何损失或损害，或任何人员（根据**第 18.4 款**[**承包商人员的保险**]规定被保险的人员除外）的任何死亡或伤害，办理每方责任险。

此类保险对发生每次事件的保险金限额应不低于**投标书附录**中规定的数额，事件发生次数不限。如果**投标书附录**中没有规定数额，本**款**应不适用。

除非**专用条件**中另有规定，本**款**规定的各项保险：

(a) 应由**承包商**作为应投保方办理和维持；

(b) 应以**各方**联合名义投保；

(c) 保险范围应扩展到因**承包商**履行**合同**引起的对**雇主**财产（根据**第 18.2 款**规定被保的物品除外）的所有损失和损害的责任；以及

(d) 但可以不包括以下事项引起的责任：

(i) **雇主**在任何土地上面、上方、下面、范围内，或穿过它实施**永久工程**，以及为了**永久工程**占用该土地的权利；

(ii) 由**承包商**实施工程和修补任何缺陷的义务造成的不可避免的损害；和

(iii)   a cause listed in Sub-Clause 17.3 [*Employer's Risks*], except to the extent that cover is available at commercially reasonable terms.

18.4

Insurance for Contractor's Personnel

The Contractor shall effect and maintain insurance against liability for claims, damages, losses and expenses (including legal fees and expenses) arising from injury, sickness, disease or death of any person employed by the Contractor or any other of the Contractor's Personnel.

The Employer and the Engineer shall also be indemnified under the policy of insurance, except that this insurance may exclude losses and claims to the extent that they arise from any act or neglect of the Employer or of the Employer's Personnel.

The insurance shall be maintained in full force and effect during the whole time that these personnel are assisting in the execution of the Works. For a Subcontractor's employees, the insurance may be effected by the Subcontractor, but the Contractor shall be responsible for compliance with this Clause.

Force Majeure

19.1

Definition of Force Majeure

In this Clause, "Force Majeure" means an exceptional event or circumstance:

(a)   which is beyond a Party's control,
(b)   which such Party could not reasonably have provided against before entering into the Contract,
(c)   which, having arisen, such Party could not reasonably have avoided or overcome, and
(d)   which is not substantially attributable to the other Party.

Force Majeure may include, but is not limited to, exceptional events or circumstances of the kind listed below, so long as conditions (a) to (d) above are satisfied:

(i)   war, hostilities (whether war be declared or not), invasion, act of foreign enemies,
(ii)   rebellion, terrorism, revolution, insurrection, military or usurped power, or civil war,
(iii)   riot, commotion, disorder, strike or lockout by persons other than the Contractor's Personnel and other employees of the Contractor and Sub-contractors,
(iv)   munitions of war, explosive materials, ionising radiation or contamination by radio-activity, except as may be attributable to the Contractor's use of such munitions, explosives, radiation or radio-activity, and
(v)   natural catastrophes such as earthquake, hurricane, typhoon or volcanic activity.

19.2

Notice of Force Majeure

If a Party is or will be prevented from performing any of its obligations under the Contract by Force Majeure, then it shall give notice to the other Party of the event or circumstances constituting the Force Majeure and shall specify the obligations, the performance of which is or will be prevented. The notice shall be given within 14 days after the Party became aware, or should have become aware, of the relevant event or circumstance constituting Force Majeure.

(iii)　第 17.3 款[*雇主的风险*]列举的某项原因，但可以按合理的商务条件得到保险的范围除外。

18.4

承包商人员的保险

承包商应对**承包商**雇用的任何人员或任何其他**承包商人员**的伤害、患病、疾病或死亡引起的索赔、损害赔偿费、损失和开支(包括法律费用和开支)的责任办理并维持保险。

除该保险可不包括由**雇主**或**雇主人员**的任何行为或疏忽引起的损失和索赔的情况以外，**雇主和工程师**也应由该项保险单得到保障。

此类保险应在这些人员参加**工程**实施的整个期间保持全面实施和有效。对于**分包商**的雇员，此类保险可以由**分包商**投保，但**承包商**应对其符合本**条**规定负责。

19　不可抗力

19.1

不可抗力的定义

在本**条**中，"不可抗力"系指某种特殊事件或情况：
(a)　一方无法控制的；
(b)　该方在签订**合同**前，不能对之进行合理防备的；

(c)　发生后，该方不能合理避免或克服的；以及

(d)　不主要归因于他方的。

只要满足上述(a)至(d)项条件，**不可抗力**可包括但不限于下列各种特殊事件或情况：

(i)　战争、敌对行动(不论宣战与否)、入侵、外敌行为；

(ii)　叛乱、恐怖主义、革命、暴动、军事政变或篡夺政权，或内战；

(iii)　**承包商人员**和承包商及其**分包商**的其他雇员以外的人员的骚动、喧闹、混乱、罢工或停工；

(iv)　战争军火、爆炸物资、电离辐射或放射性污染，但可能因**承包商**使用此类军火、炸药、辐射或放射性引起的除外；以及

(v)　自然灾害，如地震、飓风、台风或火山活动。

19.2

不可抗力的通知

如果一方因**不可抗力**使其履行**合同**规定的任何义务已或将受到阻碍，应向他方发出关于构成**不可抗力**的事件或情况的通知，并应明确说明履行已或将受到阻碍的各项义务。此项通知应在该方察觉或应已察觉到构成**不可抗力**的有关事件或情况后 14 天内发出。

The Party shall, having given notice, be excused performance of such obligations for so long as such Force Majeure prevents it from performing them.

Notwithstanding any other provision of this Clause, Force Majeure shall not apply to obligations of either Party to make payments to the other Party under the Contract.

19.3

Duty to Minimise Delay

Each Party shall at all times use all reasonable endeavours to minimise any delay in the performance of the Contract as a result of Force Majeure.

A Party shall give notice to the other Party when it ceases to be affected by the Force Majeure.

19.4

Consequences of Force Majeure

If the Contractor is prevented from performing any of his obligations under the Contract by Force Majeure of which notice has been given under Sub-Clause 19.2 [*Notice of Force Majeure*], and suffers delay and/or incurs Cost by reason of such Force Majeure, the Contractor shall be entitled subject to Sub-Clause 20.1 [*Contractor's Claims*] to:

(a) an extension of time for any such delay, if completion is or will be delayed, under Sub-Clause 8.4 [*Extension of Time for Completion*], and

(b) if the event or circumstance is of the kind described in sub-paragraphs (i) to (iv) of Sub-Clause 19.1 [*Definition of Force Majeure*] and, in the case of sub-paragraphs (ii) to (iv), occurs in the Country, payment of any such Cost.

After receiving this notice, the Engineer shall proceed in accordance with Sub-Clause 3.5 [*Determinations*] to agree or determine these matters.

19.5

Force Majeure Affecting Subcontractor

If any Subcontractor is entitled under any contract or agreement relating to the Works to relief from force majeure on terms additional to or broader than those specified in this Clause, such additional or broader force majeure events or circumstances shall not excuse the Contractor's non-performance or entitle him to relief under this Clause.

19.6

Optional Termination, Payment and Release

If the execution of substantially all the Works in progress is prevented for a continuous period of 84 days by reason of Force Majeure of which notice has been given under Sub-Clause 19.2 [*Notice of Force Majeure*], or for multiple periods which total more than 140 days due to the same notified Force Majeure, then either Party may give to the other Party a notice of termination of the Contract. In this event, the termination shall take effect 7 days after the notice is given, and the Contractor shall proceed in accordance with Sub-Clause 16.3 [*Cessation of Work and Removal of Contractor's Equipment*].

Upon such termination, the Engineer shall determine the value of the work done and issue a Payment Certificate which shall include:

(a) the amounts payable for any work carried out for which a price is stated in the Contract;

(b) the Cost of Plant and Materials ordered for the Works which have been delivered to the Contractor, or of which the Contractor is liable to accept delivery: this Plant and Materials shall become the property of (and be at the risk of) the Employer when paid for by the Employer, and the Contractor shall place the same at the Employer's disposal;

(c) any other Cost or liability which in the circumstances was reasonably incurred by the Contractor in the expectation of completing the Works;

发出通知后，该方应在该**不可抗力**阻碍其履行义务期间，免于履行该义务。

不管**本条**的其他任何规定，**不可抗力**的规定不应施用于任一**方**根据**合同**向另一**方**支付的义务。

19.3

将延误减至最小的义务

每方都应始终尽所有合理的努力，使**不可抗力**对履行**合同**造成的任何延误减至最小。

当一方不再受**不可抗力**影响时，应向另一方发出通知。

19.4

不可抗力的后果

如果**承包商**因已根据**第 19.2 款**[*不可抗力的通知*]的规定发出通知的**不可抗力**，妨碍其履行**合同**规定的任何义务，使其遭受延误和（或）招致增加**费用**，**承包商**应有权根据**第 20.1 款**[*承包商的索赔*]的规定要求：

(a) 根据**第 8.4 款**[*竣工时间的延长*]的规定，如竣工已或将受到延误，对任何此类延误给予延长期；以及

(b) 如果是**第 19.1 款**[*不可抗力的定义*]中第(i)至(iv)目所述的事件或情况，且第(ii)至(iv)目所述事件或情况发生在**工程所在国**时，对任何此类**费用**给予支付。

工程师收到此通知后，应按照**第 3.5 款**[*确定*]的规定，对这些事项进行商定或确定。

19.5

不可抗力影响分包商

如果任何**分包商**根据有关**工程**的任何**合同**或协议，有权因较**本条**规定更多或更广范围的**不可抗力**免除某些义务，此类更多或更广的不可抗力事件或情况，不应成为**承包商**不履约的借口，或有权根据**本条**规定免除其义务。

19.6

自主选择终止，付款和解除

如果因已根据**第 19.2 款**[*不可抗力的通知*]的规定发出通知的**不可抗力**，使基本上全部进展中的**工程**实施受到阻碍已连续 84 天，或由于同一通知的**不可抗力**断续阻碍几个期间累计超过 140 天，任一方可向他方发出终止**合同**的通知。在此情况下，终止应在该通知发出 7 天后生效，**承包商**应按照**第 16.3 款**[*停止工作和承包商设备的撤离*]的规定进行。

在此类终止的情况下，**工程师**应确定已完成工作的价值，并发出包括以下各项的**付款证书**：

(a) 已完成的、**合同**中有价格规定的任何工作的应付款额；

(b) 为**工程**订购的、已交付给**承包商**或**承包商**有责任接受交付的**生产设备和材料**的**费用**：当**雇主**支付上述费用后，此项**生产设备和材料**应成为**雇主**的财产（风险也由其承担），**承包商**应将其交由**雇主**处理；

(c) 在**承包商**原预期要完成**工程**的情况下，合理导致的任何其他**费用**或债务；

127

(d)   the Cost of removal of Temporary Works and Contractor's Equipment from the Site and the return of these items to the Contractor's works in his country (or to any other destination at no greater cost); and

(e)   the Cost of repatriation of the Contractor's staff and labour employed wholly in connection with the Works at the date of termination.

19.7

**Release from
Performance
under the Law**

Notwithstanding any other provision of this Clause, if any event or circumstance outside the control of the Parties (including, but not limited to, Force Majeure) arises which makes it impossible or unlawful for either or both Parties to fulfil its or their contractual obligations or which, under the law governing the Contract, entitles the Parties to be released from further performance of the Contract, then upon notice by either Party to the other Party of such event or circumstance:

(a)   the Parties shall be discharged from further performance, without prejudice to the rights of either Party in respect of any previous breach of the Contract, and

(b)   the sum payable by the Employer to the Contractor shall be the same as would have been payable under Sub-Clause 19.6 [*Optional Termination, Payment and Release*] if the Contract had been terminated under Sub-Clause 19.6.

Claim, Disputes and Arbitration

20.1
Contractor's Claims

If the Contractor considers himself to be entitled to any extension of the Time for Completion and/or any additional payment, under any Clause of these Conditions or otherwise in connection with the Contract, the Contractor shall give notice to the Engineer, describing the event or circumstance giving rise to the claim. The notice shall be given as soon as practicable, and not later than 28 days after the Contractor became aware, or should have become aware, of the event or circumstance.

If the Contractor fails to give notice of a claim within such period of 28 days, the Time for Completion shall not be extended, the Contractor shall not be entitled to additional payment, and the Employer shall be discharged from all liability in connection with the claim. Otherwise, the following provisions of this Sub-Clause shall apply.

The Contractor shall also submit any other notices which are required by the Contract, and supporting particulars for the claim, all as relevant to such event or circumstance.

The Contractor shall keep such contemporary records as may be necessary to substantiate any claim, either on the Site or at another location acceptable to the Engineer. Without admitting the Employer's liability, the Engineer may, after receiving any notice under this Sub-Clause, monitor the record-keeping and/or instruct the Contractor to keep further contemporary records. The Contractor shall permit the Engineer to inspect all these records, and shall (if instructed) submit copies to the Engineer.

Within 42 days after the Contractor became aware (or should have become aware) of the event or circumstance giving rise to the claim, or within such other period as may be proposed by the Contractor and approved by the Engineer, the Contractor shall send to the Engineer a fully detailed claim which includes full supporting particulars of the basis of the claim and of the extension of time and/or additional payment claimed. If the event or circumstance giving rise to the claim has a continuing effect:

(a)   this fully detailed claim shall be considered as interim;

(d) 将临时工程和承包商设备撤离现场，并运回承包商本国工作地点的费用(或运往任何其他目的地，但其费用不得超过)；以及

(e) 将终止日期时完全为工程雇用的承包商的员工遣返回国的费用。

19.7

根据法律解除履约

不管本条的任何其他规定，如果发生各方不能控制的任何事件或情况(包括但不限于不可抗力)，使任一方或双方完成他或他们的合同义务成为不可能或非法，或根据管理合同的法律规定，各方有权解除进一步履行合同的义务，则根据任一方向他方发出此类事件或情况的通知：

(a) 双方应解除进一步履约的义务，并不影响任一方对过去任何违反合同事项的权利；以及

(b) 雇主应支付给承包商的款额，应等于如已根据第19.6款[自主选择终止，付款和解除]的规定终止合同，按该款规定应予支付的款额。

20 索赔、争端和仲裁

20.1

承包商的索赔

如果承包商认为，根据本条件任何条款或与合同有关的其他文件，他有权得到竣工时间的任何延长期和(或)任何追加付款，承包商应向工程师发出通知，说明引起索赔的事件或情况。该通知应尽快在承包商察觉或应已察觉该事件或情况后28天内发出。

如果承包商未能在上述28天期限内发出索赔通知，则竣工时间不得延长，承包商应无权获得追加付款，而雇主应免除有关该索赔的全部责任。否则，应适用本款以下规定。

承包商还应提交所有有关此类事件或情况的、合同要求的任何其他通知，以及支持索赔的详细资料。

承包商应在现场或工程师认可的其他地点，保持用以证明任何索赔可能需要的此类同期记录。工程师收到根据本款发出的任何通知后，未承认雇主责任前，可检查记录保持情况，并可指示承包商保持进一步的当时记录。承包商应允许工程师检查所有这些记录，并应向工程师(若有指示要求)提供复印件。

在承包商察觉(或应已察觉)引起索赔的事件或情况后42天内，或在承包商可能建议并经工程师认可的其他期限内，承包商应向工程师递交一份充分详细的索赔报告，包括索赔的依据、要求延长的时间和(或)追加付款的全部详细资料。如果引起索赔的事件或情况具有连续影响，则：

(a) 上述充分详细的索赔报告应被视为是中间的；

(b)   the Contractor shall send further interim claims at monthly intervals, giving the accumulated delay and/or amount claimed, and such further particulars as the Engineer may reasonably require; and

(c)   the Contractor shall send a final claim within 28 days after the end of the effects resulting from the event or circumstance, or within such other period as may be proposed by the Contractor and approved by the Engineer.

Within 42 days after receiving a claim or any further particulars supporting a previous claim, or within such other period as may be proposed by the Engineer and approved by the Contractor, the Engineer shall respond with approval, or with disapproval and detailed comments. He may also request any necessary further particulars, but shall nevertheless give his response on the principles of the claim within such time.

Each Payment Certificate shall include such amounts for any claim as have been reasonably substantiated as due under the relevant provision of the Contract. Unless and until the particulars supplied are sufficient to substantiate the whole of the claim, the Contractor shall only be entitled to payment for such part of the claim as he has been able to substantiate.

The Engineer shall proceed in accordance with Sub-Clause 3.5 [*Determinations*] to agree or determine (i) the extension (if any) of the Time for Completion (before or after its expiry) in accordance with Sub-Clause 8.4 [*Extension of Time for Completion*], and/or (ii) the additional payment (if any) to which the Contractor is entitled under the Contract.

The requirements of this Sub-Clause are in addition to those of any other Sub-Clause which may apply to a claim. If the Contractor fails to comply with this or another Sub-Clause in relation to any claim, any extension of time and/or additional payment shall take account of the extent (if any) to which the failure has prevented or prejudiced proper investigation of the claim, unless the claim is excluded under the second paragraph of this Sub-Clause.

20.2

Appointment of the Dispute Adjudication Board

Disputes shall be adjudicated by a DAB in accordance with Sub-Clause 20.4 [*Obtaining Dispute Adjudication Board's Decision*]. The Parties shall jointly appoint a DAB by the date stated in the Appendix to Tender.

The DAB shall comprise, as stated in the Appendix to Tender, either one or three suitably qualified persons ("the members"). If the number is not so stated and the Parties do not agree otherwise, the DAB shall comprise three persons.

If the DAB is to comprise three persons, each Party shall nominate one member for the approval of the other Party. The Parties shall consult both these members and shall agree upon the third member, who shall be appointed to act as chairman.

However, if a list of potential members is included in the Contract, the members shall be selected from those on the list, other than anyone who is unable or unwilling to accept appointment to the DAB.

The agreement between the Parties and either the sole member ("adjudicator") or each of the three members shall incorporate by reference the General Conditions of Dispute Adjudication Agreement contained in the Appendix to these General Conditions, with such amendments as are agreed between them.

The terms of the remuneration of either the sole member or each of the three members, including the remuneration of any expert whom the DAB consults, shall be

（b）　**承包商**应按月递交进一步的中间索赔报告，说明累计索赔的延误时间和（或）款额，及**工程师**可能合理要求的**此类**进一步详细资料；以及

（c）　**承包商**应在引起**索赔**的事件或情况产生的影响结束后 28 天内，或在**承包商**可能建议并经**工程师**认可的此类其他期限内，递交一份最终索赔报告。

工程师在收到索赔报告或对过去索赔的任何进一步证明资料后 42 天内，或在**工程师**可能建议并经**承包商**认可的此类其他期限内，做出回应，表示批准、或不批准并附具体意见。他还可以要求任何必要的进一步资料，但他仍要在上述期限内对索赔的原则做出回应。

每份**付款证书**应包括已根据**合同**有关规定，合理证明是有依据的、对任何索赔的此类应付款额。除非并直到提供的详细资料足以证明索赔的全部要求是有依据的以前，**承包商**只有权得到索赔中他已能证明有依据部分的付款。

工程师应按照**第 3.5 款**［**确定**］的规定，就以下事项商定或确定：（i）根据**第 8.4 款**［**竣工时间的延长**］的规定，应给予竣工时间（其期满前或后）的延长期（如果有），和（或）（ii）根据**合同**，**承包商**有权得到的追加付款（如果有）。

本**款**各项要求是对适用于索赔的任何其他**条款**的追加要求。如果**承包商**未能达到本**款**或有关任何索赔的其他**条款**的要求，除非该索赔根据本**款**第二段的规定被拒绝，对给予任何延长期和（或）追加付款，应考虑**承包商**此项未达到要求对索赔的彻底调查造成阻碍或影响（如果有）的程度。

20.2

争端裁决委员会的任命

争端应按照**第 20.4 款**［**取得争端裁决委员会的决定**］的规定，由**争端裁决委员会**（简称**DAB**—译注*）裁决。双方应在**投标书附录**中规定的日期前，联合任命一个**DAB**。

DAB 应按**投标书附录**中的规定，由具有适当资格的一名或三名人员（"**成员**"）组成。如果对委员会人数没有规定，且**双方**没有另外协议，**DAB** 应由三人组成。

如果**DAB** 由三人组成，**各方**均应推荐一人，报他方认可。双方应与这些成员协商，并商定第三名成员，此人应任命为主席。

但如果**合同**中包括有备选成员名单，除有人不能或不愿接受**DAB** 的任命外，成员应从名单上的人员中选择。

双方与该唯一成员（"**裁决人**"）或该三人成员中的每个人间的协议书，应参考本**通用条件附录**的**争端裁决协议书一般条件**，结合他们间商定的此类修订意见拟定。

该唯一成员或三人成员中的每个人的报酬条件，包括**DAB** 咨询过的任何专

---

* 译注：下文中争端裁决委员会用全称或简称都按原文本。

131

mutually agreed upon by the Parties when agreeing the terms of appointment. Each Party shall be responsible for paying one-half of this remuneration.

If at any time the Parties so agree, they may jointly refer a matter to the DAB for it to give its opinion. Neither Party shall consult the DAB on any matter without the agreement of the other Party.

If at any time the Parties so agree, they may appoint a suitably qualified person or persons to replace (or to be available to replace) any one or more members of the DAB. Unless the Parties agree otherwise, the appointment will come into effect if a member declines to act or is unable to act as a result of death, disability, resignation or termination of appointment.

If any of these circumstances occurs and no such replacement is available, a replacement shall be appointed in the same manner as the replaced person was required to have been nominated or agreed upon, as described in this Sub-Clause.

The appointment of any member may be terminated by mutual agreement of both Parties, but not by the Employer or the Contractor acting alone. Unless otherwise agreed by both Parties, the appointment of the DAB (including each member) shall expire when the discharge referred to in Sub-Clause 14.12 [*Discharge*] shall have become effective.

20.3

Failure to Agree Dispute Adjudication Board

If any of the following conditions apply, namely:

(a)   the Parties fail to agree upon the appointment of the sole member of the DAB by the date stated in the first paragraph of Sub-Clause 20.2,

(b)   either Party fails to nominate a member (for approval by the other Party) of a DAB of three persons by such date,

(c)   the Parties fail to agree upon the appointment of the third member (to act as chairman) of the DAB by such date, or

(d)   the Parties fail to agree upon the appointment of a replacement person within 42 days after the date on which the sole member or one of the three members declines to act or is unable to act as a result of death, disability, resignation or termination of appointment,

then the appointing entity or official named in the Appendix to Tender shall, upon the request of either or both of the Parties and after due consultation with both Parties, appoint this member of the DAB. This appointment shall be final and conclusive. Each Party shall be responsible for paying one-half of the remuneration of the appointing entity or official.

20.4

Obtaining Dispute Adjudication Board's Decision

If a dispute (of any kind whatsoever) arises between the Parties in connection with, or arising out of, the Contract or the execution of the Works, including any dispute as to any certificate, determination, instruction, opinion or valuation of the Engineer, either Party may refer the dispute in writing to the DAB for its decision, with copies to the other Party and the Engineer. Such reference shall state that it is given under this Sub-Clause.

For a DAB of three persons, the DAB shall be deemed to have received such reference on the date when it is received by the chairman of the DAB.

Both Parties shall promptly make available to the DAB all such additional information, further access to the Site, and appropriate facilities, as the DAB may require for the

家的报酬在内，应由**双方**在协商任命条件时共同商定。每**方**应负担上述报酬的一半。

如果经**双方**同意，他们可以在任何时候联合将某事项交由**DAB**提出意见。一方未得另**一方**同意，不应与**DAB**商谈任何事项。

如果经**双方**同意，他们可以在任何时候任命一位或几位有适当资格的人员，替代**DAB**的任何一位或几位成员(或作替代人员的后备)。除非**双方**另有协议，在某一成员拒绝履行职责，或因其死亡、无行为能力、辞职或任命期满而不能履行职责时，上述替代任命即告生效。

如果发生以上情况，又无可替代人员，应按本**款**所述对被替代人员在提名或商定时所需的同样方式，任命一位替代人员。

对任何成员的任命，可以经过双方相互协议终止，但**雇主**或**承包商**都不能单独采取行动。除非双方另有协议，在**第 14.12 款**[**结清证明**]中的结清证明生效后，**DAB**(包括每位成员)的任期应即期满。

20.3

对争端裁决委员会未能取得一致

如果下列任一情况适用，即：

(a) 到**第 20.2 款**第一段规定的日期，**双方**未能就**DAB**唯一成员的任命达成一致意见；

(b) 到该日期，任一方未能提名**DAB**三人成员中的一人(供另**一方**认可)；

(c) 到该日期，**双方**未能就**DAB**第三位成员(将担任主席)的任命达成一致意见；或

(d) 在唯一成员或三人成员中的一人拒绝履行职责，或因其死亡、无行为能力、辞职或任命期满而不能履行职责后 42 天内，**双方**未能就任命一位替代人员达成一致意见；

这时，在**专用条件**中指名的任命实体或官员，应在任**一方**或**双方**的请求下，并经与双方做应有的协商后，任命**DAB**该成员。此项任命应是最终的、决定性的。每**方**将负责支付给该任命实体或官员报**酬**的一半。

20.4

取得争端裁决委员会的决定

如果**双方**间发生了有关或起因于**合同**或**工程**实施的争端(不论任何种类)，包括对**工程师**的任何证明、确定、指示、意见或估价的任何争端，任一方可以将该争端以书面形式，提交**DAB**供其裁定，并抄送另一方和**工程师**。此项委托应说明是根据本**款**规定做出的。

对于三人**DAB**，在其主席收到委托的日期应视为该**DAB**已收到该项委托。

双方应迅速向**DAB**提供，**DAB**为对此类争端做出决定可能需要的所有此

purposes of making a decision on such dispute. The DAB shall be deemed to be not acting as arbitrator(s).

Within 84 days after receiving such reference, or within such other period as may be proposed by the DAB and approved by both Parties, the DAB shall give its decision, which shall be reasoned and shall state that it is given under this Sub-Clause. The decision shall be binding on both Parties, who shall promptly give effect to it unless and until it shall be revised in an amicable settlement or an arbitral award as described below. Unless the Contract has already been abandoned, repudiated or terminated, the Contractor shall continue to proceed with the Works in accordance with the Contract.

If either Party is dissatisfied with the DAB's decision, then either Party may, within 28 days after receiving the decision, give notice to the other Party of its dissatisfaction. If the DAB fails to give its decision within the period of 84 days (or as otherwise approved) after receiving such reference, then either Party may, within 28 days after this period has expired, give notice to the other Party of its dissatisfaction.

In either event, this notice of dissatisfaction shall state that it is given under this Sub-Clause, and shall set out the matter in dispute and the reason(s) for dissatisfaction. Except as stated in Sub-Clause 20.7 [*Failure to Comply with Dispute Adjudication Board's Decision*] and Sub-Clause 20.8 [*Expiry of Dispute Adjudication Board's Appointment*], neither Party shall be entitled to commence arbitration of a dispute unless a notice of dissatisfaction has been given in accordance with this Sub-Clause.

If the DAB has given its decision as to a matter in dispute to both Parties, and no notice of dissatisfaction has been given by either Party within 28 days after it received the DAB's decision, then the decision shall become final and binding upon both Parties.

20.5

Amicable Settlement

Where notice of dissatisfaction has been given under Sub-Clause 20.4 above, both Parties shall attempt to settle the dispute amicably before the commencement of arbitration. However, unless both Parties agree otherwise, arbitration may be commenced on or after the fifty-sixth day after the day on which notice of dissatisfaction was given, even if no attempt at amicable settlement has been made.

20.6

Arbitration

Unless settled amicably, any dispute in respect of which the DAB's decision (if any) has not become final and binding shall be finally settled by international arbitration. Unless otherwise agreed by both Parties:

(a)   the dispute shall be finally settled under the Rules of Arbitration of the International Chamber of Commerce,

(b)   the dispute shall be settled by three arbitrators appointed in accordance with these Rules, and

(c)   the arbitration shall be conducted in the language for communications defined in Sub-Clause 1.4 [*Law and Language*].

The arbitrator(s) shall have full power to open up, review and revise any certificate, determination, instruction, opinion or valuation of the Engineer, and any decision of the DAB, relevant to the dispute. Nothing shall disqualify the Engineer from being called as a witness and giving evidence before the arbitrator(s) on any matter whatsoever relevant to the dispute.

Neither Party shall be limited in the proceedings before the arbitrator(s) to the evidence or arguments previously put before the DAB to obtain its decision, or to the reasons

类附加资料、进一步的**现场**进入权及相应设施。DAB 应被视为不是在进行仲裁员的工作。

DAB 应在收到此项委托后 84 天内，或在可能由 DAB 建议并经**双方**认可的此类其他期限内，提出它的决定，决定应是有理由的，并说明是根据**本款**规定提出的。决定应对**双方**具有约束力，双方都应迅速遵照实行，除非并直到如下文所述，决定在友好解决或仲裁裁决中应做出修改。除非**合同**已被放弃、拒绝、或终止，**承包商**应继续按照**合同**进行**工程**。

如果任一方对 DAB 的决定不满意，可在收到该决定通知后 28 天内，将其不满向另**一方**发出通知。如果 DAB 未能在收到此项委托后 84 天（或经认可的其他）期限内，提出其决定，则任一方可以在该期限期满后 28 天内，向另**一方**发出其不满的通知。

在上述任一情况下，表示不满的通知应说明是根据**本款**规定发出的，并说明争端的事项和不满的理由。除**第 20.7 款**[**未能遵守争端裁决委员会的决定**]和**第 20.8 款**[**争端裁决委员会任命期满**]所述的情况外，除非已按**本款**发出表示不满的通知，任一方都无权着手争端的仲裁。

如果 DAB 已就争端事项向**双方**提交了它的决定，而任一方在收到 DAB 决定后 28 天内，均未发出表示不满的通知，则该决定应成为最终的，对**双方**均具有约束力。

20.5

友好解决

如果已按上述**第 20.4 款**发出了表示不满的通知，**双方**应在着手仲裁前，努力以友好方式解决争端。但是，除非**双方**另有协议，仲裁可在表示不满的通知发出后第 56 天或其后着手进行，即使未曾做过友好解决的努力。

20.6

仲裁

经 DAB 对之做出的决定（如果有）未能成为最终的和有约束力的任何争端，除非已获得友好解决，应通过国际仲裁对其作出最终解决。除非双方另有协议：

(a) 争端应根据**国际商会仲裁规则**最终解决；

(b) 争端应由按上述**规则**任命的三位仲裁人员负责解决；以及

(c) 仲裁应以**第 1.4 款**[**法律和语言**]规定的交流语言进行。

仲裁员应有全权公开、审查和修改与该争端有关的**工程师**发出的任何证明、确定、指示、意见，或估价，以及 DAB 的任何决定。任何事项都不应否定**工程师**对不论与争端有关的任何事项被传为证人并向仲裁员提供证据的资格。

任一**方**在仲裁员面前的诉讼中，应不受以前为获得 DAB 的决定而向其提供

for dissatisfaction given in its notice of dissatisfaction. Any decision of the DAB shall be admissible in evidence in the arbitration.

Arbitration may be commenced prior to or after completion of the Works. The obligations of the Parties, the Engineer and the DAB shall not be altered by reason of any arbitration being conducted during the progress of the Works.

20.7

Failure to Comply with Dispute Adjudication Board's Decision

In the event that:

(a)   neither Party has given notice of dissatisfaction within the period stated in Sub-Clause 20.4 [Obtaining Dispute Adjudication Board's Decision],

(b)   the DAB's related decision (if any) has become final and binding, and

(c)   a Party fails to comply with this decision,

then the other Party may, without prejudice to any other rights it may have, refer the failure itself to arbitration under Sub-Clause 20.6 [Arbitration]. Sub-Clause 20.4 [Obtaining Dispute Adjudication Board's Decision] and Sub-Clause 20.5 [Amicable Settlement] shall not apply to this reference.

20.8

Expiry of Dispute Adjudication Board's Appointment

If a dispute arises between the Parties in connection with, or arising out of, the Contract or the execution of the Works and there is no DAB in place, whether by reason of the expiry of the DAB's appointment or otherwise:

(a)   Sub-Clause 20.4 [Obtaining Dispute Adjudication Board's Decision] and Sub-Clause 20.5 [Amicable Settlement] shall not apply, and

(b)   the dispute may be referred directly to arbitration under Sub-Clause 20.6 [Arbitration].

的证据或论据、或在其表示不满的通知中提出的不满意理由的限制。DAB 的任何决定都应可以作为仲裁中的证据。

仲裁在工程竣工前或竣工后，都可以着手进行。双方、工程师和DAB的义务，不得因为在工程进展过程中正在进行任何仲裁而改变。

20.7

未能遵守争端裁决委员会的决定　在以下情况下：

(a)　任一方在第 20.4 款[取得争端裁决委员会的决定]规定的期限内均未发出表示不满的通知；

(b)　DAB 的有关决定(如果有)已成为最终的、有约束力的；以及

(c)　有一方未遵守上述决定。

这时，另一方可以在不损害其可能拥有的其他权利的情况下，根据第 20.6 款[仲裁]的规定，将上述未遵守决定的事项提交仲裁。在此情况下，第 20.4 款[取得争端裁决委员会的决定]和第 20.5 款[友好解决]的规定应不适用。

20.8

争端裁决委员会任命期满　如果双方间因与合同或工程实施有关或由其引起的问题产生争端，且又因 DAB 任命期满或其他原因，没有DAB进行工作，则：

(a)　第 20.4 款[取得争端裁决委员会的决定]和第 20.5 款[友好解决]的规定应不适用；以及

(b)　此项争端可根据第 20.6 款[仲裁]的规定，直接提交仲裁。

137

APPENDIX

General Conditions of Dispute Adjudication Agreement

1

Definitions

Each "Dispute Adjudication Agreement" is a tripartite agreement by and between:
(a)   the "Employer";
(b)   the "Contractor"; and
(c)   the "Member" who is defined in the Dispute Adjudication Agreement as being:
    (i)   the sole member of the "DAB" (or "adjudicator") and, where this is the case, all references to the "Other Members" do not apply, or
    (ii)   one of the three persons who are jointly called the "DAB" (or "dispute adjudication board") and, where this is the case, the other two persons are called the "Other Members".

The Employer and the Contractor have entered (or intend to enter) into a contract, which is called the "Contract" and is defined in the Dispute Adjudication Agreement, which incorporates this Appendix. In the Dispute Adjudication Agreement, words and expressions which are not otherwise defined shall have the meanings assigned to them in the Contract.

2

General Provisions

Unless otherwise stated in the Dispute Adjudication Agreement, it shall take effect on the latest of the following dates:
(a)   the Commencement Date defined in the Contract,
(b)   when the Employer, the Contractor and the Member have each signed the Dispute Adjudication Agreement, or
(c)   when the Employer, the Contractor and each of the Other Members (if any) have respectively each signed a dispute adjudication agreement.

When the Dispute Adjudication Agreement has taken effect, the Employer and the Contractor shall each.give notice to the Member accordingly. If the Member does not receive either notice within six months after entering into the Dispute Adjudication Agreement, it shall be void and ineffective.

This employment of the Member is a personal appointment. At any time, the Member may give not less than 70 days' notice of resignation to the Employer and to the Contractor, and the Dispute Adjudication Agreement shall terminate upon the expiry of this period.

No assignment or subcontracting of the Dispute Adjudication Agreement is permitted without the prior written agreement of all the parties to it and of the Other Members (if any).

3

Warranties

The Member warrants and agrees that he/she is and shall be impartial and independent of the Employer, the Contractor and the Engineer. The Member shall promptly disclose, to each of them and to the Other Members (if any), any fact or circumstance which might appear inconsistent with his/her warranty and agreement of impartiality and independence.

When appointing the Member, the Employer and the Contractor relied upon the Member's representations that he/she is:
(a)   experienced in the work which the Contractor is to carry out under the Contract,
(b)   experienced in the interpretation of contract documentation, and
(c)   fluent in the language for communications defined in the Contract.

附录

争端裁决协议书一般条件

1
定义

每份"**争端裁决协议书**"是由下列三方间签订的三方协议书：
(a) "**雇主**"；
(b) "**承包商**"；
(c) "**成员**"，在**争端裁决协议书**中定义为：
    (i) "**DAB**"的唯一**成员**(或"**裁决员**")，在此情况下，所有"**其他成员**"的说法都不适用；或
    (ii) 联合称为"**DAB**"(或"**争端裁决委员会**"全称)的三人中的一人，在此情况下，另外两人称为"**其他成员**"。

雇主和**承包商**已(或将)签一份**合同**，在**争端裁决协议书**中称为"**合同**"，其含义是确定的，该**合同**包括本**附录**。**争端裁决协议书**中的词语和措辞，除另有规定的以外，应具有**合同**赋予它们的含义。

2
一般规定

除非**争端裁决协议书**中另有说明，**争端裁决协议书**应在以下日期中最晚的日期生效：
(a) **合同**规定的开工日期；
(b) **雇主、承包商**和**成员**分别签署**争端裁决协议书**的日期；或
(c) **雇主、承包商**和每一位**其他成员**(如果有)分别签署**争端裁决协议书**的日期。

争端裁决协议书生效后，**雇主**和**承包商**各自都应相应向**成员**发出通知。如果在签订**争端裁决协议书**6个月内，**成员**没有收到任一份通知，该协议书应作废和无效。

这种对**成员**的聘任属对个人的任命。任何时候**成员**可在不少于70天前向**雇主**和**承包商**提出辞职通知，**争端裁决协议书**应在该期限期满时终止。

事先未经涉及各方和**其他成员**(如果有)的书面同意，**争端裁决协议书**不得转让或分包。

3
保证

成员保证并同意，他(她)对**雇主、承包商**和**工程师**保持和应保持公正和独立。**成员**应将看来可能与其公正和独立的保证和同意不相符的任何事实或情况，迅速告知他们各人及**其他成员**(如果有)。

当任命**成员**时，**雇主**和**承包商**依据**成员**他(或她)的下列表现：

(a) 具有**承包商**根据**合同**要进行的工作的经验；
(b) 具有解释**合同**文件的经验；以及
(c) 能流利地使用**合同**规定的交流语言。

4
General Obligations of the Member

The Member shall:

(a)   have no interest financial or otherwise in the Employer, the Contractor or the Engineer, nor any financial interest in the Contract except for payment under the Dispute Adjudication Agreement;

(b)   not previously have been employed as a consultant or otherwise by the Employer, the Contractor or the Engineer, except in such circumstances as were disclosed in writing to the Employer and the Contractor before they signed the Dispute Adjudication Agreement;

(c)   have disclosed in writing to the Employer, the Contractor and the Other Members (if any), before entering into the Dispute Adjudication Agreement and to his/her best knowledge and recollection, any professional or personal relationships with any director, officer or employee of the Employer, the Contractor or the Engineer, and any previous involvement in the overall project of which the Contract forms part;

(d)   not, for the duration of the Dispute Adjudication Agreement, be employed as a consultant or otherwise by the Employer, the Contractor or the Engineer, except as may be agreed in writing by the Employer, the Contractor and the Other Members (if any);

(e)   comply with the annexed procedural rules and with Sub-Clause 20.4 of the Conditions of Contract;

(f)   not give advice to the Employer, the Contractor, the Employer's Personnel or the Contractor's Personnel concerning the conduct of the Contract, other than in accordance with the annexed procedural rules;

(g)   not while a Member enter into discussions or make any agreement with the Employer, the Contractor or the Engineer regarding employment by any of them, whether as a consultant or otherwise, after ceasing to act under the Dispute Adjudication Agreement;

(h)   ensure his/her availability for all site visits and hearings as are necessary;

(i)   become conversant with the Contract and with the progress of the Works (and of any other parts of the project of which the Contract forms part) by studying all documents received which shall be maintained in a current working file;

(j)   treat the details of the Contract and all the DAB's activities and hearings as private and confidential, and not publish or disclose them without the prior written consent of the Employer, the Contractor and the Other Members (if any); and

(k)   be available to give advice and opinions, on any matter relevant to the Contract when requested by both the Employer and the Contractor, subject to the agreement of the Other Members (if any).

5
General Obligations of the Employer and the Contractor

The Employer, the Contractor, the Employer's Personnel and the Contractor's Personnel shall not request advice from or consultation with the Member regarding the Contract, otherwise than in the normal course of the DAB's activities under the Contract and the Dispute Adjudication Agreement, and except to the extent that prior agreement is given by the Employer, the Contractor and the Other Members (if any). The Employer and the Contractor shall be responsible for compliance with this provision, by the Employer's Personnel and the Contractor's Personnel respectively.

The Employer and the Contractor undertake to each other and to the Member that the Member shall not, except as otherwise agreed in writing by the Employer, the Contractor, the Member and the Other Members (if any):

(a)   be appointed as an arbitrator in any arbitration under the Contract;

(b)   be called as a witness to give evidence concerning any dispute before arbitrator(s) appointed for any arbitration under the Contract; or

(c)   be liable for any claims for anything done or omitted in the discharge or purported discharge of the Member's functions, unless the act or omission is shown to have been in bad faith.

4 **成员的一般义务**	**成员**应： （a）除根据**争端裁决协议书**的付款外，与**雇主**、**承包商**或**工程师**没有财务或其他利益关系，在**合同**中没有任何财务利益； （b）以前未曾被**雇主**、**承包商**或**工程师**聘任咨询顾问或其他职务，在签订**争端裁决协议书**前，已书面告知**雇主**和**承包商**的情况除外； （c）在签订**争端裁决协议书**前，已就他（或她）的了解和记忆所及，将其与**雇主**、**承包商**或**工程师**的董事、职员或雇员间的任何业务或个人关系，以及此前在本**合同**为其组成部分的全面**工程**中的任何参与情况，书面告知**雇主**、**承包商**和**其他成员**（如果有）； （d）在执行**争端裁决协议书**期间，除经**雇主**、**承包商**和**其他成员**（如果有）的书面同意外，不接受**雇主**、**承包商**或**工程师**的聘任，担任咨询顾问或其他职位； （e）依从所附程序规则和**合同**条件第 **20.4 款**的规定； （f）除按照所附程序规则办事外，不向**雇主**、**承包商**、**雇主人员**或**承包商人员**提供有关执行**合同**的建议； （g）在担任**成员**期间，不与**雇主**、**承包商**或**工程师**，就其停止按**争端裁决协议书**任职后就任他们中任一方的咨询顾问或其他职位进行洽谈或签订任何协议； （h）保证出席任何必要的现场视察和意见听取会； （i）通过研究应保存在现有工作档案中的所有收到的文件，熟悉**合同**和**工程**（以及本**合同**作为组成一部分的某项目的任何其他部分）的进展； （j）将**合同**的所有细节、及 **DAB** 的所有活动和意见听取会情况视为私人的和机密的事项，没有**雇主**、**承包商**和**其他成员**（如果有）的事先书面同意，不将前述各事项公开发表或向外泄露；以及 （k）当**雇主**和**承包商**都提出要求，并经**其他成员**（如果有）同意，能就有关**合同**的任何事项提出建议和意见。
5 **雇主和承包商的一般义务**	除事先经**雇主**、**承包商**和**其他成员**（如果有）同意的范围以外，**雇主**、**承包商**、**雇主人员**和**承包商人员**不应在DAB 根据**合同**和本**争端裁决协议书**进行活动的正常过程之外，就**合同**有关问题要求**成员**提供建议，或与其协商。**雇主**和**承包商**应分别对**雇主人员**和**承包商人员**遵守此项规定负责。 除另经**雇主**、**承包商**、**成员**和**其他成员**（如果有）书面同意外，**雇主**和**承包商**应互相并向**成员**承诺，**成员**不应： （a）在根据**合同**进行的任何仲裁中，被任命为仲裁员； （b）在根据**合同**进行的任何仲裁中任命的仲裁员面前，被请来作为就任何争端提供证据的证人；或 （c）对因执行或据称执行**成员**任务中的任何行为或遗漏提出的任何索赔负责，除非该行为或遗漏表明是不诚实的。

The Employer and the Contractor hereby jointly and severally indemnify and hold the Member harmless against and from claims from which he/she is relieved from liability under the preceding paragraph.

Whenever the Employer or the Contractor refers a dispute to the DAB under Sub-Clause 20.4 of the Conditions of Contract, which will require the Member to make a site visit and attend a hearing, the Employer or the Contractor shall provide *appropriate security for a sum equivalent to the reasonable expenses to be incurred* by the Member. No account shall be taken of any other payments due or paid to the Member.

6

Payment

The Member shall be paid as follows, in the currency named in the Dispute Adjudication Agreement:

(a)   a retainer fee per calendar month, which shall be considered as payment in full for:

    (i)   being available on 28 days' notice for all site visits and hearings;

    (ii)   becoming and remaining conversant with all project developments and maintaining relevant files;

    (iii)   all office and overhead expenses including secretarial services, photocopying and office supplies incurred in connection with his duties; and

    (iv)   all services performed hereunder except those referred to in sub-paragraphs (b) and (c) of this Clause.

The retainer fee shall be paid with effect from the last day of the calendar month in which the Dispute Adjudication Agreement becomes effective; until the last day of the calendar month in which the Taking-Over Certificate is issued for the whole of the Works.

With effect from the first day of the calendar month following the month in which Taking-Over Certificate is issued for the whole of the Works, the retainer fee shall be reduced by 50%. This reduced fee shall be paid until the first day of the calendar month in which the Member resigns or the Dispute Adjudication Agreement is otherwise terminated.

(b)   a daily fee which shall be considered as payment in full for:

    (i)   each day or part of a day up to a maximum of two days' travel time in each direction for the journey between the Member's home and the site, or another location of a meeting with the Other Members (if any);

    (ii)   each working day on site visits, hearings or preparing decisions; and

    (iii)   each day spent reading submissions in preparation for a hearing.

(c)   all reasonable expenses incurred in connection with the Member's duties, including the cost of telephone calls, courier charges, faxes and telexes, travel expenses, hotel and subsistence costs: a receipt shall be required for each item in excess of five percent of the daily fee referred to in sub-paragraph (b) of this Clause;

(d)   any taxes properly levied in the Country on payments made to the Member (unless a national or permanent resident of the Country) under this Clause 6.

The retainer and daily fees shall be as specified in the Dispute Adjudication Agreement. Unless it specifies otherwise, these fees shall remain fixed for the first 24 calendar months, and shall thereafter be adjusted by agreement between the Employer, the Contractor and the Member, at each anniversary of the date on which the Dispute Adjudication Agreement became effective.

雇主和承包商在此共同并各自负责保障和保持成员免受因上段中他（或她）已被解除的责任引起的索赔带来的损害。

每当雇主或承包商根据合同条件第20.4款向DAB委托一项争端，要求成员进行现场视察与出席意见听取会时，雇主或承包商应为该成员提供与其招致的合理开支相等的款额的适当担保。其他应付或已付给成员的费用应不予考虑。

6 报酬

成员应按争端裁决协议书中规定的货币，得到以下付款：

(a) 每个日历月的聘请费，应认为对以下事项的全部付款：

  (i) 出席所有提前28天通知的现场视察和意见听取会；
  (ii) 做到和保持熟悉所有项目进展情况，并保存有关文档；

  (iii) 所有办公和管理费开支，包括履行其任务而发生的秘书服务费、复印和办公用品费；以及

  (iv) 除本条(b)和(c)项提出的以外，下文所述的所有服务。

聘请费应从争端裁决协议书生效的日历月的最后一天起支付，直至颁发整个工程的接收证书的日历月的最后一天为止。

从颁发整个工程的接收证书的月份的下一个日历月的第一天起，聘请费应减少50%。此项减少后的费用应继续支付，直到成员辞职，或争端裁决协议书因其他原因终止的日历月的第一天为止。

(b) 日酬金，此项费用应被视为对下列事项的全部付款：
  (i) 在成员住所与现场，或与其他成员(如果有)开会的其他地点之间，单向一天或不足一天，最多至2天时间的旅程；

  (ii) 现场视察和意见听取会或准备决定意见的每个工作日；和
  (iii) 用于准备意见听取会而阅读提交资料的每一天；
(c) 因履行成员义务而发生的所有合理开支，包括电话费、信差等服务费、传真和电传费、差旅费、旅馆和生活补助费。每项超过本条(b)项所述日酬金的百分之五时，应提交费用的收据；

(d) 在工程所在国对成员(如果不是工程所在国的国民或永久居民)根据本第6条取得的付款，合理征收的任何税款。

聘请费和日酬金应按争端裁决协议书的规定执行。除非另有规定，这些费用在开始的24个日历月内应保持不变，其后应在争端裁决协议书生效日的每个周年，在雇主、承包商和成员同意后调整。

The Member shall submit invoices for payment of the monthly retainer and air fares quarterly in advance. Invoices for other expenses and for daily fees shall be submitted following the conclusion of a site visit or hearing. All invoices shall be accompanied by a brief description of activities performed during the relevant period and shall be addressed to the Contractor.

The Contractor shall pay each of the Member's invoices in full within 56 calendar days after receiving each invoice and shall apply to the Employer (in the Statements under the Contract) for reimbursement of one-half of the amounts of these invoices. The Employer shall then pay the Contractor in accordance with the Contract.

If the Contractor fails to pay to the Member the amount to which he/she is entitled under the Dispute Adjudication Agreement, the Employer shall pay the amount due to the Member and any other amount which may be required to maintain the operation of the DAB; and without prejudice to the Employer's rights or remedies. In addition to all other rights arising from this default, the Employer shall be entitled to reimbursement of all sums paid in excess of one-half of these payments, plus all costs of recovering these sums and financing charges calculated at the rate specified in Sub-Clause 14.8 of the Conditions of Contract.

If the Member does not receive payment of the amount due within 70 days after submitting a valid invoice, the Member may (i) suspend his/her services (without notice) until the payment is received, and/or (ii) resign his/her appointment by giving notice under Clause 7.

7

Termination

At any time: (i) the Employer and the Contractor may jointly terminate the Dispute Adjudication Agreement by giving 42 days' notice to the Member; or (ii) the Member may resign as provided for in Clause 2.

If the Member fails to comply with the Dispute Adjudication Agreement, the Employer and the Contractor may, without prejudice to their other rights, terminate it by notice to the Member. The notice shall take effect when received by the Member.

If the Employer or the Contractor fails to comply with the Dispute Adjudication Agreement, the Member may, without prejudice to his/her other rights, terminate it by notice to the Employer and the Contractor. The notice shall take effect when received by them both.

Any such notice, resignation and termination shall be final and binding on the Employer, the Contractor and the Member. However, a notice by the Employer or the Contractor, but not by both, shall be of no effect.

8

Default of the Member

If the Member fails to comply with any obligation under Clause 4, he/she shall not be entitled to any fees or expenses hereunder and shall, without prejudice to their other rights, reimburse each of the Employer and the Contractor for any fees and expenses received by the Member and the Other Members (if any), for proceedings or decisions (if any) of the DAB which are rendered void or ineffective.

9

Disputes

Any dispute or claim arising out of or in connection with this Dispute Adjudication Agreement, or the breach, termination or invalidity thereof, shall be finally settled under the Rules of Arbitration of the International Chamber of Commerce by one arbitrator appointed in accordance with these Rules of Arbitration.

成员应按季度先提交月份聘请费和航空费的发票。其他开支和日酬金的发票，应在每次现场视察和意见听取会后提交。所有发票应附相应时期从事活动的简要说明，一并提交承包商。

承包商应在收到每个发票后56天内，对成员的每个发票进行足额付款，并向雇主申请(在根据合同提交的报表中)付还这些发票金额的一半。这时，雇主应按照合同付给承包商。

如果承包商未能向成员支付他(或她)根据争端裁决协议书的规定应得的款额，雇主应向成员支付其应得款额和维持DAB运作可能需要的任何其他款额；此项支付不损害雇主的权利或应得补偿。除由此项违约引起的所有其他权利外，雇主对他支付的超过这些付款一半部分的所有款额应有权获得偿还，还应加上回收这些款项的全部费用和按合同条件第14.8款规定的利率计算的融资费用。

如果成员在提交有效发票70天内，没有收到应付款额的支付，成员可(i)暂停他(或她)的服务(不需通知)，直到收到付款为止，和(或)(ii)根据本第7条发出通知辞去他(或她)的职务。

7

终止

在任何时候，(i)雇主和承包商可在42天前联合向成员发出通知终止争端裁决协议书，或(ii)成员可按照第2条辞职。

如果成员未能遵守争端裁决协议书，雇主和承包商可通知成员终止该协议，而不损害他们的其他权利。该通知应在成员收到时生效。

如果雇主或承包商未能遵守争端裁决协议书，成员可通知雇主和承包商终止该协议，而不损害他(或她)的其他权利。该通知应在该双方都收到时生效。

任何这类通知、辞职和终止，将是最终的，对雇主、承包商和成员都有约束力。但由雇主或承包商单独，而不是两者发出的通知，应属无效。

8

成员的违约

如果成员未能遵守第4条规定的任何义务，他(或她)应无权得到在此所述的任何酬金和开支，并应在不损害雇主和承包商其他权利的条件下，将该成员和其他成员(如果有)为已导致作废和无效的DAB的工作和决定(如果有)收到的任何费用和开支，分别付还雇主和承包商。

9

争端

因本争端裁决协议书或与之有关的，或因对其违反或其终止或无效而引起的任何争端或索赔，应根据国际商会仲裁规则，由一位按这些仲裁规则任命的仲裁员最终解决。

Annex   PROCEDURAL RULES

1   Unless otherwise agreed by the Employer and the Contractor, the DAB shall visit the site at intervals of not more than 140 days, including times of critical construction events, at the request of either the Employer or the Contractor. Unless otherwise agreed by the Employer, the Contractor and the DAB, the period between consecutive visits shall not be less than 70 days, except as required to convene a hearing as described below.

2   The timing of and agenda for each site visit shall be as agreed jointly by the DAB, the Employer and the Contractor, or in the absence of agreement, shall be decided by the DAB. The purpose of site visits is to enable the DAB to become and remain acquainted with the progress of the Works and of any actual or potential problems or claims.

3   Site visits shall be attended by the Employer, the Contractor and the Engineer and shall be co-ordinated by the Employer in co-operation with the Contractor. The Employer shall ensure the provision of appropriate conference facilities and secretarial and copying services. At the conclusion of each site visit and before leaving the site, the DAB shall prepare a report on its activities during the visit and shall send copies to the Employer and the Contractor.

4   The Employer and the Contractor shall furnish to the DAB one copy of all documents which the DAB may request, including Contract documents, progress reports, variation instructions, certificates and other documents pertinent to the performance of the Contract. All communications between the DAB and the Employer or the Contractor shall be copied to the other Party. If the DAB comprises three persons, the Employer and the Contractor shall send copies of these requested documents and these communications to each of these persons.

5   If any dispute is referred to the DAB in accordance with Sub-Clause 20.4 of the Conditions of Contract, the DAB shall proceed in accordance with Sub-Clause 20.4 and these Rules. Subject to the time allowed to give notice of a decision and other relevant factors, the DAB shall:

(a)   act fairly and impartially as between the Employer and the Contractor, giving each of them a reasonable opportunity of putting his case and responding to the other's case, and

(b)   adopt procedures suitable to the dispute, avoiding unnecessary delay or expense.

6   The DAB may conduct a hearing on the dispute, in which event it will decide on the date and place for the hearing and may request that written documentation and arguments from the Employer and the Contractor be presented to it prior to or at the hearing.

7   Except as otherwise agreed in writing by the Employer and the Contractor, the DAB shall have power to adopt an inquisitorial procedure, to refuse admission to hearings or audience at hearings to any persons other than representatives of the Employer, the Contractor and the Engineer, and to proceed in the absence of any party who the DAB is satisfied received notice of the hearing; but shall have discretion to decide whether and to what extent this power may be exercised.

附件 程序规则

1 　　除非**雇主**和**承包商**另有商定，**DAB** 现场视察的时间间隔应不大于 140 天，其中包括应**雇主**或**承包商**要求进行的各次重要施工事件的视察。除非**雇主**、**承包商**和 **DAB** 另有商定，连续视察之间的时间间隔应不小于 70 天，但下述需要召集意见听取会的情况除外。

2 　　每次现场视察的时间和日程，应得到 **DAB**、**雇主**和**承包商**的一致同意，或在没有一致同意的情况下，由 **DAB** 作出决定。现场视察的目的，是使 **DAB** 做到并保持熟悉工程，以及任何实际的或潜在的问题或索赔的进展情况。

3 　　现场视察应有**雇主**、**承包商**和**工程师**出席，并应由**雇主**在**承包商**协助下进行协调。**雇主**应确保提供适当的会议设施以及秘书和复印服务。每次现场视察结束时，在离开**现场**前，**DAB** 应编写一份视察期间的活动报告，并抄送**雇主**和**承包商**。

4 　　**雇主**和**承包商**应向 **DAB** 提供一份其可能要求的所有文件，包括合同文件、进度报告、变更指示、证明和与履行**合同**有关的其他文件。**DAB** 和**雇主**或**承包商**间的所有函件，都应抄送另一方。如果 **DAB** 由三人组成，**雇主**和**承包商**应将这些要求的文件和这些信函抄送给他们每人。

5 　　如有任何争端按照**合同条件第 20.4 款**委托给 **DAB**，**DAB** 应按照**第 20.4 款**和本**规则**进行工作。根据提出决定和其他有关因素的通知所允许的时间，**DAB** 应：

（a） 公平、公正地对待**雇主**和**承包商**，对每方都给予合理的机会陈述己方的论据，回应他方的论据；以及

（b） 采用对争端事项适宜的程序，避免不必要的延误或开支。

6 　　**DAB** 可以就争端事项召开意见听取会，在此情况下，它将决定意见听取会的日期和地点，并可要求**雇主**和**承包商**在意见听取会前或开会时向它递交书面文件和论据。

7 　　除另经**雇主**和**承包商**书面同意外，**DAB** 应有权采用讯问调查程序，拒绝除**雇主**、**承包商**和**工程师**的代表以外的任何人参加或旁听意见听取会；并有权在任一方缺席，且 **DAB** 确信其已收到意见听取会通知的情况下，进行会议；但对是否实施这一权力和可能实施的范围，应有权自主做出决定。

8   The Employer and the Contractor empower the DAB, among other things, to:

(a)   establish the procedure to be applied in deciding a dispute,

(b)   decide upon the DAB's own jurisdiction, and as to the scope of any dispute referred to it,

(c)   conduct any hearing as it thinks fit, not being bound by any rules or procedures other than those contained in the Contract and these Rules,

(d)   take the initiative in ascertaining the facts and matters required for a decision,

(e)   make use of its own specialist knowledge, if any,

(f)   decide upon the payment of financing charges in accordance with the Contract,

(g)   decide upon any provisional relief such as interim or conservatory measures, and

(h)   open up, review and revise any certificate, decision, determination, instruction, opinion or valuation of the Engineer, relevant to the dispute.

9   The DAB shall not express any opinions during any hearing concerning the merits of any arguments advanced by the Parties. Thereafter, the DAB shall make and give its decision in accordance with Sub-Clause 20.4, or as otherwise agreed by the Employer and the Contractor in writing. If the DAB comprises three persons:

(a)   it shall convene in private after a hearing, in order to have discussions and prepare its decision;

(b)   it shall endeavour to reach a unanimous decision: if this proves impossible the applicable decision shall be made by a majority of the Members, who may require the minority Member to prepare a written report for submission to the Employer and the Contractor; and

(c)   if a Member fails to attend a meeting or hearing, or to fulfil any required function, the other two Members may nevertheless proceed to make a decision, unless:

(i)   either the Employer or the Contractor does not agree that they do so, or

(ii)   the absent Member is the chairman and he/she instructs the other Members to not make a decision.

8   在其他方面，**雇主**和**承包商**给予DAB 以下权力：

(a)   确定在决定争端中应用的程序；
(b)   决定**DAB**自身的权限，及委托其处理的任何争端涉及的范围；

(c)   召开其认为适宜的任何意见听取会，除包括在**合同**和本**规则**中的规定外，不受任何规则或程序的约束；
(d)   主动确定为**做出决定**所需的事实和情况；
(e)   利用其自身的专家知识，如果有；
(f)   按照**合同**规定，决定融资费用的支付；

(g)   决定任何暂时补救办法，如暂时的或保护性的措施；以及

(h)   公开、审查和修正**工程师**发出的与争端有关的任何证明、决定、确定、指示、意见或估价。

9   **DAB**在任何意见听取会期间，不应就各方提出的任何论据的是非表示任何意见。其后，**DAB**应按照合同条件第 **20.4 款**，或经**雇主**和**承包商**书面同意的其他规定，作出决定，并发出通知。如果**DAB**由三人组成，则：

(a)   为讨论和做出其决定，应在意见听取会后召开秘密会议；

(b)   应努力做出一致决定：如果不可能，应由多数**成员**做出合适的决定，并要求少数**成员**编写一份书面报告，提交给**雇主**和**承包商**；以及

(c)   如果某一**成员**未参加会议或意见听取会，或未履行其应尽的职责，另外两名**成员**仍可继续作出决定，除非：
    (i)   **雇主**或**承包商**不同意他们这样做，或
    (ii)   该缺席**成员**是主席，并且他（或她）通知其他**成员**不要作出决定。

INDEX OF SUB-CLAUSES

154

条款索引

（原文按英文字母顺序排列，中译文按汉语拼音字母顺序排列）

投标函、合同协议书和
争端裁决协议书格式
FORMS OF LETTER OF
TENDER, CONTRACT
AGREEMENT AND
DISPUTE ADJUDICATION
AGREEMENT

施工合同条件

Conditions of Contract
for CONSTRUCTION

用于由雇主设计的建筑和工程

FOR BUILDING AND ENGINEERING WORKS
DESIGNED BY THE EMPLOYER

专用条件编写指南

Guidance for the Preparation of Particular
Conditions

国 际 咨 询 工 程 师 联 合 会

FEDERATION INTERNATIONALE DES INGENIEURS-CONSEILS
INTERNATIONAL FEDERATION OF CONSULTING ENGINEERS
INTERNATIONALE VEREINIGUNG BERATENDER INGENIEURE
FEDERACION INTERNACIONAL DE INGENIEROS CONSOLTORES

FIDIC

161

Guidance
for the Preparation of Particular Conditions

CONTENTS

GENERAL
CONDITIONS

GUIDANCE

FORMS

专用条件编写指南

目　　录

Guidance for the Preparation of Particular Conditions

INTRODUCTION

The terms of the Conditions of Contract for Construction have been prepared by the Fédération Internationale des Ingénieurs-Conseils (FIDIC) and are recommended for general use for the purpose of the construction (excluding most design) of building or engineering works where tenders are invited on an international basis. Modifications to the Conditions may be required in some legal jurisdictions, particularly if they are to be used on domestic contracts.

Under the usual arrangements for this type of contract, the Contractor constructs the works in accordance with design details provided by the Employer or his representative, the Engineer. Although these Conditions allow for the possibility that the Contractor may be required to design parts of the permanent works, they are not intended for use where most of the works are designed by the Contractor. For these Works, it would be more appropriate to utilise FIDIC's Conditions of Contract for Plant and Design-Build or Conditions of Contract for EPC/Turnkey Projects.

The guidance hereafter is intended to assist writers of the Particular Conditions by giving options for various sub-clauses where appropriate. As far as possible, example wording is included, between lines. In some cases, however, only an aide-memoire is given.

Before incorporating any example wording, it must be checked to ensure that it is wholly suitable for the particular circumstances. Unless it is considered suitable, example wording should be amended before use.

Where example wording is amended, and in all cases where other amendments or additions are made, care must be taken to ensure that no ambiguity is created, either with the General Conditions or between the clauses in the Particular Conditions.

In the preparation of the Conditions of Contract to be included in the tender documents for a contract, the following text can be used:

> The Conditions of Contract comprise the "General Conditions", which form part of the "Conditions of Contract for Construction" First Edition 1999 published by the Fédération Internationale des Ingénieurs-Conseils (FIDIC), and the following "Particular Conditions", which include amendments and additions to such General Conditions.

There are no Sub-Clauses in the General Conditions which require data to be included in the Particular Conditions. As noted in sub-paragraph (ii) of the Foreword, the General Conditions refer to any necessary data being contained in the Appendix to Tender or (for technical matters) in the Specification.

FIDIC has published a document entitled "Tendering Procedure" which presents a systematic approach to the selection of tenderers and the obtaining and evaluation of tenders; the second edition was published in 1994. The document is intended to assist the Employer to receive sound competitive tenders with a minimum of qualifications. FIDIC intends to update Tendering Procedure and to publish a guide to the use of these Conditions of Contract for Construction.

专用条件编写指南

引　　言

国际咨询工程师联合会(FIDIC 菲迪克)已编制了**《施工合同条件》**的条款，推荐用于进行国际招标的建筑或工程(大部分不包括设计)。在某些法律管辖地区，特别是用于国内合同时，可能需要对**条件**做些修改。

根据这类合同的通常安排，**承包商**按照**雇主**或其代表(**工程师**)提供的详细设计，进行工程的施工。虽然本**条件**考虑了可能要求**承包商**进行部分永久工程设计的可能性，但它们不是为大部分工程都由**承包商**设计的情况下使用的。FIDIC 的**《生产设备和设计-施工合同条件》**或**《设计采购施工(EPC)/交钥匙工程合同条件》**，可能对此类工程更为合适。

下述指南旨在通过在适当处给出各类备选条款，为**专用条件**的编写人提供帮助。尽可能包括一些文字间的范例措辞。但在有些情况下只给出备忘要点。

在使用任何范例措辞前，必须核实，以确保完全适用于特定的情况。除非认为是适合的，使用前应对范例措辞进行修改。

当对范例措辞进行修改时，以及在所有其他修改和补充的情况下，必须注意确保不与**通用条件**产生歧义，或在**专用条件**条款间产生歧义。

在编写包括在一项合同的招标文件中的**合同条件**时，可以使用下列文字：

> **合同条件**包括 "通用条件"，和"专用条件"，通用条件是国际咨询工程师联合会(FIDIC)1999年出版的**《施工合同条件》**第一版的组成部分，其后的"**专用条件**"包括对上述**通用条件**的修改和补。

通用条件没有条款要求将数据包括在**专用条件**中。如前言(ii)项中所述，**通用条件**提及的任何必要数据都包含在**投标书附录**中，或(有关技术事项)在**规范要求**中。

菲迪克(FIDIC)已出版了名为"**招标程序**"的文件，为选择投标人以及招标和评标，提供了一套系统的办法；其第 2 版已于 1994 年出版。这一文件是为了帮助**雇主**在最低资格要求下收到可靠而有竞争力的投标书。菲迪克(FIDIC)准备更新"**招标程序**"，并出版本**施工合同条件**的使用指南。

Notes on the Preparation of Tender Documents

The tender documents should be prepared by suitably-qualified engineers who are familiar with the technical aspects of the required works, and a review by suitably-qualified lawyers may be advisable. The tender documents issued to tenderers will consist of the Conditions of Contract, the Specification, the Drawings, and the Letter of Tender and Schedules for completion by the Tenderer. For this type of contract, where the Works are valued by measurement, the Bill of Quantities will usually be the most important Schedule. A Daywork Schedule may also be necessary, to cover minor works to be evaluated at cost. In addition, each of the Tenderers should receive the data referred to in Sub-Clause 4.10, and the Instructions to Tenderers to advise them of any special matters which the Employer wishes them to take into account when pricing the Bill of Quantities but which are not to form part of the Contract. When the Employer accepts the Letter of Tender, the Contract (which then comes into full force and effect) includes these completed Schedules.

The Specification may include the matters referred to in some or all of the following Sub-Clauses:

1.8	Requirements for Contractor's Documents
1.13	Permissions being obtained by the Employer
2.1	Phased possession of foundations, structures, plant or means of access
4.1	Contractor's designs
4.6	Other contractors (and others) on the Site
4.7	Setting-out points, lines and levels of reference
4.14	Third parties
4.18	Environmental constraints
4.19	Electricity, water, gas and other services available on the Site
4.20	Employer's Equipment and free-issue material
5.1	Nominated Subcontractors
6.6	Facilities for Personnel
7.2	Samples
7.4	Testing during manufacture and/or construction
9.1	Tests on Completion
13.5	Provisional Sums

Many Sub-Clauses in the General Conditions make reference to data being contained in the Appendix to Tender, providing a convenient location for the data which is usually required. The example form in this publication thus provides a check-list of the data required; but there is no indication, either in the General Conditions or in the example Appendix to Tender, that this data is either prescribed by the Employer or inserted by the Tenderer. The Employer should prepare the Appendix to Tender, based on this example form, with the elements completed to the extent of his requirements.

The Employer may also require other data from Tenderers, and include a questionnaire in the Schedules.

The Instructions to Tenderers may need to specify any constraints on the completion of the Appendix to Tender and/or Schedules, and/or specify the extent of other information which each Tenderer is to include with his Tender. If each Tenderer is to produce a parent company guarantee and/or a tender security, these requirements (which apply prior to the Contract becoming effective) should be included in the Instructions to Tenderers: example forms are annexed to this document as Annexes A and B. The Instructions may include matters referred to in some or all of the following Sub-Clauses:

4.3	Contractor's Representative (name and curriculum vitae)
4.9	Quality Assurance system
9.1	Tests on Completion
18	Insurances
20	Resolution of disputes

166

编写招标文件注意事项

招标文件应由具有适当资质、熟悉要建工程技术情况的工程师编写，并请有适当资质的律师进行审核可能是明智的。发给投标人的招标文件将由**合同条件**、**规范要求**、图纸及需由投标人填写的**投标函和资料表**组成。对此类合同，**工程**是通过测量来进行估价，**工程量表**通常是最重要的**资料表**。计日工作计划表也可能是必需的，以便包括需要估价的次要工作。此外，每位投标人都应**款**中提到的资料，以及**投标人须知**，以告诉他们**雇主**希望他们在给**工程量表**定价时要考虑的任何收到在**第 4.10** 特定事项，但这些事项不构成**合同**的一部分。当**雇主**接受**投标函**时，**合同**(此时全面实施和生效)包括这些填写好的**资料表**。

规范要求中可能包括下列部分或全部**条款**中提出的事项：
    1.8 对**承包商文件**的要求
    1.13 **雇主**取得的许可
    2.1 基础、结构、生产设备分阶段的占用权或进入的方法
    4.1 **承包商**的设计
    4.6 在**现场**的其他承包商(和其他人员)
    4.7 放线的基准点、基准线和基准标高
    4.14 第三方
    4.18 环境约束
    4.19 **现场**可供的电、水、燃气和其他服务
    4.20 **雇主设备**和免费供应的材料
    5.1 **指定的分包商**
    6.6 为人员提供设施
    7.2 样品
    7.4 制造和(或)施工期间的试验
    9.1 **竣工试验**
    13.5 **暂列金额**

通用条件中的许多条款提到**投标书附录**中要包括的数据，为常用数据提供了方便的查阅地址。本文本中的示范格式，提供了所需数据的核查表；但在**通用条件**和**投标书附录**范例中，都没有表明此项数据是由**雇主**指定，还是由**投标人**填入。**雇主**应根据此范例格式，编写**投标书附录**，按其要求填写各项内容。

雇主还可以要求**投标人**提供其他数据，并在要求的**资料表**中包括一份问卷调查。

投标人须知可能需要规定填写**投标书附录**和(或)**资料表**的任何约束条件，和(或)每位**投标人**需在其**投标书**中包括的其他资料的范围。如果要每位投标人取得母公司保函和(或)投标保函，这些要求(将在**合同**生效前应用)应包括在**投标人须知**中：其范例格式见本文件**附件**A 和 B。**须知**中可包括下列部分或全部**条款**中提出的事项：

    4.3 **承包商代表**(姓名和简历)
    4.9 **质量保证体系**
    9.1 **竣工试验**
    18 **保险**
    20 争端的解决

Clause 1 General Provisions

Sub-Clause 1.1 Definitions

It may be necessary to amend some of the definitions. For example:

1.1.3.1	the Base Date could be defined as a particular calendar date
1.1.4.6	one particular Foreign Currency may be required by the financing institution
1.1.4.8	a different currency may be required to be the contract Local Currency
1.1.6.2	the references to "Country" may be inappropriate for a cross-border Site

Sub-Clause 1.2 Interpretation

If the references to "profit" are to be more precisely specified, this Sub-Clause may be varied:

EXAMPLE At the end of Sub-Clause 1.2, insert:

In these Conditions, provisions including the expression "Cost plus reasonable profit" require this profit to be one-twentieth (5%) of this Cost.

Sub-Clause 1.5 Priority of Documents

An order of precedence is usually necessary, in case a conflict is subsequently found among the contract documents. If no order of precedence is to be prescribed, this Sub-Clause may be varied:

EXAMPLE Delete Sub-Clause 1.5 and substitute:

The documents forming the Contract are to be taken as mutually explanatory of one another. If an ambiguity or discrepancy is found, the priority shall be such as may be accorded by the governing law. The Engineer has authority to issue any instruction which he considers necessary to resolve an ambiguity or discrepancy.

Sub-Clause 1.6 Contract Agreement

The form of Agreement should be included in the tender documents as an annex to the Particular Conditions: an example form is included at the end of this publication. If lengthy tender negotiations were necessary, it may be considered advisable for the Contract Agreement to record the Accepted Contract Amount, Base Date and/or Commencement Date. Entry into an Agreement may be necessary under applicable law.

Sub-Clause 1.14 Joint and Several Liability

For a major contract, detailed requirements for the joint venture may need to be specified. For example, it may be desirable for each member to produce a parent company guarantee: an example form is annexed to this document as Annex A.

These requirements, which apply prior to the Contract becoming effective, should be included in the Instructions to Tenderers. The Employer will wish the leader of the joint venture to be appointed at an early stage, providing a single point of contact thereafter, and will not wish to be

第1条　　　　　　　　　一般规定

第1.1款　　　　　定义

可能需要对一些定义进行修改。例如：

1.1.3.1　**基准日期**可规定为某一特定日历日期
1.1.4.6　融资机构可能要求某种特定**外币**
1.1.4.8　合同**当地货币**可能要求另一种货币
1.1.6.2　对于跨边界的**现场**，"工程所在国"的提法可能不适宜

第1.2款　　　　　解释

如果对"利润"的提法要更明确地规定，本**款**可改为：

范例　　　　　　　在第1.2**款**末尾插入：

在本**条件**中，包括"**费用**加合理利润"词语的规定，要求该利润为该**费用**的二十分之一(5%)。

第1.5款　　　　　文件优先次序

由于随后合同文件间可能发现矛盾，优先次序通常是需要的。如果不拟规定优先次序，本**款**可改为：

范例　　　　　　　删除第1.5**款**，代之以：

组成**合同**的各项文件将被认为是互作说明的。如出现含糊或歧义时，应按管辖的法律确定先后次序。**工程师**有权发出他认为必要的任何指示，以解决此含糊或歧义。

第1.6款　　　　　合同协议书

协议书的格式应作为**专用条件**的附件，包含在招标文件中：在本文本的后面有其范例格式。如投标谈判需要较长时间，在**合同协议书**中最好写入**中标合同金额**、**基准日期**和(或)开工日期。根据适用的法律可能要求签订**协议书**。

第1.14款　　　　　共同的和各自的责任

对于大型合同，可能需要对联营体规定一些具体要求。如可能希望每位成员提交一份母公司保函：本文件附有范例格式，见**附件A**。

这些在**合同**生效前适用的要求，应包含在**投标人须知**中。**雇主**将希望早期指定联营体的负责方，以便此后有一个单独的联系方，以避免卷入联营体成员间的争端。**雇主**应仔细审查联营

involved in a dispute between the members of a joint venture. The Employer should scrutinise the joint venture agreement carefully, and it may have to be approved by the project's financing institutions.

Additional Sub-Clause   Details to be Confidential

If confidentiality is required, an additional sub-clause may be added:

EXAMPLE SUB-CLAUSE

> The Contractor shall treat the details of the Contract as private and confidential, except to the extent necessary to carry out obligations under it or to comply with applicable Laws. The Contractor shall not publish, permit to be published, or disclose any particulars of the Works in any trade or technical paper or elsewhere without the previous agreement of the Employer.

Clause 2   The Employer

Sub-Clause 2.1   Right of Access to the Site

If right of access cannot be granted, both early and thereafter exclusively, details should be given in the Specification.

Sub-Clause 2.3   Employer's Personnel

These provisions should be reflected in the Employer's contracts with any other contractors on the Site.

Clause 3   The Engineer

Sub-Clause 3.1   Engineer's Duties and Authority

Any requirements for Employer's approval should be set out in the Particular Conditions:

EXAMPLE

> The Engineer shall obtain the specific approval of the Employer before taking action under the following Sub-Clauses of these Conditions:
>
> (a)   Sub-Clause _____   **
>
> (b)   Sub-Clause _____   **
>
> ** (insert number; describe action, unless all require approval)

This list should be extended or reduced as necessary. If the obligation to obtain the approval of the Employer only applies beyond certain limits, financial or otherwise, the example wording should be varied.

Additional Sub-Clause   Management Meetings

EXAMPLE SUB-CLAUSE

> The Engineer or the Contractor's Representative may require the other to attend a management meeting in order to review the arrangements for future work. The Engineer shall record the business of management meetings and supply copies of the record to those attending the meeting

体的协议书，此类协议书可能须经项目融资机构批准。

附加条款　　　　　　**需保密的细节**

如需要保密，可另加条款：

范例条款

除了根据**合同**履行义务或遵守适用法律所必需的以外，**承包商**应以私人的和保密的方式处理**合同**的细节。没有**雇主**事先同意，**承包商**不得在任何商业、技术论文或其他场合出版、允许出版或透露任何**工程**的详情。

第 2 条　　　　　　雇主

第 2.1 款　　　　　现场进入权

如果不能给予早期和以后独享的现场进入权，应在**规范要求**中列出详情。

第 2.3 款　　　　　雇主人员

这些规定应反映在**雇主**与**现场**的其他承包商间的合同中。

第 3 条　　　　　　工程师

第 3.1 款　　　　　工程师的任务和权力

任何需经**雇主**批准的要求应在**专用条件**中列出：

范例

工程师在根据**本条件**的以下各**款**采取行动前，应得到**雇主**的专门批准：

(a)　第 ＿＿＿＿＿＿＿ 款＊＊

(b)　第 ＿＿＿＿＿＿＿ 款＊＊

　　　　　　　　　　　＊＊（填入各款款号；除非条款的全部行动均要批准，说明要批准的行动）

此表应视需要增减。如要获得**雇主**批准的义务仅在超过一定的财务或其他限度时才适用，范例的措辞应予修改。

附加条款　　　　　　**管理会议**

范例条款

工程师或**承包商**代表可要求对方出席管理会议，以审查未来工作的安排。**工程师**应记录管理会议的内容，并向与会人员和**雇主**提供记

171

and to the Employer. In the record, responsibilities for any actions to be taken shall be in accordance with the Contract.

Clause 4   The Contractor

Sub-Clause 4.1   Contractor's General Obligations

Occasionally, there may be an item of Temporary Works for which the Contractor will not be fully responsible. For example, the Contract may specify temporary arrangements for river diversion which have been designed by the Engineer. In these cases, the Sub-Clause may require amendment, taking account of the type of this item of Temporary Works, and of the extent of the Employer's responsibility.

Sub-Clause 4.2   Performance Security

The acceptable form(s) of Performance Security should be included in the tender documents, annexed to the Particular Conditions. Example forms are annexed to this document as Annex C and Annex D. They incorporate two sets of Uniform Rules published by the International Chamber of Commerce (the "ICC", which is based at 38 Cours Albert 1er, 75008 Paris, France), which also publishes guides to these Uniform Rules. These example forms and the wording of the Sub-Clause may have to be amended to comply with applicable law.

EXAMPLE

At the end of the second paragraph of Sub-Clause 4.2, insert:

If the Performance Security is in the form of a bank guarantee, it shall be issued either (a) by a bank located in the Country, or (b) directly by a foreign bank acceptable to the Employer. If the Performance Security is not in the form of a bank guarantee, it shall be furnished by a financial entity registered, or licensed to do business, in the Country.

Sub-Clause 4.3   Contractor's Representative

If the Representative is known at the time of submission of the Tender, the Tenderer may propose the Representative. The Tenderer may wish to propose alternatives, especially if the contract award seems likely to be delayed. If the ruling language is not the same as the language for day to day communications (under Sub-Clause 1.4), or if for any other reason it is necessary to stipulate that the Contractor's Representative shall be fluent in a particular language, one of the following sentences may be added.

EXAMPLE

At the end of Sub-Clause 4.3, add:

The Contractor's Representative and all these persons shall also be fluent in _____ (insert name of language)

EXAMPLE

At the end of Sub-Clause 4.3, add:

If the Contractor's Representative, or these persons, is not fluent in _____ (insert name of language), the Contractor shall make a competent interpreter available during all working hours.

Sub-Clause 4.4   Subcontractors

The wording in the General Conditions includes the conditions which will usually be applicable. If less (or no) consent is required, some (or all) of sub-paragraphs (a) to (d) may be deleted, or qualified in the Particular Conditions:

录的副本。记录中所列需要采取行动的职责，应与**合同**一致。

第4条   承包商

第4.1款   承包商的一般义务

有时，**临时工程**的某一项目可能不是完全由**承包商**负责的。例如，**合同**可能规定由**工程师**设计的河流改道的临时安排。在此类情况下，**本款**可能需要修改，要考虑**临时工程**中该项目的类型及**雇主**职责的范围。

第4.2款   履约担保

认可的**履约担保**格式应包括在招标文件中，附在**专用条件**后面。范例格式作为**附件** C 和**附件** D，附于本文件后。它们体现**国际商会**(ICC，总部位于法国巴黎 38 Cours Albert 1er，75008 Paris, France)出版的两套**统一规则**，**国际商会**还出版了这些**统一规则**的指南。这些范例格式及**条款**的措辞可能需要进行修改，以符合适用法律。

范例   在**第4.2款**第二段末尾插入：

> 如果**履约担保**是银行保函的形式，它应(a)由工程所在国内的银行，或(b)直接由**雇主**认可的外国银行出具。如**履约担保**不是银行保函的形式，应由在**工程所在**国注册或取得营业执照的金融实体提供。

第4.3款   承包商代表

如果在递交**投标书**时已确定**代表**人选，**投标人**可提出代表人选的建议。**投标人**可能希望提出替代人选，特别是看来要推迟授予**合同**时。如果主导语言不是日常交流的语言(根据**第1.4款**)，或由于其他任何原因需要规定**承包商代表**能流利使用某种语言时，可增加下列句子之一：

范例   在**第4.3款**末尾增加：

> **承包商代表**及所有此类人员还应能流利使用 _____ (填入语言名称)

范例   在**第4.3款**末尾增加：

> 如果**承包商代表**或此类人员不能流利地使用 _____ (填入语言名称)，**承包商**应派一名胜任的译员在所有工作时间随时在场。

第4.4款   分包商

通用条件的措辞包括通常适用的条件。如果要经同意的较少(或不要)，(a)至(d)项的某些(或全部)内容可删除，或在**专用条件**中附加条件：

Prior consent shall not be required if the value of the subcontract is less than 0.01% of the Accepted Contract Amount.

A sentence may be added to increase the extent to which consent is required:

The prior consent of the Engineer shall be obtained to the suppliers of the following Materials:

(insert details: for example, specific manufactured or prefabricated items)

A sentence may be added in order to encourage the Contractor to use local contractors:

Where practicable, the Contractor shall give a fair and reasonable opportunity for contractors from the Country to be appointed as Sub-contractors.

Sub-Clause 4.8   Safety Procedures

If the Contractor is sharing occupation of the Site with others, it may not be appropriate for him to provide some of the listed items. In these circumstances, the Employer's obligations should be specified.

Sub-Clause 4.9   Quality Assurance

The wording in the General Conditions imposes the requirement of a quality assurance system in accordance with details specified in the Contract. If inappropriate, this Sub-Clause may be deleted.

Sub-Clause 4.12   Unforeseeable Physical Conditions

In the case of major sub-surface works, the allocation of the risk of sub-surface conditions is an aspect which should be considered when tender documents are being prepared. If this risk is to be shared between the parties, the Sub-Clause may be amended:

Delete sub-paragraph (b) of Sub-Clause 4.12 and substitute:

(b)   payment for any such Cost, _____ per cent (_____ %) of which shall be included in the Contract Price (the balance _____ percent of the Cost shall be borne by the Contractor).

Sub-Clause 4.17   Contractor's Equipment

If the Contractor is not to provide all the Contractor's Equipment necessary to complete the Works, the Employer's obligations should be specified: see Sub-Clause 4.20. If vesting of Contractor's Equipment is required, further paragraphs may be added, subject to their being consistent with applicable laws:

At the end of Sub-Clause 4.17, add the following paragraphs:

Contractor's Equipment which is owned by the Contractor (either directly or indirectly) shall be deemed to be the property of the Employer with effect from its arrival on the Site. This vesting of property shall not:

范例	如分包合同的价值小于**中标合同金额**的 0.01%，则无需得到事先同意。

如要增加同意的范围，可加一句：

范例	对以下**材料**的供应商应事先得到**工程师**的同意： （填入细节：如具体的制成品或预制件）

为鼓励**承包商**使用当地的**承包商**，可加一句：

范例	只要实际可行，**承包商**应对**工程所在国**的**承包商**，提供公正合理的指派为**分包商**的机会。

第 4.8 款　　　　**安全程序**

如**承包商**和他人共同占用**现场**，由他提供某些所列事项可能不适当。在这些情况下，应规定**雇主**的义务。

第 4.9 款　　　　**质量保证**

在**通用条件**中按照合同规定的细节，提出了对质量保证体系的要求。如果不适当，**本款**可删去。

第 4.12 款　　　　**不可预见的物质条件**

对于重要的地下工程，编写招标文件时，应考虑的一个方面是各种地下条件的风险分配。如果此风险由双方分担，**本款**可作如下修改：

范例	删除**第 4.12 款**(b)项，代之以： (b)　对任何此类**费用**的付款，其百分之 _____（_____%）将计入**合同价格**（此**费用**的其余百分之 _____，应由**承包商**承担）。

第 4.17 款　　　　**承包商设备**

如果**承包商**不提供完成工程所需的所有**承包商设备**，应规定**雇主**的义务：见**第 4.20 款**。如果**承包商设备**需要明确归属，可增加进一步的与适用法律相一致的内容：

范例	在**第 4.17 款**末尾加入以下内容： **承包商**（直接或间接）拥有的**承包商设备**，从到达**现场**起，应被视为**雇主**的财产。此项财产归属不应：

(a)   affect the responsibility or liability of the Employer,

(b)   prejudice the right of the Contractor to the sole use of the vested Contractor's Equipment for the purpose of the Works, or

(c)   affect the Contractor's responsibility to operate and maintain Contractor's Equipment.

The property in each item shall be deemed to revest in the Contractor when he is entitled either to remove it from the Site or to receive the Taking-Over Certificate for the Works, whichever occurs first.

Sub-Clause 4.19   **Electricity, Water and Gas**

If services are to be available for the Contractor to use, the Specification should give details, including locations and prices.

Sub-Clause 4.20   **Employer's Equipment and Free-Issue Material**

For this Sub-Clause to apply, the Specification should describe each item which the Employer will provide and/or operate and should specify all necessary details. With some types of facilities, further provisions may be necessary, in order to clarify aspects such as liability and insurance.

Sub-Clause 4.22   **Security of the Site**

If the Contractor is sharing occupation of the Site with others, it may not be appropriate for him to be responsible for its security. In these circumstances, the Employer's obligations should be specified.

Clause 5   Nominated Subcontractors

In most cases under Sub-Clause 4.4, the Contractor selects Subcontractors, subject to any constraints specified in the Contract. Clause 5 provides for the particular situation whereby the Employer may select a Subcontractor, although the second sentence of Sub-Clause 4.4 should still apply.

The sub-paragraphs of Sub-Clause 5.2 indicate some of the problems which may have to be overcome.

If a nominated Subcontractor is to be required, full details should be included in the tender documents. If the Employer anticipates that a Subcontractor is to be instructed under Clause 13 but is not to be a nominated Subcontractor, Clause 5 should be amended, describing the particular circumstances.

Clause 6   Staff and Labour

Sub-Clause 6.5   **Working Hours**

If the Employer does not wish to specify working hours in the Appendix to Tender, or to restrict them to the times specified by the Tenderer (in order to plan the Engineer's supervision, for example), this Sub-Clause may be deleted.

Sub-Clause 6.6   **Facilities for Staff and Labour**

If the Employer will make some accommodation available, his obligations to do so should be specified.

(a) 影响**雇主**的职责或责任；

(b) 损害**承包商**为**工程**单独使用已归属的**承包商设备**的权利；或

(c) 影响**承包商**操作和维护**承包商设备**的职责。

当**承包商**有权从**现场**撤离每项设备，或有权得到**工程**的**接收证书**时，按两者中发生较早者，该设备应视为重归**承包商**的财产。

第 4.19 款   电、水和燃气

如果这些服务可供**承包商**使用，应在**规范要求**中给出细节，包括供应地点和价格。

第 4.20 款   雇主设备和免费供应的材料

如要适用本**款**，**规范要求**中应描述**雇主**将提供和(或)操作的每项内容，并应规定所有必要的细节。对有些类型的设施，可能需要做出进一步规定，以明确责任和保险等方面的事项。

第 4.22 款   现场保安

如果**承包商**与其他人员共同占用**现场**，由他对安全负责可能不合适。在此情况下，应规定**雇主**的义务。

第 5 条   指定的分包商

在大多数情况下，根据**第 4.4 款**，**承包商**按照**合同**规定的约束选择**分包商**。**第 5 条**规定了**雇主**可以选择**分包商**的特定情况，但是**第 4.4 款**第二句仍应适用。

第 5.2 款说明了某些需要克服的问题。

如果需要指定**分包商**，招标文件中应包括全部细节。如果**雇主**预期**分包商**按照**第 13 条**接受指示，而不算指定的**分包商**，**第 5 条**应进行修改，说明此特定情况。

第 6 条   员工

第 6.5 款   工作时间

如果**雇主**不希望在**投标书附录**中规定工作时间，或不希望限于**投标人**规定的时间内(例如为了安排**工程师**的监督)，本**款**可删除。

第 6.6 款   为员工提供设施

如果**雇主**将提供某些食宿设施，其此类义务应予以规定。

Sub-Clause 6.8   Contractor's Superintendence

If the ruling language is not the same as the language for day to day communications (under Sub-Clause 1.4), or if for any other reason it is necessary to stipulate that the Contractor's superintending staff shall be fluent in a particular language, the following sentence may be added.

EXAMPLE

Insert at the end of Sub-Clause 6.8:

A reasonable proportion of the Contractor's superintending staff shall have a working knowledge of

(insert name of language),

or the Contractor shall have a sufficient number of competent interpreters available on Site during all working hours.

Additional Sub-Clauses

It may be necessary to add a few sub-clauses to take account of the circumstances and locality of the Site:

EXAMPLE SUB-CLAUSE

Foreign Staff and Labour

The Contractor may import any personnel who are necessary for the execution of the Works. The Contractor must ensure that these personnel are provided with the required residence visas and work permits. The Contractor shall be responsible for the return to the place where they were recruited or to their domicile of imported Contractor's Personnel. In the event of the death in the Country of any of these personnel or members of their families, the Contractor shall similarly be responsible for making the appropriate arrangements for their return or burial.

EXAMPLE SUB-CLAUSE

Measures against Insect and Pest Nuisance

The Contractor shall at all times take the necessary precautions to protect all staff and labour employed on the Site from insect and pest nuisance, and to reduce their danger to health. The Contractor shall provide suitable prophylactics for the Contractor's Personnel and shall comply with all the regulations of the local health authorities, including use of appropriate insecticide.

EXAMPLE SUB-CLAUSE

Alcoholic Liquor or Drugs

The Contractor shall not, otherwise than in accordance with the Laws of the Country, import, sell, give, barter or otherwise dispose of any alcoholic liquor or drugs, or permit or allow importation, sale, gift, barter or disposal by Contractor's Personnel.

178

第 6.8 款　　　　　　　　**承包商的监督**

如果主导语言不同于日常交流的语言(根据**第 1.4 款**规定)，或由于任何其他原因，有必要规定**承包商**的监督职员应能流利使用某种语言，可增加下列句子：

范例

　　　　　　　第 6.8 款末尾插入：

　　　　　　　承包商监督职员中应有合理比例的人员能使用

　　　　　　　(填入语言名称)作工作语言；

　　　　　　　或**承包商**应有足够数量的胜任的译员在所有工作时间随时在**现场**。

附加条款

可能需要增加一些条款，以考虑**现场**环境和位置的需要：

范例条款

　　　　　　　外国员工

　　　　　　　承包商可引进实施**工程**所需要的任何人员。**承包商**必须确保此类人员所需的居住签证和工作许可。**承包商**应负责引进的**承包商人员**返回他们的招聘地点或户籍所在地。在任何此类人员或他们的家属在**工程所在国**死亡的情况下，**承包商**同样应负责对他们的送回或安葬作出适当的安排。

范例条款

　　　　　　　防止昆虫和害虫侵扰的**措施**

　　　　　　　承包商任何时候都应采取必要的预防措施，保护**现场**雇用的所有员工免于昆虫和害虫的侵扰，减少它们对健康的危害。**承包商**应为**承包商人员**提供适当的预防药品，遵从当地卫生当局的所有规定，包括使用适当的杀虫剂。

范例条款

　　　　　　　酒精饮料或**毒品**

　　　　　　　承包商除遵照**工程所在国**法律外，不得进口、销售、给予、易货交换或以其他方式处理任何酒精饮料或毒品；或许可或容许**承包商人员**进口、销售、馈赠、易货交换或处理上述物品。

EXAMPLE SUB-CLAUSE

Arms and Ammunition

The Contractor shall not give, barter or otherwise dispose of to any person, any arms or ammunition of any kind, or allow Contractor's Personnel to do so.

EXAMPLE SUB-CLAUSE

Festivals and Religious Customs

The Contractor shall respect the Country's recognised festivals, days of rest and religious or other customs.

Clause 7   Plant, Materials and Workmanship

Additional Sub-Clause

If the Contract is being financed by an institution whose rules or policies require a restriction on the use of its funds, a further sub-clause may be added:

EXAMPLE SUB-CLAUSE

All Goods shall have their origin in eligible source countries as defined in

(insert name of published guidelines for procurement).

Goods shall be transported by carriers from these eligible source countries, unless exempted by the Employer in writing on the basis of potential excessive costs or delays. Surety, insurance and banking services shall be provided by insurers and bankers from the eligible source countries.

Clause 8   Commencement, Delays and Suspension

Sub-Clause 8.2   Time for Completion

If the Works are to be taken-over in stages, these stages should be defined as Sections, in the Appendix to Tender.

Sub-Clause 8.7   Delay Damages

Under many legal systems, the amount of these pre-defined damages must represent a reasonable pre-estimate of the Employer's probable loss in the event of delay. If the Accepted Contract Amount is to be quoted as the sum of figures in more than one currency, it may be preferable to define these damages (per day) as the percentage reduction which would be applied to each of these figures. If the Accepted Contract Amount is expressed in the Local Currency, the damages per day may either be defined as a percentage or be defined as a figure in Local Currency: see Sub-Clause 14.15(b).

Additional Sub-Clause

Incentives for early completion may be included in the tender documents (although Sub-Clause 13.2 refers to accelerated completion):

武器和弹药

承包商不得向任何人给予、易货交换或以其他方式处理任何种类的任何武器和弹药，或容许**承包商**人员这样做。

节日和宗教习惯

承包商应尊重工程所在国公认的节日、休息日，以及宗教或其他习惯。

第7条　　　　　　　　生产设备、材料和工艺

如果**合同**由某一机构提供资金，其规则或政策要求对资金的使用加以限制，可增加进一步条款：

所有**货物**应产自 _____

(填写公布的采购指南的名称)中规定的合格来源国。

除非是**雇主**基于可能造成过高费用或延迟的考虑，书面通知的免例，**货物**应由这些合格来源国的承运人运输。担保、保险和银行服务应由合格来源国的保险人和银行提供。

第8条　　　　　　　　开工、延误和暂停

第 8.2 款　　　　　竣工时间

如工程要分阶段接收，这些阶段应在**投标书附录**中定义为单位工程。

第 8.7 款　　　　　误期损害赔偿费

根据许多法律体系，此类事先规定的损害赔偿费款额，必须是在延误情况下**雇主**可能遭受的损失的合理预估额。如果**中标合同金额**是多种货币数额的总和，最好规定这些损害赔偿费(每天)按每种货币数额的减少百分比。如果**中标合同金额**是用当地货币表示的，则每天的损害赔偿费可规定为一个百分比，或当地货币的数额：见**第 14.15 款**(b)项。

在招标文件中可包括对提前竣工的鼓励(虽然**第 13.2 款**提到加快竣工)：

EXAMPLE SUB-CLAUSE

Sections are required to be completed by the dates given in the Appendix to Tender in order that these Sections may be occupied and used by the Employer in advance of the completion of the whole of the Works. Details of the work required to be executed to entitle the Contractor to bonus payments and the amount of the bonuses are stated in the Specification.

For the purposes of calculating bonus payments, the dates given in the Appendix to Tender for completion of Sections are fixed. No adjustments *of the dates by reason of granting an extension of the Time for* Completion will be allowed.

Clause 9 Tests on Completion

Sub-Clause 9.1 Contractor's Obligations

The Specification should describe the tests which the Contractor is to carry out before being entitled to a Taking-Over Certificate. If the Works are to be tested and taken-over in stages, the tests requirements may have to take account of the effect of some parts of the Works being incomplete.

Clause 10 Employer's Taking Over

Sub-Clause 10.1 Taking-Over Certificate

If the Works are to be taken-over in stages, these stages should to be defined as Sections, in the Appendix to Tender. Precise geographical definitions are advisable, and the Appendix should include a table, so as to define the Time for Completion and delay damages: the table is shown in the example Appendix.

Clause 11 Defects Liability

Sub-Clause 11.10 Unfulfilled Obligations

It may be necessary to review this Sub-Clause in relation to the period of liability under the applicable law.

Clause 12 Measurement and Evaluation

Sub-Clause 12.1 Works to be Measured

If any part of the Permanent Works is to be measured according to records of its construction, details should be specified in the tender documents, including any records for which the Contractor is to be responsible.

Clause 13 Variations and Adjustments

Variations can be initiated by any of three ways:

(a) the Engineer may instruct the variation under Sub-Clause 13.1, without prior agreement as

为了在整个**工程**竣工前**雇主**能提前占有和使用某些单位**工程**,这些单位**工程**要求在**投标书附录**中规定的日期前竣工。**承包商**能获得奖金所需实施的工作细节,以及奖金数额,都要在**规范要求**中写明。

为了计算奖金数额,**投标书附录**中的这些单位**工程**的完工日期固定不变。不许以**竣工时间**获准延长为由,对这些日期进行调整。

第 9 条　　　　　　　　竣工试验

第 9.1 款　　　　　　承包商的义务

规范要求中应说明**承包商**在有权得到**接收证书**前要进行的试验。如果**工程**要分阶段进行试验和接收, 试验要求可能要考虑**工程**的某些部分尚未完成的影响。

第 10 条　　　　　　　雇主的接收

第 10.1 款　　　　　　接收证书

如果**工程**要分阶段接收,这些阶段应在**投标书附录**中定义为**单位工程**。最好规定它们的精确的地理定界,**投标书附录**中应有一张表,规定**竣工时间**和误期损害赔偿费。该表见下面的范例**附录**。

第 11 条　　　　　　　缺陷责任

第 11.10 款　　　　　　未履行的义务

可能需要根据适用法律关于责任期限的要求,审核本**款**的规定。

第 12 条　　　　　　　测量和估价

第 12.1 款　　　　　　需测量的工程

如果**永久工程**的任何部分需要按照其施工记录来进行测量,其细节,包括**承包商**应负责的记录,应在招标文件中作出规定。

第 13 条　　　　　　　变更和调整

变更可通过以下三种中任一种方式提出:

(a) **工程师**可根据第 **13.1 款**的规定指示进行变更,对**变更**的可行性或价格无需事先协议;

183

to feasibility or price;

(b)   the Contractor may initiate his own proposals under Sub-Clause 13.2, which are intended to benefit both Parties; or

(c)   the Engineer may request a proposal under Sub-Clause 13.3, seeking prior agreement so as to minimise dispute.

Sub-Clause 13.8   Adjustments for Changes in Cost

These provisions for adjustments may be required if it would be unreasonable for the Contractor to bear the risk of escalating costs due to inflation. Unless this Sub-Clause is not to apply, the Appendix to Tender should include a table for each of the currencies of payment: the appropriate table is shown in the example Appendix. Particular care should be taken in the calculation of the weightings/coefficients ("a", "b", "c", ..., the total of which must not exceed unity) and in the selection and verification of cost indices. Expert advice may be appropriate.

Clause 14   Contract Price and Payment

Sub-Clause 14.1   The Contract Price

When writing the Particular Conditions, consideration should be given to the amount and timing of payment(s) to the Contractor. A positive cash flow is clearly of benefit to the Contractor, and tenderers will take account of the interim payment procedures when preparing their tenders.

Additional Sub-Clauses may be required to cover any exceptions to the options set out in Sub-Clause 14.1, and any other matters relating to payment.

Cost-plus contracts, under which the actual Costs are determined and paid, are unusual and only used when (for reasons of urgency or otherwise) the Employer is willing to accept the risks involved. If the Contractor is to be paid actual Costs, Clause 12 should be replaced by provisions describing the method of determining the Costs and Contract Price. As a result, the provisions in the General Conditions which entitle the Contractor to payment of additional Costs will generally be of no effect.

Sub-Clause 14.1(a) would not apply if payment is to be made on a lump sum basis.

Lump sum contracts may be suitable if the tender documents include details which are sufficiently complete for construction and for Variations to be unlikely. From the information supplied in the tender documents, the Contractor can prepare any other details necessary, and construct the Works, without having to refer back to the Engineer for clarification or further information.

Further design by the Contractor (under sub-paragraphs (a) to (d) of Sub-Clause 4.1) is not precluded. However, these Conditions would be inappropriate if significant design input by the Contractor is required. In those cases, FIDIC's other forms may be more appropriate: see FIDIC's Conditions of Contract for Plant and Design-Build or Conditions of Contract for EPC/Turnkey Projects.

For a lump sum contract, the tender documents should include a schedule of payments (see Sub-Clause 14.4), and any drawings required for construction may be specified as being Contractor's Documents. The Specification should describe the procedures under which the Contractor submits these Documents for the Engineer to approve.

EXAMPLE PROVISIONS FOR A LUMP SUM CONTRACT

Delete Clause 12.

(b)　承包商可以根据第 13.2 款的规定，提出他自己认为有利于双方的建议；或

(c)　为尽量减少争端，寻求事先协议，工程师可根据第 13.3 款的规定，要求提出一份建议书。

第 13.8 款　　　　因成本改变的调整

如果考虑要承包商承担因通货膨胀的成本上升的风险是不合理的，可能需要这些调整的规定。除非本款不适用，投标书附录中应包括列有每种支付货币的表：在下面的范例附录中有适用的表。在计算权重因子/系数（"a"、"b"、"c"、…，其总和不能超过 1）及选择和核实成本指数时应特别予以注意。吸取专家的建议可能是适宜的。

第 14 条　　　　　　合同价格和付款

第 14.1 款　　　　合同价格

在编写专用条件时，应考虑向承包商支付的款额和时间安排。一个正的现金流量是明显有利于承包商的，投标人在编制其投标书时，将会考虑到期中付款的程序。

为了包含第 14.1 款提出的可选内容以外的任何其他内容，以及有关付款的任何其他事项，可能需要一些附加条款。

成本加利合同，是按实际成本进行确定和支付的，通常不用，仅当雇主愿意接受所涉及的风险（由于紧急情况或其他原因）时才采用。如果支付给承包商的是实际成本，则应以说明成本和合同价格的确定方法的规定代替第 12 条。因此，通用条件中使承包商有权获得附加费用付款的规定，通常将失效。

如果是按总额支付的，第 14.1 款(a)项将不适用。

如果招标文件包括的细节，对于施工和不大可能的变更已足够完善，则总额合同可能是合适的。承包商从招标文件提供的资料，可以编写其他必要的细节、对工程进行施工，而不需要找工程师澄清情况或取得其他资料。

不排除由承包商做进一步的设计（根据第 4.1 款(a)至(d)项的规定）。但是，如果承包商承担重要的设计时，使用本条件可能不合适。在这种情况下，FIDIC 的其他合同格式可能更为合适：见 FIDIC 的《生产设备和设计-施工合同条件》或《设计采购施工(EPC)/交钥匙工程合同条件》。

对总额合同，招标文件应包括付款计划表（见第 14.4 款），施工所需任何图纸可规定为承包商文件。规范要求应说明承包商提交这些文件请工程师批准的程序。

总额合同范例条款

删去第 12 条。

Delete the last sentence of Sub-Clause 13.3 and substitute:

Upon instructing or approving a Variation, the Engineer shall proceed in accordance with Sub-Clause 3.5 to agree or determine adjustments to the Contract Price and to the schedule of payments under Sub-Clause 14.4. These adjustments shall include reasonable profit, and shall take account of the Contractor's submissions under Sub-Clause 13.2 if applicable.

Delete sub-paragraph (a) of Sub-Clause 14.1 and substitute:

(a)   the Contract Price shall be the lump sum Accepted Contract Amount and be subject to adjustments in accordance with the Contract;

If Sub-Clause 14.1(b) is not to apply, additional Sub-Clause(s) should be added.

EXAMPLE SUB-CLAUSE ON EXEMPTION FROM DUTIES

All Goods imported by the Contractor into the Country shall be exempt from customs and other import duties, if the Employer's prior written approval is obtained for import. The Employer shall endorse the necessary exemption documents prepared by the Contractor for presentation in order to clear the Goods through Customs, and shall also provide the following exemption documents:

(describe the necessary documents, which the Contractor will be unable to prepare)

If exemption is not then granted, the customs duties payable and paid shall be reimbursed by the Employer.

All imported Goods, which are not incorporated in or expended in connection with the Works, shall be exported on completion of the Contract. If not exported, the Goods will be assessed for duties as applicable to the Goods involved in accordance with the Laws of the Country.

However, exemption may not available for:

(a)   Goods which are similar to those locally produced, unless they are not available in sufficient quantities or are of a different standard to that which is necessary for the Works; and

(b)   any element of duty or tax inherent in the price of goods or services procured in the Country, which shall be deemed to be included in the Accepted Contract Amount.

Port dues, quay dues and, except as set out above, any element of tax or duty inherent in the price of goods or services shall be deemed to be included in the Accepted Contract Amount.

EXAMPLE SUB-CLAUSE ON EXEMPTION FROM TAXES

Expatriate (foreign) personnel shall not be liable for income tax levied in the Country on earnings paid in any foreign currency, or for income tax

删去第 **13.3 款**最后一句，代以：

工程师指示或批准**变更**时，应按照**第 3.5 款**对**合同价格**和**第 14.4 款**的付款计划表的调整，进行商定或确定。此类调整应包括合理利润，如果适用还应考虑**承包商**根据**第 13.2 款**的的有益建议。

删去**第 14.1 款**(a)项，代以：

(a)　**合同价格**应是**中标合同金额**的总额，可根据**合同**加以调整；

如果第 14.1 款　　　(b)　项不适用，应增加以下一款(或几款)附加条款。

免除关税范例条款

如果事先取得**雇主**对进口的书面的批准，**承包商**进口到**工程所在国**的所有货物都应免关税和其他进口税。**雇主**应签署支持**承包商**编制的为**货物**结关出示的必要免税文件，还应提供下列免税文件：

(描述**承包商**不能编制的必需的文件)

如果未能获准免税，应付和已付的关税应由**雇主**补偿。

所有未用在**工程**上或消耗在有关**工程**方面的进口**货物**，在**合同**完成时应予出口。如 不出口，该**货物**应按**工程所在国**的**法律**就涉及**货物**的适用税种估价纳税。

但对下列情况，免税规定可能不适用：

(a)　与当地产品相类似的**货物**，除非因数量不足或标准不同不能满足**工程**需要；以及

(b)　在**工程所在国**采购的货物或服务的价格中，原本含有的任何关税或其他税收因素，应被视为已包括在**中标合同金额**中。

港口税、码头税及上述情况以外的任何原本含在货物或服务价格中的关税或其他税收因素，应被视为已包括在**中标合同金额**中。

免除税收范例条款

外侨(外籍)人员不应负担**工程所在国**对其任何外币收入征收的所得税，或对由**承包商**直接向**承包商人员**提供的生活费、租金和类似服

levied on subsistence, rentals and similar services directly furnished by the Contractor to Contractor's Personnel, or for allowances in lieu. If any Contractor's Personnel have part of their earnings paid in the Country in a foreign currency, they may export (after the conclusion of their term of service on the Works) any balance remaining of their earnings paid in foreign currencies.

The Employer shall seek exemption for the purposes of this Sub-Clause. If it is not granted, the relevant taxes paid shall be reimbursed by the Employer.

Sub-Clause 14.2   Advance Payment

When writing the Particular Conditions, consideration should be given to the benefits of advance payment(s). Unless this Sub-Clause is not to apply, the total advance payment (and the number of instalments if more than one) must be specified in the Appendix to Tender. The rate of deduction for the repayments should be checked to ensure that repayment is achieved before completion. The typical figures in sub-paragraphs (a) and (b) of the General Conditions Sub-Clause are based on the assumption that the total advance payment is less than 22% of the Accepted Contract Amount.

The acceptable form(s) of guarantee should be included in the tender documents, annexed to the Particular Conditions: an example form is annexed to this document, as Annex E.

Sub-Clause 14.7   Payment

If a different period for payment is to apply, the Sub-Clause may be amended:

EXAMPLE

In sub-paragraph (b) of Sub-Clause 14.7, delete "56" and substitute "42"

If the country/countries of payment need to be specified, details may be included in a Schedule.

Sub-Clause 14.8   Delayed Payment

If the discount rate of the central bank in the country of the currency of payment is not a reasonable basis for assessing the Contractor's financing costs, a new rate may have to be defined. Alternatively, the actual financing Costs could be paid, taking account of local financing arrangements.

Sub-Clause 14.9   Payment of Retention Money

If part of the Retention Money is to be released and substituted by an appropriate guarantee, an additional Sub-Clause may be added. The acceptable form(s) of guarantee should be included in the tender documents, annexed to the Particular Conditions: an example form is annexed to this document, as Annex F.

EXAMPLE SUB-CLAUSE FOR RELEASE OF RETENTION

When the Retention Money has reached three-fifths (60%) of the limit of Retention Money stated in the Appendix to Tender, the Engineer shall certify and the Employer shall make payment of half (50%) of the limit of Retention Money to the Contractor if he obtains a guarantee, in a form and provided by an entity approved by the Employer, in amounts and currencies equal to the payment.

The Contractor shall ensure that the guarantee is valid and enforceable until the Contractor has executed and completed the Works and

务费，或替代上述费用的津贴征收的所得税。如果**承包商人员**在**工程所在国**的部分收入是用外币支付的，他们(在**工程**的服务期结束后)可以将以外币支付的收入的剩余部分汇出或带出境。

雇主应为本**款**目标争取免税。如未能获准，支付的相关税款应由**雇主**补偿。

第 14.2 款　　　　　　**预付款**

在编写**专用条件**时，应考虑到预付款的利益。除非本**款**不适用，预付款总额(以及分期次数，如多于一次)必须在**投标书附录**中规定。对付还的扣减率应予核查，以确保在竣工前得到付还。**通用条件**本款(a)和(b)项中的代表性数字，是以预付款总额小于**中标合同金额** 22% 的假定为基础的。

可接受的保函格式，应包括在招标文件中，附在**专用条件**后：本文件附有范例格式，见**附件 E**。

第 14.7 款　　　　　　**付款**

如果要施用不同的付款期间，本**款**可以修改如下：

范例　　　　　　在第 **14.7 款**的(b)项中，删除"42"代之以"56"。

如果需要规定付款的国家(或几个国家)，可在**资料表**中包括其细节。

第 14.8 款　　　　　　**延误的付款**

如果支付货币的国家中央银行的贴现率不是评定**承包商**融资成本的合理依据，可能需要另定利率。或参照当地融资情况，按实际融资**成本**支付。

第 14.9 款　　　　　　**保留金的支付**

如果要放还部分**保留金**，代之以适当的保函，可增加附加**条款**。招标文件中应包括认可的保函格式，附在**专用条件**后：本文件附有范例格式，见**附件 F**。

放还保留金范例条款

当**保留金**达到**投标书附录**规定的**保留金**限额的五分之三(60%)时，如果**雇主**已得到由其批准的实体，以其认可的格式，出具的金额和货币与付款相同的保函。则**工程师**应确认、**雇主**应付给**承包商**保留金限额的一半(50%)，

承包商应确保该保函如**第 4.2 款**对**履约担保**的规定，直到他完成

remedied any defects, as specified for the Performance Security in Sub-Clause 4.2, and shall be returned to the Contractor accordingly. This release of retention shall be in lieu of the release of the second half of the Retention Money under the second paragraph of Sub-Clause 14.9.

Sub-Clause 14.15   Currencies of Payment

If all payments are to be made in Local Currency, it must be named in the Letter of Tender, and only the first sentence of this Sub-Clause will apply. Alternatively, the Sub-Clause may then be replaced:

EXAMPLE SUB-CLAUSE FOR A SINGLE CURRENCY CONTRACT

The currency of account shall be the Local Currency and all payments made in accordance with the Contract shall be in Local Currency. The Local Currency payments shall be fully convertible, except those for local costs. The percentage attributed to local costs shall be as stated in the Appendix to Tender.

Financing Arrangements

For major contracts in some markets, there may be a need to secure finance from entities such as aid agencies, development banks, export credit agencies, or other international financing institutions. If financing is to be procured from any of these sources, the Particular Conditions may need to incorporate its special requirements. The exact wording will depend on the relevant institution, so reference will need to be made to them to ascertain their requirements, and to seek approval of the draft tender documents.

These requirements may include tendering procedures which need to be adopted in order to render the eventual contract eligible for financing, and/or special Sub-Clauses which may need to be incorporated into the Particular Conditions. The following examples indicate some of the topics which the institution's requirements may cover:

(a)   prohibition from discrimination against the shipping companies of any one country;

(b)   ensuring that the Contract is subject to a widely-accepted neutral law;

(c)   provision for arbitration under recognised international rules and at a neutral location;

(d)   giving the Contractor the right to suspend/terminate in the event of default under the financing arrangements;

(e)   restricting the right to reject Plant;

(f)   specifying the payments due in the event of termination;

(g)   specifying that the Contract does not become effective until certain conditions precedent have been satisfied, including pre-disbursement conditions for the financing arrangements; and

(h)   obliging the Employer to make payments from his own resources if, for any reason, the funds under the financing arrangements are insufficient to meet the payments due to the Contractor, whether due to a default under the financing arrangements or otherwise.

In addition, the financing institution or bank may wish the Contract to include references to the financing arrangements, especially if funding from more than one source is to be arranged to finance different elements of supply. It is not unusual for the Particular Conditions to include special provisions identifying different categories of Plant and specifying the documents to be presented to

工程的施工、竣工及修补完任何缺陷时一直有效和可执行，届时保函应相应退还给承包商。保留金此项放还应代替根据第 14.9 款第 2 段规定的放还保留金后一半的要求。

第 14.15 款	支付的货币

如果所有付款都用当地货币支付，应在投标书附录中说明本款中仅第一句话还适用。代替地，本款可代之以：

单一货币合同范例条款

结算货币应为当地货币，按照合同支付的所有款项都应为当地货币。除当地开支的费用外，所有当地货币的付款应全部可以兑换。当地开支的费用所占百分比应按投标书附录中的规定。

融资安排

对于某些市场上的重要合同，可能需要从一些实体，如援助机构、开发银行、出口信贷机构、或其他国际融资组织获取资金。如果从任何这类来源获取资金，专用条件可能需要编入这些机构的特定要求。准确的措辞要依靠这些相关机构，因此需征求他们的意见以确定其要求，使招标文件草案得到其批准。

这些要求可能包括，为使最终合同具有融资资格要采用的招标程序，和（或）需要编入专用条件的某些特定条款。下列范例指出了贷款机构的要求可能涉及的一些问题：

(a)   禁止歧视任一国家的航运公司；

(b)   确保合同受广泛接受的中立法律管辖；

(c)   在中立地点按公认的国际规则进行仲裁的规定；

(d)   根据融资安排发生违约时，给予承包商暂停或终止的权利；

(e)   限制拒收生产设备权利的；

(f)   规定终止应付款项；

(g)   规定直到一些先决条件，包括融资安排中提前支付的条件得到满足后，合同才能生效；以及

(h)   规定如果由于任何原因，不论是根据融资安排发生违约还是其他原因，造成融资安排的资金不能满足应付承包商的款项时，雇主有义务以其自有资金支付承包商。

此外，融资机构或银行可能希望合同中包括融资安排的内容，尤其是对不同部分供货安排一个以上来源提供资金时。通常情况是，在专用条件中包括一些特定的规定，分别不同种类的

the relevant financing institution to obtain payment. If the financing institution's requirements are not met, it may be difficult (or even impossible) to secure suitable financing for the project, and/or the institution may decline to provide finance for part or all of the Contract.

However, where the financing is not tied to the export of goods and services from any particular country but is simply provided by commercial banks lending to the Employer, those banks may be concerned to ensure that the Contractor's rights are very restricted. These banks may wish the Contract to exclude any reference to the financing arrangements, and/or to restrict the Contractor's rights under Clause 16.

FORM OF SUB-CLAUSE WHICH A FINANCING INSTITUTION MAY REQUIRE

The Accepted Contract Amount is made up as follows:

(breakdown into items and/or into supply/delivery/etc)

and shall be payable by the Employer to the Contractor as set out below.

(a) _____ % of the Accepted Contract Amount shall be payable by a direct payment from the Employer to the Contractor within 28 days of receipt by the Employer of the following documents:

(i) commercial invoice addressed to the Employer specifying the amount of the payment now due,
(ii) advance payment security guarantee issued by _____ Bank in the form annexed,
(iii) performance security guarantee issued by _____ Bank in the form annexed, and
(iv) Interim Payment Certificate confirming the payment due and specifying the amount.

(b) _____ % of the contract price for the supply of Plant shall be payable as follows:

(i) _____ % of the estimated contract value of the Plant supplied, by direct payment from the Employer to the Contractor on shipment of each item, against the following documents:
(original) commercial invoice,
(original) shipping documents,
(original) certificate of origin,
(original) insurance certificate, and
(original) Interim Payment Certificate confirming the payment due and specifying the amount.

(ii) _____ % of the estimated contract value of the Plant supplied, by disbursement from the Loan Agreement to the Contractor on shipment of each item, on presentation of a Qualifying Certificate in the form annexed and copies of the documents listed in sub-paragraph (b)(i) above.

(c) the balance of the Contract Price shall be payable as follows:

(i) _____ % of the estimated contract value of the services rendered, by direct payment from the Employer to the Contractor on execution of the relevant service, against the following documents:

192

生产设备，规定要向相关融资机构提交的申请付款的文件。如果融资机构的要求得不到满足，则可能很难(或甚至不可能)为项目获得适当的资金，并且(或)该机构可能拒绝对整个或部分**合同**提供资金。

但如果融资不与从任何特定国家出口货物和服务相联系，只是由商业银行简单地贷款给**雇主**，那些银行关注的可能是要确保严格限制**承包商**的权利。这些银行可能希望**合同**不包括任何融资安排，和(或)希望**合同**限制**承包商**根据第 **16** 条的规定所拥有的权利。

融资机构可能要求的条款格式

中标合同金额由以下内容构成：

(将**中标合同金额**内容分解为细目,和(或)分解为供货/交付/等)

将按下列规定由**雇主**向**承包商**支付。

(a)　在**雇主**收到下列文件后 28 天内，应由**雇主**向**承包商**直接支付**中标合同金额**的 ＿＿＿ %：

　　(i)　致**雇主**的列明现已到期的应付金额的商业发票，

　　(ii)　由 ＿＿＿ **银行**按附件所列格式出具的预付款担保函，

　　(iii)　由 ＿＿＿ **银行**按附件所列格式出具的履约担保函，以及

　　(iv)　确认到期款项，列明金额的**期中付款证书**。

(b)　用于**生产设备**供货的合同价格的 ＿＿＿ %应如下支付：

　　(i)　在每项设备装船后，**雇主**根据以下文件，向**承包商**直接支付已供**生产设备**估算合同价值的 ＿＿＿ %：
　　　(原始)商业发票，
　　　(原始)装运单证，
　　　(原始)原产地证书，
　　　(原始)保险证书，以及
　　　(原始)确认应付款项，列明金额的**期中付款证书**。

　　(ii)在每项设备装船后，**雇主**根据提交的按所附格式出具的**资格合格证书**，以及上述(b)项第(i)目所列文件的复制件，从**贷款协议**中向**承包商**支付已供**生产设备**估算合同价值的 ＿＿＿ %。

(c)　**合同价格**的余额应如下支付：

　　(i)　对实施的相关服务，**雇主**根据下列文件，向**承包商**直接支付已提供服务的估算合同价值的 ＿＿＿ %：
　　　(原始)商业发票，以及

(original) commercial invoice, and

(original) Interim Payment Certificate confirming the payment due and specifying the amount.

(ii) _____ % of the estimated contract value of the services rendered, by disbursement from the Loan Agreement to the Contractor, on presentation of a Qualifying Certificate in the form annexed and copies of the documents listed in sub-paragraph (c)(i) above.

(d) The direct payments by the Employer specified in sub-paragraph (b) shall be made by an irrevocable letter of credit established by the Employer in favour of the Contractor and confirmed by a bank acceptable to the Contractor.

The above arrangements (involving financing institution(s), Employer and Contractor) may be initiated by the Employer; or by the Contractor, before submitting the Tender. Alternatively, the Contractor may be prepared to initiate financing arrangements and retain responsibility for them, although he would probably be unable or unwilling to provide finance from his own resources. His financing bank's requirements would then affect his attitude in contract negotiations. They might well require the Employer to make interim payments, although a large proportion of the Contract Price might be withheld until the Works are complete.

This payment arrangement can be achieved either by a high Percentage of Retention; or by a suitably completed schedule of payments (see Sub-Clause 14.4), with the Instructions to Tenderers specifying the criteria with which the Tenderer should comply. Since the Contractor would then have to arrange his own financing to cover the shortfall between the payments and his outgoings, he (and his financing bank) would probably require some form of security, guaranteeing payment when due.

It may be appropriate for the Employer, when preparing the tender documents, to anticipate the latter requirement by undertaking to provide a guarantee for the element of payment which the Contractor is to receive when the Works are complete. The acceptable form(s) of guarantee should be included in the tender documents, annexed to the Particular Conditions: an example form is annexed to this document, as Annex G. The following Sub-Clause may be added.

EXAMPLE PROVISIONS FOR CONTRACTOR FINANCE

The Employer shall obtain (at his cost) a payment guarantee in the amount and currencies, and provided by an entity, as stated in the Appendix to Tender. The Employer shall deliver the guarantee to the Contractor within 28 days after both Parties have entered into the Contract Agreement. The guarantee shall be in the form annexed to these Particular Conditions, or in another form acceptable to the Contractor. Unless and until the Contractor receives the guarantee, the Engineer shall not give the notice under Sub-Clause 8.1.

The guarantee shall be returned to the Employer at the earliest of the following dates:

(a) when the Contractor has been paid the Accepted Contract Amount;

(b) when obligations under the guarantee expire or have been discharged; or

(c) when the Employer has performed all obligations under the Contract.

(原始)确认应付款项，列明金额的**期中付款证书**。

    (ii)   **雇主**根据提交的按所附格式出具的**资格合格证书**，以及上述(c)项第(i)目所列文件的复制件，从**贷款协议**中向**承包商**支付已提供服务的估算合同价值的 _____ %。

    (d)   本款(b)项规定的**雇主**的直接付款方式应为，由**雇主**出具的、经**承包商**认可的银行保兑的、以**承包商**为受益人的不可撤销信用证。

上述安排(涉及融资机构、**雇主**和**承包商**)可以由**雇主**，或由**承包商**在提交**投标书**前提出。另外的作法是，虽然**承包商**可能没有能力或不愿自己提供资金，但他可能愿意主动着手融资安排，并对之保持责任。因而他的融资银行的要求，会影响他在**合同**谈判中的态度。他们可能尽力要求**雇主**支付期中付款，尽管大部分**合同价格**直到**工程**竣工后才能支付。

可以通过采用高**保留金百分比**，或通过适当制定**付款计划表**(参见**第 14.4 款**)，并在**投标人须知**中规定**投标人**应遵守的标准等方式，完成此项付款安排。由于**承包商**随后必须自筹资金以弥补其所得付款与其开支之间的差额，他(及其融资银行)可能要求某种形式的担保，以保证到期能得到付款。

对于**雇主**来说可能适宜的作法是，在编制招标文件时，就预计到上述后一项要求，承诺为**承包商**在**工程**竣工时应得到的付款提供保函。可接受的保函格式应包括在招标文件中，附在**专用条件**后：本文件附有范例格式，见**附件**G。这里可增加以下**条款**。

承包商融资范例条款

    雇主应(自费)取得一份按**投标书附录**规定的金额和币种，由某实体出具的支付保函。**雇主**应在双方签署**合同协议书**后 28 天内，将保函提交给**承包商**。保函应采用本**专用条件**所附格式，或**承包商**认可的其他格式。除非并直到**承包商**收到此保函时，**工程师**不应根据**第8.1款**规定发出通知。

    保函应在下列日期中的最早日期退回**雇主**：

    (a)   已向**承包商**支付**中标合同金额**时；

    (b)   根据保函的义务已期满或已解除时；或

    (c)   **雇主**已根据合同履行了其全部义务时。

Clause 15   Termination by Employer

Sub-Clause 15.2   **Termination by Employer**

Before inviting tenders, the Employer should verify that the wording of this Sub-Clause, and each anticipated ground for termination, is consistent with the law governing the Contract.

Sub-Clause 15.5   **Employer's Entitlement to Termination**

Unless inconsistent with the requirements of the Employer and/or financing institutions, a further sentence may be added.

EXAMPLE   Insert at the end of Sub-Clause 15.5:

The Employer shall also pay to the Contractor the amount of any other loss or damage resulting from this termination.

Clause 16   Suspension and Termination by Contractor

Sub-Clause 16.2   **Termination by Contractor**

Before inviting tenders, the Employer should verify that the wording of this Sub-Clause is consistent with the law governing the Contract. The Contractor should verify that each anticipated ground for termination is consistent with such law.

Clause 17   Risk and Responsibility

Sub-Clause 17.6   **Limitation of Liability**

EXAMPLE

In Sub-Clause 17.6, the sum referred to in the penultimate sentence shall be _____

Additional Sub-Clause   Use of Employer's Accommodation/Facilities

If the Contractor is to occupy the Employer's facilities temporarily, an additional sub-clause may be added:

EXAMPLE SUB-CLAUSE

The Contractor shall take full responsibility for the care of the items detailed below, from the respective dates of use or occupation by the Contractor, up to the respective dates of hand-over or cessation of occupation (where hand-over or cessation of occupation may take place after the date stated in the Taking-Over Certificate for the Works):

(insert details)

If any loss or damage happens to any of the above items while the Contractor is responsible for their care, arising from any cause whatsoever other than those for which the Employer is liable, the Contractor shall, at his own cost, rectify the loss or damage to the satisfaction of the Engineer.

第 15 条　　　　　　　由雇主终止

第 15.2 款　　　　　由雇主终止

招标前，**雇主**应核实本**款**规定的措辞和每项预计终止的依据，符合管辖**合同**的法律。

第 15.5 款　　　　　雇主终止的权利

除非与**雇主**和(或)融资机构的要求不符，可增加一句。

范例　　　　　　　在**第 15.5 款**末尾插入：

雇主还应向**承包商**支付由于此项终止产生的任何其他损失或损害的金额。

第 16 条　　　　　　　由承包商暂停和终止

第 16.2 款　　　　　由承包商终止

招标前，**雇主**应核实本**款**规定的措辞符合管辖**合同**的法律。**承包商**应核实每项预计终止的依据符合此类法律。

第 17 条　　　　　　　风险与职责

第 17.6 款　　　　　责任限度

范例

第 17.6 款倒数第二句提到的总额应为

附加条款使用雇主提供的住宿/设施

如果**承包商**要临时占用**雇主**的设施，可增加附加条款：

范例条款

　　承包商应自使用或占用下列各项设施的各自日期起，至移交或停止占用(此处移交或停止占用可发生在**工程接收证书**注明的日期之后)的各自日期止，承担对各项设施的全部照管职责：

(插入设施细节)

如果在**承包商**负责照管期间，由于**雇主**应负责的以外的任何原因，使上述设施发生任何损失或损害，**承包商**应自费修正此类损失或损害，达到**工程师**满意。

Clause 18   Insurance

The wording in the General Conditions describes the insurances which are to be arranged by the "insuring Party", who is to be the Contractor unless otherwise stated in the Particular Conditions. Insurances so provided by the Contractor are to be consistent with the general terms agreed with the Employer. The Instructions to Tenderers may therefore require tenderers to provide details of the proposed terms.

If the Employer is to arrange any of the insurances under this Clause, the tender documents should include details as an annex to the Particular Conditions (so that tenderers can estimate what other insurances they wish to have for their own protection), including the conditions, limits, exceptions and deductibles; preferably in the form of a copy of each policy. The Employer may find it difficult to effect the insurances described in the third paragraph of Sub-Clause 18.2 (for Contractor's Equipment, which includes Subcontractor's equipment), because the Employer may not know the amount or value of these items of equipment. The following sentence may be included in the Particular Conditions:

EXAMPLE   Delete the final paragraph of Sub-Clause 18.2 and substitute:

However, the insurances described in the first two paragraphs of Sub-Clause 18.2 shall be effected and maintained by the Employer as insuring Party, and not by the Contractor.

Clause 19   Force Majeure

Before inviting tenders, the Employer should verify that the wording of this Clause is compatible with the law governing the Contract.

Clause 20   Claims, Disputes and Arbitration

Sub-Clause 20.2   Appointment of the Dispute Adjudication Board

Unless the Engineer (although appointed by the Employer) is to make the pre-arbitral decisions under this Clause 20, in accordance with the alternative option described below, the Contract should include the provisions under Clause 20 which, whilst not discouraging the Parties from reaching agreement on disputes as the works proceed, allow them to refer contentious matters to an impartial dispute adjudication board ("DAB").

The adjudication procedure depends for its success on, amongst other things, the Parties' confidence in the agreed individual(s) who will serve on the DAB. Therefore, it is essential that candidates for this position are not imposed by either Party on the other Party; and that, if the individual is selected under Sub-Clause 20.3, the selection is made by a wholly impartial entity. FIDIC is prepared to perform this role, if this authority has been delegated in accordance with the example wording in the Appendix to Tender.

It is preferable, but not essential, for the individual(s) to be agreed before the Letter of Acceptance is issued, and for the DAB to visit the Site on a regular basis. Under the example text in the Appendix to Tender, the Parties may either so agree before the Letter of Acceptance is issued or agree the appointment within the specified period thereafter. Alternatively, the Parties may prefer to defer the appointment until a dispute has arisen, in which case Sub-Clause 20.2 plus the Appendix - General Conditions of Dispute Adjudication Agreement with its Annex (Procedural Rules) and the Dispute Adjudication Agreement should be amended to comply with the wording contained in the corresponding sections of FIDIC's Conditions of Contract for Plant and Design - Build.

第 18 条 保险

通用条件描述要由"应投保方"办理的保险的措辞中,该应投保方除非在**专用条件**中另有说明,将是**承包商**。**承包商**提供的这些保险都要符合与**雇主**达成一致的一般条款的规定。因此**投标人须知**可要求投标人提供建议条件的细节。

如果**雇主**要根据本**条**办理任何保险,招标文件应包括保险的细节,作为**专用条件**的附件(以使投标人能够估计为保护自己需要的其他保险),此类细节包括保险条件、限额、除外责任和免赔额;最好采用每份保险单抄件的形式。**雇主**可能感到难以对**第 18.2 款**第 3 段所述的(对**承包商设备**,包括**分包商设备**的)保险投保,因为**雇主**可能不知道这些各类设备的数量或价值。在**专用条件**中可包括下列句子:

范例	删去**第 18.2 款**最后一段,代之以: 但**第 18.2 款**开头两段所述的保险,应由**雇主**而不是**承包商**作为应投保方办理并保持。

第 19 条 不可抗力

招标前,**雇主**应核实本**条**措辞与管辖**合同**的法律不相矛盾。

第 20 条 索赔、争端和仲裁

第 20.2 款 争端裁决委员会的任命

除非**工程师**(虽然是**雇主**任命的)将按照下述另一种选择,根据**第 20 条**做出仲裁前的决定,合同应包括根据**第 20 条**在不劝阻**双方**在工程进行过程中就争端达成协议的同时,允许他们将争端事项提交公正的争端裁决委员会("DAB")的各项规定。

裁决程序的成功,在许多因素中主要取决于**双方**对商定的将服务于 DAB 的人员的信任。因此重要的是,该职位的候选人不是由某方强加于另一方;如果是根据**第 20.3 款**的规定选择人员,由一个完全公正的实体来选择。如果已按照**投标书附录**中的范例措辞委托授权,菲迪克(FIDIC)愿承担此任。

要在**中标函**发出前就人选取得一致,以及 DAB 要定期视察现场,这两点是可取的,但不是必要的。根据**投标书附录**中的范例条文,**双方**可在**中标函**发出前,或在其后一定时间内同意其任命。另一种办法是,双方可能愿意推迟到发生争端时才进行任命,在这种情况下,**第 20.2 款**加上**附录——争端裁决协议书一般条件**及其**附件(程序规则)**和**争端裁决协议书**,应加以修改,以符合菲迪克(FIDIC)的《**生产设备和设计-施工合同条件**》相应部分的条文。

Sub-Clause 20.2 provides for two alternative arrangements for the DAB:

(a)   one person, who acts as the sole member of the DAB, having entered into a tripartite agreement with both Parties; or

(b)   a DAB of three persons, each of whom has entered into a tripartite agreement with both Parties.

The form of this tripartite agreement could be one of the two alternatives shown at the end of this publication, as appropriate to the arrangement adopted. Both of these forms incorporate (by reference) the General Conditions of Dispute Adjudication Agreement, which are included as the Appendix to the General Conditions because they are also referred to in Sub-Clause 20.2. Under either of these alternative forms of Dispute Adjudication Agreement, each individual person is referred to as a Member.

At an early stage, consideration should be given as to whether a one-person or three-person DAB is preferable for a particular project, taking account of its size, duration and the fields of expertise which will be involved. For some projects, it may be considered appropriate to appoint a one-person DAB for each major field of expertise relevant to the Works; however, this may give rise to problems if, when a dispute arises, the Parties cannot agree which field is applicable and, there-fore, to whom the dispute should be referred.

For a one-person DAB to be mutually agreed, the Employer (or the tenderer) could propose the names and curriculum vitae of suitable persons, for the tenderer (or the Employer) to accept. It may be advisable to propose alternates in case some subsequently decline the appointment, assuming that they have not previously indicated their willingness to accept. Each Party may be reluctant to choose names from a list of people who have already been contacted by the other Party.

For a three-person DAB, the Employer and the tenderer may each propose one member, similar to the above procedure, for the tenderer and the Employer respectively to accept. For the chairman, the Employer (or the tenderer) could similarly propose suitable persons for the tenderer (or the Employer) to accept. It may be appropriate for the chairman's retainer fee to be more than that of the other two members, reflecting the additional administrative tasks which a chairman will have to perform.

The appointment of the DAB may be facilitated, especially if the members are not to be appointed at the commencement of the Contract, by including an agreed list of potential members in the Contract: in a Schedule.

Alternatively, the Engineer may make these pre-arbitral decisions. This alternative, which has been the Engineer's traditional role in common law countries, may be appropriate if the Engineer is an independent professional consulting engineer with the experience and resources required for the administration of all aspects of the contract. The Employer should recognise that, although the Engineer generally acts for the Employer as specified in Sub-Clause 3.1(a), the Engineer will make these pre-arbitral decisions impartially and the Employer must not prejudice this impartiality. If this alternative is considered appropriate, the Sub-Clause may be varied:

EXAMPLE SUB-CLAUSE FOR PRE-ARBITRAL DECISIONS BY THE ENGINEER

Delete Sub-Clauses 20.2 and 20.3.

Delete the second paragraph of Sub-Clause 20.4 and substitute:

The Engineer shall act as the DAB in accordance with this Sub-Clause 20.4, acting fairly, impartially and at the cost of the Employer. In the event that the Employer intends to replace the Engineer, the Employer's notice under Sub-Clause 3.4 shall include detailed proposals for the appointment of a replacement DAB.

第 20.2 款对 DAB 提供了两种备选安排：

(a)   一人，作为 DAB 的唯一成员，已与**双方**签订了三方协议书；或

(b)   三人 DAB，其中每人都与**双方**签订三方协议书。

此三方协议书的格式，根据选用的适宜安排方式，可从本文本最后附的两种备选格式中选择一种。这两种格式体现(参考)了**争端裁决协议书一般条件**，该一般条件因为在**第 20.2 款**规定中也谈到，作为**附录**附在**通用条件**后。在这两种**争端裁决协议书**的备选格式中，每位个人都**称为成员**。

对于具体项目，要根据项目的大小、历时长短和涉及的专业技术领域，早期就考虑是选用一人还是三人 DAB 更好。对于某些项目，对与**工程**有关的每个主要专业领域任命一个一人 DAB 可能被视为是合适的；但如果发生争端时双方不能就应适用哪一领域，以致争端应委托给谁达成一致，就会发生问题。

对于需得到双方同意的一人 DAB，**雇主**(或投标人)可提出合适人选的姓名和简历，以供投标人(或**雇主**)认可。如果此后可能有人以原未表示愿意认可为由而拒绝该任命，提出一些替代人选可能是明智的。每**方**可能都不太愿意从已与另一**方**有过接触的人员的名单中选择。

对于三人 DAB，**雇主**和投标人可以每人提出一位人选，经过前述相似的程序，供投标人和**雇主**分别认可。对委员会主席，**雇主**(或投标人)也可类似地提出合适人选，以供投标人(或**雇主**)认可。主席的聘请费高于其他两位成员可能是合适的，因为主席还要做额外的管理工作。

为了便于 DAB 的任命，尤其是成员不在**合同**开始实施时任命的情况下，可以在**合同：资料表**中包括一个商定的备选成员名单。

替代地，**工程师**可以作出这些仲裁前的决定。这种作法，在实行普通法的国家，已是**工程师**的传统角色，如果**工程师**是一个独立的专业咨询**工程师**，具有管理**合同**所有方面需要的经验和资源，这一作法可能是合适的。**雇主**应认识到，虽如**第 3.1 款**(a)项的规定，**工程师**一般代表**雇主**行动，**工程师**将公正地作出这些仲裁前的决定，**雇主**不应影响其公正性。如认为这一作法合适，**本款**可改变如下：

工程师仲裁前决定的范例条款

> 删除**第 20.2 款**和**第 20.3 款**。
>
> 删除**第 20.4 款**的第二段，代之以：
>
> **工程师**应按照本**第 20.4 款**的规定，公平、公正地进行 DAB 的工作，其费用由**雇主**承担。如果**雇主**想要替换**工程师**，**雇主**根据**第 3.4 款**的规定发出的通知应包括任命替代 DAB 的详细建议。

Sub-Clause 20.5   Amicable Settlement

The provisions of this Sub-Clause are intended to encourage the parties to settle a dispute amicably, without the need for arbitration: for example, by direct negotiation, conciliation, mediation, or other forms of alternative dispute resolution. Amicable settlement procedures often depend, for their success, on confidentiality and on both Parties' acceptance of the procedure. Therefore, neither Party should seek to impose the procedure on the other Party.

Sub-Clause 20.6   Arbitration

The Contract should include provisions for the resolution by international arbitration of any disputes which are not resolved amicably. In international construction contracts, international commercial arbitration has numerous advantages over litigation in national courts, and may be more acceptable to the Parties.

Careful consideration should be given to ensuring that the international arbitration rules chosen are compatible with the provisions of Clause 20 and with the other elements to be set out in the Appendix to Tender. The Rules of Arbitration of the International Chamber of Commerce (the "ICC", which is based at 38 Cours Albert 1er, 75008 Paris, France) are frequently included in international contracts. In the absence of specific stipulations as to the number of arbitrators and the place of arbitration, the International Court of Arbitration of the ICC will decide on the number of arbitrators (typically three in any substantial construction dispute) and on the place of arbitration.

If the UNCITRAL (or other non-ICC) arbitration rules are preferred, it may be necessary to designate, in the Appendix to Tender, an institution to appoint the arbitrators or to administer the arbitration, unless the institution is named (and their role specified) in the arbitration rules. It may also be necessary to ensure, before so designating an institution in the Appendix to Tender, that it is prepared to appoint or administer.

For major projects tendered internationally, it is desirable that the place of arbitration be situated in a country other than that of the Employer or Contractor. This country should have a modern and liberal arbitration law and should have ratified a bilateral or multilateral convention (such as the 1958 New York Convention on the Recognition and Enforcement of Foreign Arbitral Awards), or both, that would facilitate the enforcement of an arbitral award in the states of the Parties.

It may be considered desirable in some cases for other Parties to be joined into any arbitration between the Parties, thereby creating a multi-party arbitration. While this may be feasible, multi-party arbitration clauses require skilful drafting, and usually need to be prepared on a case-by-case basis. No satisfactory standard form of multi-party arbitration clause for international use has yet been developed.

第 20.5 款　　　　　　友好解决

本款规定的目的是鼓励双方友好解决争端，避免对仲裁的需要。例如，通过直接谈判、和解、调解或其他解决争端的替代作法。友好解决程序的成功，常常取决于其保密性和双方对程序的认可。因此任何一方都不应寻求将程序强加于另一方。

第 20.6 款　　　　　　仲裁

合同中应包括，对未能友好解决的任何争端通过国际仲裁解决的规定。在国际施工合同中，国际商事仲裁比国内法庭诉讼具有很多优点，因而可能更易为双方接受。

应认真考虑，确保选用的国际仲裁规则与第 20 条的规定和投标书附录中规定的其他内容相一致。国际商会(ICC,其总部设在法国巴黎75008, 38 Cours Albert 1er,)的仲裁规则常被写入国际合同中。在对仲裁员人数、仲裁地点没有具体规定的情况下，ICC的国际仲裁庭将决定仲裁员人数(在各种重大施工争端中一般为三人)和仲裁地点。

如果倾向采用联合国国际贸易法委员会(UNCITRAL)(或国际商会以外的其他组织)的仲裁规则，在投标书附录中可能需要指定一个提名仲裁员或执行仲裁的机构，除非在仲裁规则中已指明该机构(并规定了其任务)。在指定某一机构前，还需要确保该机构愿意承担提名或执行仲裁的任务。

对国际招标的大型项目，仲裁地点最好选在雇主或承包商所在国以外的国家。该国应有现代的、开放的仲裁法，并已批准了双边或多边公约(如 1958 年纽约承认及执行外国仲裁裁决公约)，或两者都被批准，这样有利于仲裁裁决在双方所在国执行。

在某些情况下，可能认为请其他方加入双方间的任何仲裁，形成一个多边仲裁比较好。尽管这可能是可行的，但多边仲裁条款需要起草技巧，且需要根据逐个案情而定。目前还没有编制出令人满意的、国际通用的多边仲裁条款的标准格式。

Annexes   FORMS OF SECURITY

Acceptable form(s) of security should be included in the tender documents: for Annex A and/or B, in the Instructions to Tenderers; and for Annexes C to G, annexed to the Particular Conditions. The following example forms, which (except for Annex A) incorporate Uniform Rules published by the International Chamber of Commerce (the "ICC", which is based at 38 Cours Albert 1er, 75008 Paris, France), may have to be amended to comply with the applicable law. Although the ICC publishes guides to these Uniform Rules, legal advice should be taken before the securities are written. Note that the guaranteed amounts should be quoted in all the currencies, as specified in the Contract, in which the guarantor pays the beneficiary.

附件　担保函格式

招标文件中应包括认可的担保函格式：**附件**A 和(或)B 附于**投标人须知**；**附件**C 至 G 附于**专用条件**。下列范例格式(**附件**A 除外)体现了**国际商会**(ICC,总部设在法国巴黎 75008，38 Cours Albert 1er,)公布的**统一规则**，应用时可能需要修改，以符合适用的法律。虽然**国际商会**出版了对这些**统一规则**的指南，在起草担保函前还应听取法律咨询建议。还应注意，保证金额应按**合同**中规定的，担保人向受益人支付的所有币种分别列出。

Annex A   EXAMPLE FORM OF PARENT COMPANY GUARANTEE

[See page 166, and the comments on Sub-Clause 1.14]

Brief description of Contract ....

Name and address of Employer ....

.... (together with successors and assigns).

We have been informed that .... (hereinafter called the "Contractor") is submitting an offer for such Contract in response to your invitation, and that the conditions of your invitation require his offer to be supported by a parent company guarantee.

In consideration of you, the Employer, awarding the Contract to the Contractor, we (*name of parent company*) .... irrevocably and unconditionally guarantee to you, as a primary obligation, the due performance of all the Contractor's obligations and liabilities under the Contract, including the Contractor's compliance with all its terms and conditions according to their true intent and meaning.

If the Contractor fails to so perform his obligations and liabilities and comply with the Contract, we will indemnify the Employer against and from all damages, losses and expenses (including legal fees and expenses) which arise from any such failure for which the Contractor is liable to the Employer under the Contract.

This guarantee shall come into full force and effect when the Contract comes into full force and effect. If the Contract does not come into full force and effect within a year of the date of this guarantee, or if you demonstrate that you do not intend to enter into the Contract with the Contractor, this guarantee shall be void and ineffective. This guarantee shall continue in full force and effect until all the Contractor's obligations and liabilities under the Contract have been discharged, when this guarantee shall expire and shall be returned to us, and our liability hereunder shall be discharged absolutely.

This guarantee shall apply and be supplemental to the Contract as amended or varied by the Employer and the Contractor from time to time. We hereby authorise them to agree any such amendment or variation, the due performance of which and compliance with which by the Contractor are likewise guaranteed hereunder. Our obligations and liabilities under this guarantee shall not be discharged by any allowance of time or other indulgence whatsoever by the Employer to the Contractor, or by any variation or suspension of the works to be executed under the Contract, or by any amendments to the Contract or to the constitution of the Contractor or the Employer, or by any other matters, whether with or without our knowledge or consent.

This guarantee shall be governed by the law of the same country (or other jurisdiction) as that which governs the Contract and any dispute under this guarantee shall be finally settled under the Rules of Arbitration of the International Chamber of Commerce by one or more arbitrators appointed in accordance with such Rules. We confirm that the benefit of this guarantee may be assigned subject only to the provisions for assignment of the Contract.

Date .... Signature(s) ....

附件 A　母公司保函范例格式

[见第 167 页和对第 1.14 款解释]

合 同 简 述 ....

雇主名称和地址 ....

....（连同继承人和受让人）。

我方已获知，＿＿＿＿＿（以下称"**承包商**"）正响应你方**邀请**对以上**合同**提交报价，你方邀请条件要求报价应附一份母公司保函支持。

考虑到你方，**雇主**，将向**承包商**授予**合同**，我方（母公司名称）＿＿＿＿不可撤销和无条件地，作为一项首要义务向你方保证，**承包商**根据**合同**规定的所有应履行的义务和责任，包括**承包商**按照其真实意图和含义遵守所有合同条款和条件。

如果**承包商**未能如上履行其义务和责任，未能遵守**合同**，我方将保障**雇主**免受因任何**承包商**根据**合同**应对**雇主**负责的任何此类违约造成的所有损害赔偿费、损失和开支（包括法律费用和开支）。

本保函将在**合同**全面实施和生效时，全面实施和生效。如果在本保函日期后一年内，**合同**没有全面实施和生效，或如果你方表明不想与**承包商**签订合同，本保函将作废和无效。本保函将持续全面实施和有效直到**承包商**根据**合同**规定的义务和责任全部解除为止，届时本保函将期满，应退还我方，我方在其下的责任应完全解除。

当**雇主**和**承包商**有时对**合同**进行修改或变更时，本保函仍适用并作为**合同**的补充。我方在此授权他们同意此类任何修改或变更，对**承包商**应履行和应遵守的修改或变更部分同样予以保证。我方根据本保函规定的义务和责任，不因**雇主**对**承包商**做出的任何时限允许或其他宽让，或根据**合同**要实施的工程的任何变更或暂停，或对**合同**或**承包商**或**雇主**的组成的任何修改，或任何其他事项而解除，不论这些事项我方是否知晓或同意。

本保函应由管辖**合同**的同一国家（或其他司法管辖区）的法律管辖，关于本保函的任何争端，应根据**国际商会仲裁规则**，由按该**规则**任命的一位或几位仲裁员最终解决。我方确认，本保函的权益仅可按照**合同**转让的条款进行转让。

日期 ＿＿＿＿＿　　　签字 ＿＿＿＿＿＿＿＿＿＿

Annex B   EXAMPLE FORM OF TENDER SECURITY

[See page 166]

Brief description of Contract ....

Name and address of Beneficiary ....

.... (whom the tender documents define as the Employer).

We have been informed that .... (hereinafter called the "Principal") is submitting an offer for such Contract in response to your invitation, and that the conditions of your invitation (the "conditions of invitation", which are set out in a document entitled Instructions to Tenderers) require his offer to be supported by a tender security.

At the request of the Principal, we (*name of bank*) .... hereby irrevocably undertake to pay you, the Beneficiary/Employer, any sum or sums not exceeding in total the amount of .... (say: ....) upon receipt by us of your demand in writing and your written statement (in the demand) stating that:

(a)   the Principal has, without your agreement, withdrawn his offer after the latest time specified for its submission and before the expiry of its period of validity, or

(b)   the Principal has refused to accept the correction of errors in his offer in accordance with such conditions of invitation, or

(c)   you awarded the Contract to the Principal and he has failed to comply with sub-clause 1.6 of the conditions of the Contract, or

(d)   you awarded the Contract to the Principal and he has failed to comply with sub-clause 4.2 of the conditions of the Contract.

Any demand for payment must contain your signature(s) which must be authenticated by your bankers or by a notary public. The authenticated demand and statement must be received by us at this office on or before (*the date 35 days after the expiry of the validity of the Letter of Tender*) .... , when this guarantee shall expire and shall be returned to us.

This guarantee is subject to the Uniform Rules for Demand Guarantees, published as number 458 by the International Chamber of Commerce, except as stated above.

Date ....   Signature(s) ....

附件 B　投标保函范例格式

［见第 167 页］

合同简述 ....

受益人名称和地址 ....

.... （招标文件中称为**雇主**）。

我方已获知，_____（以下称"**委托人**"）正响应你方**邀请**对上述**合同**提交报价，你方**邀请**条件(在题为**投标人须知**的文件中规定的"**邀请条件**")要求投标人报价要有一份投标保函支持。

应**委托人**请求，我方(银行名称)_____在此不可撤销地承诺，在我方收到你方的书面要求和关于(在要求中)下列事项的书面说明后，向你方，**受益人/雇主**，支付总额不超过_____（即：_____）的任何一笔或几笔款额：

(a)　**委托人**未经你方同意，在规定的提交报价的最终时间后和其有效期限期满前，已撤回其报价；或

(b)　**委托人**已拒绝接受对其按照上述**邀请条件**所做报价中错误的改正；或

(c)　你方将**合同**授予了**委托人**，但**委托人**未能遵守合同条件的**第1.6款**；或

(d)　你方将**合同**授予了**委托人**，但**委托人**未能遵守合同条件的**第4.2款**。

任何付款的要求，都必须有经你方银行或公证人确证的你方签字。经确证的要求和说明必须在(**投标函**有效期期满后 35 天的日期)_____或其以前，由我方在本办公地点收到，届时本保函应期满，应退还我方。

本保函除上述要求外，应遵守**国际商会**以 458 号文公布的**即付保函统一规则**的规定。

日期 _____　签字 ....

Annex C   EXAMPLE FORM OF PERFORMANCE SECURITY - DEMAND GUARANTEE

[See comments on Sub-Clause 4.2]

Brief description of Contract ....

Name and address of Beneficiary ....

.... (whom the Contract defines as the Employer).

We have been informed that ....(hereinafter called the "Principal") is your contractor under such Contract, which requires him to obtain a performance security.

At the request of the Principal, we (*name of bank*)................................. hereby irrevocably undertake to pay you, the Beneficiary/Employer, any sum or sums not exceeding in total the amount of ....(the "guaranteed amount", say:........................) upon receipt by us of your demand in writing and your written statement stating:

(a)   that the Principal is in breach of his obligation(s) under the Contract, and

(b)   the respect in which the Principal is in breach.

[Following the receipt by us of an authenticated copy of the taking-over certificate for the whole of the works under clause 10 of the conditions of the Contract, such guaranteed amount shall be reduced by.........% and we shall promptly notify you that we have received such certificate and have reduced the guaranteed amount accordingly.] [1]

Any demand for payment must contain your [minister's/directors'] [1] signature(s) which must be authenticated by your bankers or by a notary public. The authenticated demand and statement must be received by us at this office on or before (*the date 70 days after the expected expiry of the Defects Notification Period for the Works*) .... (the "expiry date"), when this guarantee shall expire and shall be returned to us.

We have been informed that the Beneficiary may require the Principal to extend this guarantee if the performance certificate under the Contract has not been issued by the date 28 days prior to such expiry date. We undertake to pay you such guaranteed amount upon receipt by us, within such period of 28 days, of your demand in writing and your written statement that the performance certificate has not been issued, for reasons attributable to the Principal, and that this guarantee has not been extended.

This guarantee shall be governed by the laws of .... and shall be subject to the Uniform Rules for Demand Guarantees, published as number 458 by the International Chamber of Commerce, except as stated above.

Date ....   Signature(s) ....

---

[1]   *When writing the tender documents, the writer should ascertain whether to include the optional text, shown in parentheses [ ]*

附件 C　履约担保函 – 即付保函范例格式

[见第 4.2 款解释]

合同简述 ....

受益人名称和地址 ....

.... **(合同中称为雇主)。**

我方已获知, _____ (以下称"**委托人**")是你方根据上述合同的**承包商, 合同**要求其取得一份履约担保函。

应**委托人**请求, 我方(银行名称) _____ 在此不可撤销地承诺, 在我方收到你方的书面要求和关于以下情况的书面说明后, 向你方, **受益人/雇主**, 支付总额不超过 _____

("保证金额", 即: _____)的任何一笔或几笔款额:

　(a)　**委托人**违反**合同**规定的义务; 以及

　(b)　**委托人**违反的方面。

[在我方收到经确证的根据**合同**条件第 10 条规定颁发的整个工程接收证书的抄件后, 此项保证金额应减少 _____ %, 我方将立即通知你方, 我方已收到该证书并已相应减少了保证金额。][1]

任何付款的要求都必须有经你方银行或公证人确证的你方[部长/局长][1]的签字。经确证的要求和说明都必须在(预定工程缺陷通知期限期满后 70 天的日期) _____ ("期满日期")或其以前, 由我方在本办公地点收到, 届时本保函应期满, 应退还我方。

我方已获知, 如果到上述期满日期 28 天前, 还没有颁发根据**合同**规定的履约证书, **受益人**可要求**委托人**延长本保函。我方承诺, 将在该 28 天期限内, 根据我方收到的你方书面要求, 以及关于未颁发履约证书是由于**委托人**应负责的原因造成的、及本保函尚未延长的书面说明, 向你方支付该项保证金额。

本保函除上述要求外, 应受 _____ 法律管辖, 并应遵守**国际商会**以 458 号文公布的**即付保函统一规则**的规定。

日期 _____ 　　签字 ....

___
(1) 起草人在起草招标文件时, 应确定是否要包括方括号[　]中的备选文字。

Annex D   EXAMPLE FORM OF PERFORMANCE SECURITY - SURETY BOND

[See comments on Sub-Clause 4.2]

Brief description of Contract   ....

Name and address of Beneficiary   ....

.... (together with successors and assigns, all as defined in the Contract as the Employer).

By this Bond, (*name and address of contractor*) ....
(who is the contractor under such Contract) as Principal and (*name and address of guarantor*)
.... as Guarantor are irrevocably held and firmly bound
to the Beneficiary in the total amount of .... (the "Bond Amount", say:
...............................) for the due performance of all such Principal's obligations and liabilities
under the Contract. [Such Bond Amount shall be reduced by .... % upon the issue of the taking-
over certificate for the whole of the works under clause 10 of the conditions of the Contract.][1]

This Bond shall become effective on the Commencement Date defined in the Contract.

Upon Default by the Principal to perform any Contractual Obligation, or upon the occurrence of any of
the events and circumstances listed in sub-clause 15.2 of the conditions of the Contract, the Guarantor
shall satisfy and discharge the damages sustained by the Beneficiary due to such Default, event or
circumstances.[2] However, the total liability of the Guarantor shall not exceed the Bond Amount.

The obligations and liabilities of the Guarantor shall not be discharged by any allowance of time or
other indulgence whatsoever by the Beneficiary to the Principal, or by any variation or suspension
of the works to be executed under the Contract, or by any amendments to the Contract or to the
constitution of the Principal or the Beneficiary, or by any other matters, whether with or without the
knowledge or consent of the Guarantor.

Any claim under this Bond must be received by the Guarantor on or before (*the date six months after
the expected expiry of the Defects Notification Period for the Works*) .... (the "Expiry
Date"), when this Bond shall expire and shall be returned to the Guarantor.

The benefit of this Bond may be assigned subject to the provisions for assignment of the Contract,
and subject to the receipt by the Guarantor of evidence of full compliance with such provisions.

This Bond shall be governed by the law of the same country (or other jurisdiction) as that which
governs the Contract. This Bond incorporates and shall be subject to the Uniform Rules for
Contract Bonds, published as number 524 by the International Chamber of Commerce, and words
used in this Bond shall bear the meanings set out in such Rules.

Wherefore this Bond has been issued by the Principal and the Guarantor on (*date*) ....

Signature(s) for and on behalf of the Principal ....

Signature(s) for and on behalf of the Guarantor ....

[1] *When writing the tender documents, the writer should ascertain whether to include the optional text,
     shown in parentheses [ ]*

[2] *Insert:* [and shall not be entitled to perform the Principal's obligations under the Contract.]
     Or: [or at the option of the Guarantor (to be exercised in writing within 42 days of receiving the claim
             specifying such Default) perform the Principal's obligations under the Contract.]

附件 D   履约担保函 – 担保保证范例格式

[见第 4.2 款解释]

合同简述 _____

受益人名称和地址 _____

_____ （连同继承人和**受让人**,在**合同**中都称为**雇主**)。

根据本**保证**,（承包商名称和地址） _____ （根据上述**合同**的**承包商**)作为**委托人**
与（担保人名称和地址） _____ 作为**担保人**, 对该**委托人**根据**合同**应履行的全部义务和
责任, 以总金额 _____ （"**保证金额**",即: _____)向**受益人**不可撤销地保持和坚定地
担保。[上述**保证金额**在根据**合同条件第 10 条**颁发整个工程接收证书后,应减少 _____ %。][(1)

本**保证**自**合同**中规定的开工**日期**起生效。

在**委托人**履行任何**合同**义务中发生**违约**, 或出现任何**合同条件第 15.2 款**所列举的事件和情况
时, **担保人**应满足并偿清**受益人**因该项**违约**、事件或情况遭受的损害赔偿费[(2)], 但**担保人**的
全部责任不应超过**保证金额**。

担保人的义务和责任不因**受益人**对**委托人**做出的任何时限允许或其他宽让、或对根据**合同**应
实施的工程的任何变更或暂停、或对**合同**或对**委托人**或**受益人**的组成的任何修改、或任何其
他事项而解除, 不论是否经**担保人**知晓或同意。

根据本**保证**提出的任何索赔必须由**担保人**在（预定**工程缺陷通知期限**期满后 6 个月的日期) _____
_____ （"**期满日期**"）或其以前收到, 届时本**保证**应期满, 应退还**担保人**。

本**保证**的权益可依照**合同**转让的条款, 以及**担保人**收到完全符合上述条款的证据, 进行转让。

本**保证**应由管辖**合同**的同一国家（或其他司法管辖区)的法律管辖。本**保证**体现并应遵守**国际
商会第 524 号文**公布的**合同保证统一规则**的规定, 本**保证**使用的词语应具有该**规则**规定的含
义。

本**保证**于   年   月 日期由**委托人**和**担保人**签署。

委托人代表签字 _____

担保人代表签字 _____

(1) 起草人起草招标文件时, 应确定是否要包括方括号[　]内的备选文字。

(2) 此处插入:［并不得履行**委托人**根据**合同**规定的义务。］
　或:［或由**担保人**选择(要在收到提出该项违约索赔 42 天内用书面提出)履行**委托人**根据**合同**规定的义务。］

Annex E   EXAMPLE FORM OF ADVANCE PAYMENT GUARANTEE

[See comments on Sub-Clause 14.2]

Brief description of Contract ....

Name and address of Beneficiary ....

.... (whom the Contract defines as the Employer).

We have been informed that .... (hereinafter called the "Principal") is your contractor under such Contract and wishes to receive an advance payment, for which the Contract requires him to obtain a guarantee.

At the request of the Principal, we (*name of bank*) .... hereby irrevocably undertake to pay you, the Beneficiary/Employer, any sum or sums not exceeding in total the amount of .... (the "guaranteed amount", say: ....) upon receipt by us of your demand in writing and your written statement stating:

    (a)   that the Principal has failed to repay the advance payment in accordance with the conditions of the Contract, and

    (b)   the amount which the Principal has failed to repay.

This guarantee shall become effective upon receipt [of the first instalment] of the advance payment by the Principal. Such guaranteed amount shall be reduced by the amounts of the advance payment repaid to you, as evidenced by your notices issued under sub-clause 14.6 of the conditions of the Contract. Following receipt (from the Principal) of a copy of each purported notice, we shall promptly notify you of the revised guaranteed amount accordingly.

Any demand for payment must contain your signature(s) which must be authenticated by your bankers or by a notary public. The authenticated demand and statement must be received by us at this office on or before (*the date 70 days after the expected expiry of the Time for Completion*) .... (the "expiry date"), when this guarantee shall expire and shall be returned to us.

We have been informed that the Beneficiary may require the Principal to extend this guarantee if the advance payment has not been repaid by the date 28 days prior to such expiry date. We undertake to pay you such guaranteed amount upon receipt by us, within such period of 28 days, of your demand in writing and your written statement that the advance payment has not been repaid and that this guarantee has not been extended.

This guarantee shall be governed by the laws of .... and shall be subject to the Uniform Rules for Demand Guarantees, published as number 458 by the International Chamber of Commerce, except as stated above.

Date ....   Signature(s) ....

附件 E　预付款保函范例格式

［见第 14.2 款解释］

合同简述 _____

受益人名称和地址 _____

_____**（合同中称为雇主）**

我方已获知，_____（以下称"**委托人**"）是你方根据上述**合同**的**承包商**，希望得到一笔预付款，为此，**合同**要求其取得一份保函。

应**委托人**请求，我方（银行名称）_____在此不可撤销地**承诺**，在我方收到你方书面的要求和关于以下情况的书面说明后，向你方，**受益人/雇主**，支付总额不超过_____（"**保证金额**"，即：_____）的任何一笔或几笔款额：

(a)　**委托人**未能按照**合同**条件付还预付款；以及

(b)　**委托人**未能付还的款额。

本保函在**委托人**收到预付款［首次分期付款］时开始生效。该保证金额应按你方根据合同条件第 14.6 款规定发出的通知中证明已向你方付还的款额，逐步减少。我方每次收到（自**委托人**处）据称是该通知的抄件后，将立即将相应修改的保证金额通知你方。

任何关于付款的要求都必须有经你方银行或公证人确证的你方签字。经确证的要求和说明必须在（预定**竣工时间**期满后 70 天的日期）_____（"期满日期"）或其以前，由我方在本办公地点收到，届时本保函应期满，应退还我方。

我方已获知，如果到上述期满日期 28 天前，预付款还没有付还，**受益人**可以要求**委托人**延长本保函。我方承诺，根据我方在该 28 天期限内收到你方的书面要求，以及关于预付款还没有付还、本保函还没有延期的书面说明，向你方支付该保证金额。

本保函除上述要求外，应受_____的法律管辖，并应遵守**国际商会**以 458 号文公布的**即付保函统一规则**的规定。

日期 _____　　签字 _____

Annex F   EXAMPLE FORM OF RETENTION MONEY GUARANTEE

[See comments on Sub-Clause 14.9]

Brief description of Contract ....

Name and address of Beneficiary ....

.... (whom the Contract defines as the Employer).

We have been informed that .... (hereinafter called the "Principal") is your contractor under such Contract and wishes to receive early payment of [part of] the retention money, for which the Contract requires him to obtain a guarantee.

At the request of the Principal, we (*name of bank*) .... hereby irrevocably undertake to pay you, the Beneficiary/Employer, any sum or sums not exceeding in total the amount of .... (the "guaranteed amount", say: ....) upon receipt by us of your demand in writing and your written statement stating:

(a)   that the Principal has failed to carry out his obligation(s) to rectify certain defect(s) for which he is responsible under the Contract, and

(b)   the nature of such defect(s).

At any time, our liability under this guarantee shall not exceed the total amount of retention money released to the Principal by you, as evidenced by your notices issued under sub-clause 14.6 of the conditions of the Contract with a copy being passed to us.

Any demand for payment must contain your signature(s) which must be authenticated by your bankers or by a notary public. The authenticated demand and statement must be received by us at this office on or before (*the date 70 days after the expected expiry of the Defects Notification Period for the Works*) .... (the "expiry date"), when this guarantee shall expire and shall be returned to us.

We have been informed that the Beneficiary may require the Principal to extend this guarantee if the performance certificate under the Contract has not been issued by the date 28 days prior to such expiry date. We undertake to pay you such guaranteed amount upon receipt by us, within such period of 28 days, of your demand in writing and your written statement that the performance certificate has not been issued, for reasons attributable to the Principal, and that this guarantee has not been extended.

This guarantee shall be governed by the laws of .... and shall be subject to the Uniform Rules for Demand Guarantees, published as number 458 by the International Chamber of Commerce, except as stated above.

Date ....   Signature(s) ....

附件 F 保留金保函范例格式

[见第 14.9 款解释]

合同简述 ....

受益人名称和地址 ....

....

（合同中称为**雇主**）

我方已获知，_____（以下称"**委托人**"）是你方根据上述**合同**的**承包商**，希望收到提前付给的[部分]保留金，为此，**合同**要求他取得一份保函。

应**委托人**请求，我方（*银行名称*）_____在此不可撤销地承诺，在我方收到你方的书面要求和关于以下情况的书面说明后，向你方，**受益人/雇主**，支付总额不超过_____（"**保证金额**"，即：_____）的任何一笔或几笔款额：

（a）**委托人**未能履行根据**合同**规定他应负责的修正某些缺陷的义务；以及

（b）此类缺陷的性质。

我方根据本保函的责任任何时候都不应超过，经你方根据**合同**条件第 14.6 款发出的通知，并给我方一份抄件证明的，你方放还给**委托人**的保留金的总额。

任何关于付款的要求都必须有经你方银行或公证人确证的你方签字。经确证的要求和说明必须在（*预定工程缺陷通知期限期满日期后 70 天的日期*）_____（"**期满日期**"）或其以前，由我方在本办公地点收到，届时本保函应期满，应退还我方。

我方已获知，如果到该期满日期 28 天前还没有颁发**合同**规定的履约证书，**受益人**可以要求**委托人**延长本保函。我方承诺，根据我方在该 28 天期限内收到你方书面要求和关于履约证书因**委托人**应负责的原因尚未颁发，以及本保函尚未延长的书面说明，向你方支付该保证金额。

本保函除上述要求外，应受_____法律管辖，并应遵守**国际商会**以 458 号文公布的**即付保函统一规则**的规定。

日期_____ 签字_____

Annex G   EXAMPLE FORM OF PAYMENT GUARANTEE BY EMPLOYER

[See page 17: Contractor Finance]

Brief description of Contract ....

Name and address of Beneficiary ....

.... (whom the Contract defines as the Contractor).

We have been informed that .... (whom the Contract defines as the Employer and who is hereinafter called the "Principal") is required to obtain a bank guarantee.

At the request of the Principal, we (*name of bank*) .... hereby irrevocably undertake to pay you, the Beneficiary/Contractor, any sum or sums not exceeding in total the amount of .... (say: ....) upon receipt by us of your demand in writing and your written statement stating:

(a)   that, in respect of a payment due under the Contract, the Principal has failed to make payment in full by the date fourteen days after the expiry of the period specified in the Contract as that within which such payment should have been made, and

(b)   the amount(s) which the Principal has failed to pay.

Any demand for payment must be accompanied by a copy of [*list of documents evidencing entitlement to payment*] ...., in respect of which the Principal has failed to make payment in full.

Any demand for payment must contain your signature(s) which must be authenticated by your bankers or by a notary public. The authenticated demand and statement must be received by us at this office on or before (*the date six months after the expected expiry of the Defects Notification Period for the Works*) .... when this guarantee shall expire and shall be returned to us.

This guarantee shall be governed by the laws of .... and shall be subject to the Uniform Rules for Demand Guarantees, published as number 458 by the International Chamber of Commerce, except as stated above.

Date ....   Signature(s) ....

附件 G 雇主支付保函范例格式

[见第 18 页:承包商融资]

合 同 简 述 ....

受益人名称和地址 ....

....**(合同中称为承包商)**

我方已获知，_____**(合同中称雇主,以下称"委托人")**被要求取得银行保函。

应**委托人**请求，我方(银行名称)_____在此不可撤销地承诺，在我方收到你方的书面要求和关于以下情况的书面说明后，向你方，**受益人/承包商**，支付总额不超过_____

(即:_____)的任何一笔或几笔款额:

    (a) **委托人**对于根据**合同**应付的某笔款项，未能在**合同**规定的该笔款项应付清的期限期满后 14 天内，全部付清；以及

    (b) **委托人**未能支付的款额。

任何关于付款的要求，都必须附一份关于**委托人**未能付清款项的[有权收款证明文件清单]_____的抄件。

任何关于付款的要求，都必须有经你方银行或公证人确证的你方签字。经确证的要求和说明必须在(预定**工程缺陷通知期限**期满后 6 个月的日期)_____或其以前，由我方在本办公地点收到，届时本保函应期满，应退还我方。

本保函除上述要求外，应受_____法律管辖，并应遵守**国际商会**以 458 号文公布的**即付保函统一规则**的规定。

日期_____ 签字_____

通用条件
GENERAL CONDITIONS

专用条件编写指南
GUIDANCE FOR THE
PREPARATION OF
PARTICULAR CONDITIONS

投标函、合同协议书和
争端裁决协议书格式
FORMS OF LETTER OF
TENDER, CONTRACT
AGREEMENT AND
DISPUTE ADJUDICATION
AGREEMENT

施工合同条件

Conditions of Contract for CONSTRUCTION

用于由雇主设计的建筑和工程
FOR BUILDING AND ENGINEERING WORKS
DESIGNED BY THE EMPLOYER

投标函、合同协议书和争端裁决协议书格式
Forms of Letter of Tender, Contract Agreement and
Dispute Adjudication Agreement

国 际 咨 询 工 程 师 联 合 会
FEDERATION INTERNATIONALE DES INGENIEURS-CONSEILS
INTERNATIONAL FEDERATION OF CONSULTING ENGINEERS
INTERNATIONALE VEREINIGUNG BERATENDER INGENIEURE
FEDERACION INTERNACIONAL DE INGENIEROS CONSOLTORES

FIDIC

LETTER OF TENDER

NAME OF CONTRACT:

TO:

We have examined the Conditions of Contract, Specification, Drawings, Bill of Quantities, the other Schedules, the attached Appendix and Addenda Nos .... for the execution of the above-named Works. We offer to execute and complete the Works and remedy any defects therein in conformity with this Tender which includes all these documents, for the sum of (in currencies of payment) ....

or such other sum as may be determined in accordance with the Conditions of Contract.

We accept your suggestions for the appointment of the DAB, as set out in Schedule ....

> [*We have completed the Schedule by adding our suggestions for the other Member of the DAB, but these suggestions are not conditions of this offer*].*

We agree to abide by this Tender until .... and it shall remain binding upon us and may be accepted at any time before that date. We acknowledge that the Appendix forms part of this Letter of Tender.

If this offer is accepted, we will provide the specified Performance Security, commence the Works as soon as is reasonably practicable after the Commencement Date, and complete the Works in accordance with the above-named documents within the Time for Completion.

Unless and until a formal Agreement is prepared and executed this Letter of Tender, together with your written acceptance thereof, shall constitute a binding contract between us.

We understand that you are not bound to accept the lowest or any tender you may receive.

Signature .... in the capacity of ....

duly authorised to sign tenders for and on behalf of ....

Address: ....

....

Date: ....

* If the Tenderer does not accept, this paragraph may be deleted and replaced by:

> We do not accept your suggestions for the appointment of the DAB. We have included our suggestions in the Schedule, but these suggestions are not conditions of this offer. If these suggestions are not acceptable to you, we propose that the DAB be jointly appointed in accordance with Sub-Clause 20.2 of the Conditions of Contract.

投标函

合同名称：

致：

我方已研究了为实施上述工程的**合同条件**、**规范要求**、**图纸**、**工程量表**、其他**资料表**、所附的**附录**
及第_____号(填文件编号)**补充文件**。我方愿以
_____
_____的总额(用支付货币填写)，或按照**合同条件**
可能确定的此项其他总额的报价，按照本**投标书**，包括所有这些文件，实施和完成**工程**并修补其
中任何缺陷。

我方接受你方在**资料表**_____中列出的关于任命争端裁决委员会(以下简称**DAB**)的建议。

　　[我方已填写该资料表，增加了我方对**DAB**另一成员的建议，但这些建议不是本报价的条
　　件]。*

我方同意遵守本**投标书**直至_____，在该日期前，本**投标书**对我方一直具有约束力，随
时可接受中标。我方承认所附**附录**为本**投标函**的一部分。

如果我方中标，我方将提供规定的**履约担保**，将在**开工日期**后，尽早开工，并在**竣工时间**内，
按照上述文件完成**工程**。

除非并直到制定正式**协议书**并生效，本**投标函**以及你方书面中标通知，应构成你我双方间具
有约束力的合同。

我方理解你方没有必须接受你方可能收到的最低标或任何投标的义务。

签字_____　　　　　　　　　职务_____

正式授权代表_____
　　　　　　　　　　　　　　　　签署投标书_____

地址：_____
_____

日期：_____

* 如果**投标人**不接受该建议，可删除本段，并以下文代替：

　　我方不接受你方关于任命**DAB**的建议。我方已在**资料表**中提出我方的建议，但该建议
　　不是本报价的条件。如果你方不能接受这些建议，我方建议按照**合同条件**第 **20.2 款**的
　　规定共同任命**DAB**。

APPENDIX TO TENDER

[Note: with the exception of the items for which the Employer's requirements have been inserted, the following information must be completed before the Tender is submitted]

Item	Sub-Clause	Data
Employer's name and address	1.1.2.2 & 1.3	
Contractor's name and address	1.1.2.3 & 1.3	
Engineer's name and address	1.1.2.4 & 1.3	
Time for Completion of the Works	1.1.3.3	_____ days
Defects Notification Period	1.1.3.7	365 days
Electronic transmission systems	1.3	
Governing Law	1.4	
Ruling language	1.4	
Language for communications	1.4	
Time for access to the Site	2.1	_____ days after Commencement Date
Amount of Performance Security	4.2	_____ % of the Accepted Contract Amount, in the currencies and proportions in which the Contract Price is payable
Normal working hours	6.5	
Delay damages for the Works	8.7 & 14.15(b)	_____ % of the final Contract Price per day, in the currencies and proportions in which the Contract Price is payable
Maximum amount of delay damages . .	8.7	_____ % of the final Contract Price
If there are Provisional Sums: Percentage for adjustment of Provisional Sums	13.5(b)	_____ %

Initials of signatory of Tender

投标书附录

[注:除已填入**雇主**要求的各项目外,以下资料必须在提交**投标书**前填写]

项目	条款	填入内容
雇主名称和地址	1.1.2.2 和 1.3	
承包商名称和地址	1.1.2.3 和 1.3	
工程师名称和地址	1.1.2.4 和 1.3	
工程竣工时间	1.1.3.3	_____ 天
缺陷通知期限	1.1.3.7	365 天
电子传输系统	1.3	
管辖法律	1.4	
主导语言	1.4	
交流语言	1.4	
进入**现场**的时间	2.1	**开工日期**后 _____ 天
履约担保金额	4.2	**中标合同金额**的 _____ %,按**合同价格**的应付币种和比例
正常工作时间	6.5	
工程的误期损害赔偿费	8.7 和 14.15(b)	每天为**最终合同价格**的 _____ %,按**合同价格**的应付币种和比例
误期损害赔偿费的最高限额	8.7	**最终合同价格**的 _____ %
如有暂列金额: **暂列金额**中对实际支出的调整百分比	13.5(b)	_____ %

投标书签字人签姓名缩写 _____

If Sub-Clause 13.8 applies:
  Adjustments for Changes in Cost;
  Table(s) of adjustment data . . . . . . 13.8 . . . . . . for payments each
  month/[*YEAR*] in .... (*currency*)

Coefficient; scope of index	Country of origin; currency of index	Source of index; Title/definition	Value on stated date(s)*	
			Value	Date
a= 0.10 Fixed				
b= Labour				
c=				
d=				
e=				

* These values and dates confirm the definition of each index, but do not define Base Date indices

Total advance payment . . . . 14.2 . . . . % of the Accepted Contract Amount

Number and timing of instalments . . . . 14.2 . . . .

Currencies and proportions . . . . 14.2 . . . . % in
...... % in

Start repayment of advance payment . 14.2(a) when payments are .... %
of the Accepted Contract Amount
less Provisional Sums

Repayment amortisation of advance
payment . . . . 14.2(b) . . . . %

Percentage of retention . . . . 14.3 . . . . %

Limit of Retention Money . . . . 14.3 . . . . % of the Accepted Contract Amount

If Sub-Clause 14.5 applies:
  Plant and Materials for payment
  when shipped en route to the Site . . 14.5(b) . . . . [list]
.... [list]

  Plant and Materials for payment
  when delivered to the Site . . . . 14.5(c) . . . . [list]
.... [list]

Minimum amount of Interim Payment
Certificates . . . . 14.6 . . . . % of the Accepted Contract Amount

If payments are only to be made in a currency/currencies named on the first page of the Letter of Tender:

  Currency/currencies of payment . . . . 14.15 . . . . . . as named in the Letters of Tender

Initials of signatory of Tender

如第 13.8 款适用：

因成本改变的调整；

数据调整表　　　　　　　13.8　　　　　每月/[年]以＿＿＿＿＿（货币）支付

系数： 指数范围	来源国家； 指数对应的货币	指数来源； 名称/定义	所述日期的指数值* 指数值　　日期
a = 0.10　固定系数			
b = 　　劳动力			
c =			
d =			
e =			

*这些指数值和日期确定各指数的定义，但不定义**基准日期**的指数。

预付款总额　　　　　　　　　　　14.2　　　　　　中标合同金额的＿＿＿%

分期付款的次数和时间安排　　　　14.2

货币和比例　　　　　　　　　　　14.2　　　　　　＿＿＿＿＿＿＿＿＿＿＿＿＿%
　　　　　　　　　　　　　　　　　　　　　　　　　＿＿＿＿＿＿＿＿＿＿＿＿＿%

开始付还预付款　　　　　　　　　14.2（a）　　　　当付款额为**中标合同金额**减去**暂列
　　　　　　　　　　　　　　　　　　　　　　　　　金额**之差的＿＿＿%时

预付款分期摊还比率　　　　　　　14.2（b）　　　　　　　　　　　　　　　　　　＿＿＿%

保留金的百分比　　　　　　　　　14.3　　　　　　　　　　　　　　　　　　　　＿＿＿%

保留金限额　　　　　　　　　　14.3　　　　　　　　　　　　　　　**中标合同金额**的＿＿＿%

如第 14.5 款适用：

运往**现场**途中付费的
生产设备和**材料**　　　　　　14.5（b）　　　　　　　　　　　　　　　　　＿＿＿[列名]
　　　　　　　　　　　　　　　　　　　　　　　　　　　　　　　　　　　　　　＿＿＿[列名]

现场交付时付费的
生产设备和**材料**　　　　　　14.5（c）　　　　　　　　　　　　　　　　　＿＿＿[列名]
　　　　　　　　　　　　　　　　　　　　　　　　　　　　　　　　　　　　　　＿＿＿[列名]

期中付款证书的最低额　　　　　14.6　　　　　　　　　　　　　　　中标合同金额的＿＿＿%

如付款仅以投标函第一页中指定的一种或几种货币支付：

支付的货币（或几种货币）14.15　　　　　如**投标函**中指定的

投标书签字人签姓名缩写＿＿＿＿＿＿＿＿＿＿＿＿

If some payments are to be made in a currency/currencies not named on the first page of the Letter of Tender:

Currencies of payment 14.15

Currency Unit	Percentage payable in the Currency	Rate of exchange: number of Local per unit of Foreign
Local: _____ [name]		1.000
Foreign: _____ [name]		
_____ [name]		

Periods for submission of insurance:
    (a) evidence of insurance . . . . 18.1 . . . . _____ days
    (b) relevant policies . . . . 18.1 . . . . _____ days

Maximum amount of deductibles for
insurance of the Employer's risks . . . . 18.2(d) . . . . . _____

Minimum amount of third party
insurance . . . . 18.3 . . . . _____

Date by which the DAB shall be appointed . 20.2 . . . . 28 days after the Commencement Date

The DAB shall be . . . . 20.2 . . . . *Either:*
                                         _____ One sole Member/adjudicator
                                       Or:
                                       _____ A DAB of three Members

Appointment (if not agreed) to be
made by . . . . 20.3 . . . . The President of FIDIC or a person appointed by the President

If there are Sections:
   Definition of Sections:

Description (Sub-Clause 1.1.5.6)	Time for Completion (Sub-Clause 1.1.3.3)	Delay Damages (Sub-Clause 8.7)

[*In the above Appendix, the text shown in italics is intended to assist the drafter of a particular contract by providing guidance on which provisions are relevant to the particular contract. This italicised text should not be included in the tender documents, as it will generally appear inappropriate to tenderers.*]

Initials of signatory of Tender _____

如某些付款是以投标函第一页中未指定的一种或几种货币支付：

支付的货币   14.15

货币单位	货币应付百分比	汇率：单位外币当地货币
当地货币：　［名称］		1.000
外币　　：　［名称］		
［名称］		

提交有关保险文件的期限：
 （a） 保险证明   18.1   天
 （b） 相关保险单 18.1   天

雇主风险保险免赔额的最大金额 18.2（d）

第三方保险的最小金额   18.3

应任命 DAB 的最晚日期   20.2   **开工日期**后 28 天

DAB 应为   20.2   或：
                    唯一成员/裁决员
                 或：
                    三位成员 DAB

（如未能达成一致）
 提名的人员是   20.3   菲迪克（FIDIC）主席或其指定的人员

如有单位工程：
 单位工程定义：

说明 （第 1.1.5.6 款）	竣工时间 （第 1.1.3.3 款）	误期损害赔偿费 （第 8.7 款）

［在以上附录中，斜体文字（中译文楷体文字）旨在通过对具体合同相关规定提供指南，为具体合同起草人提供帮助。这段斜体文字一般对投标人显得不合适，不应将其包括在招标文件中。］

投标书签字人签姓名缩写

CONTRACT AGREEMENT

This Agreement made the .... day of .... 19 ....

Between .... of .... (hereinafter called "the Employer") of the one part,
and .... of .... (hereinafter called "the Contractor") of the other
part

Whereas the Employer desires that the Works known as .... should be executed by
the Contractor, and has accepted a Tender by the Contractor for the execution and completion of
these Works and the remedying of any defects therein,

The Employer and the Contractor agree as follows:

1.   In this Agreement words and expressions shall have the same meanings as are respectively
     assigned to them in the Conditions of Contract hereinafter referred to.

2.   The following documents shall be deemed to form and be read and construed as part of this
     Agreement:

     (a)   The Letter of Acceptance dated ....

     (b)   The Letter of Tender dated ....

     (c)   The Addenda nos. ....

     (d)   The Conditions of Contract

     (e)   The Specification

     (f)   The Drawings, and

     (g)   The completed Schedules.

3.   In consideration of the payments to be made by the Employer to the Contractor as
     hereinafter mentioned, the Contractor hereby covenants with the Employer to execute and
     complete the Works and remedy any defects therein, in conformity with the provisions of the
     Contract.

4.   The Employer hereby covenants to pay the Contractor, in consideration of the execution and
     completion of the Works and the remedying of defects therein, the Contract Price at the
     times and in the manner prescribed by the Contract.

In Witness whereof the parties hereto have caused this Agreement to be executed the day and
year first before written in accordance with their respective laws.

SIGNED by: ....   SIGNED by: ....

for and on behalf of the Employer in the presence   for and on behalf of the Contractor in the presence
of   of

Witness: ....   Witness: ....
Name: ....   Name: ....
Address: ....   Address: ....
Date: ....   Date: ....

230

合同协议书

本协议书于 _____ 年 _____ 月 _____ 日由 _____ 的 _____ （以下简称"**雇主**"）为一方，与 _____ 的 _____ （以下简称"**承包商**"）为另一方签订。

鉴于**雇主**愿将名称为 _____ 的**工程**交由**承包商**实施，并已接受了**承包商**提交的关于实施和完成这些**工程及**修补其中任何缺陷的**投标书**，

雇主和**承包商**达成协议如下：

1. 本**协议书**中的词语和措辞的含义应与下文提到的**合同条件**中分别赋予它们的含义相同。

2. 下列文件应被视为本**协议书**的组成部分，并应作为其一部分阅读和解释：

   (a) _____ （日期）的**中标函**；

   (b) _____ （日期）的**投标函**；

   (c) 新**补充文件**编号 _____ ；（填编号）

   (d) **合同条件**；

   (e) **规范要求**；

   (f) **图纸**；以及

   (g) 已填写的**资料表**。

3. 鉴于**雇主**将按下文所述付给**承包商**各种款项，**承包商**特此与**雇主**签约，保证遵照**合同**的各项规定，实施和完成本**工程**及修补其任何缺陷。

4. 鉴于**承包商**将承担上述**工程**的实施、竣工及**修补**其任何缺陷，**雇主**特此立约，保证按**合同**规定的时间和方式，向**承包商**支付**合同价格**。

本**协议书**由**双方**根据各自法律签字之日起生效，**特立此据**。

签字人签字：_____   签字人签字：_____

在下列证人在场下，代表**雇主**签字   在下列证人在场下，代表**承包商**签字

见证人：_____   见证人：_____
姓名：_____   姓名：_____
地址：_____   地址：_____
日期：_____   日期：_____

DISPUTE ADJUDICATION AGREEMENT

[for a one-person DAB]

Name and details of Contract ....
Name and address of Employer ....
Name and address of Contractor ....
Name and address of Member ....

Whereas the Employer and the Contractor have entered into the Contract and desire jointly to appoint the Member to act as sole adjudicator who is also called the "DAB".

The Employer, Contractor and Member jointly agree as follows:

1. The conditions of this Dispute Adjudication Agreement comprise the "General Conditions of Dispute Adjudication Agreement", which is appended to the General Conditions of the "Conditions of Contract for Construction" First Edition 1999 published by the Fédération Internationale des Ingénieurs-Conseils (FIDIC), and the following provisions. In these provisions, which include amendments and additions to the General Conditions of Dispute Adjudication Agreement, words and expressions shall have the same meanings as are assigned to them in the General Conditions of Dispute Adjudication Agreement.

2. [*Details of amendments to the General Conditions of Dispute Adjudication Agreement, if any. For example:*

    In the procedural rules annexed to the General Conditions of Dispute Adjudication Agreement, Rule _ is deleted and replaced by: " ... "]

3. In accordance with Clause 6 of the General Conditions of Dispute Adjudication Agreement, the Member shall be paid as follows:

    A retainer fee of .... per calendar month,
    plus a daily fee of .... per day.

4. In consideration of these fees and other payments to be made by the Employer and the Contractor in accordance with Clause 6 of the General Conditions of Dispute Adjudication Agreement, the Member undertakes to act as the DAB (as adjudicator) in accordance with this Dispute Adjudication Agreement.

5. The Employer and the Contractor jointly and severally undertake to pay the Member, in consideration of the carrying out of these services, in accordance with Clause 6 of the General Conditions of Dispute Adjudication Agreement.

6. This Dispute Adjudication Agreement shall be governed by the law of ....

SIGNED by: ....   SIGNED by: ....   SIGNED by: ....

for and on behalf of the Employer   for and on behalf of the Contractor   the Member in the presence of
in the presence of   in the presence of

Witness: ....   Witness: ....   Witness ....
Name: ....   Name: ....   Name: ....
Address: ....   Address: ....   Address: ....
Date: ....   Date: ....   Date: ....

争端裁决协议书

合同名称和内容 ....

雇主名称和地址 ....

承包商名称和地址 ....

成员名称和地址 ....

鉴于雇主与**承包商**已签订**合同**，并希望共同聘请**成员**作为唯一裁决员，也称"DAB"。

雇主、承包商和成员共同达成协议如下：

1. 本**争端裁决协议书**条件由**国际咨询工程师联合会**（FIDIC）出版的《**施工合同条件**》1999 年第 1 版所附的"**争端裁决协议书一般条件**"，及下列条款规定组成。这些规定，包括对**争端裁决协议书一般条件**的修改和补充，其用语和措辞应与其在**争端裁决协议书一般条件**中赋予相同的含义。

2. [对**争端裁决协议书一般条件**的修改的细节（如果有）。例如：

   附在**争端裁决协议书一般条件**后的程序规则中，删去规则 – – –，代以下文："…"]

3. 依照**争端裁决协议书一般条件**第 6 条，应向**成员**支付如下：

   每个日历月的聘请费 ....

   加上每日酬金 ....。

4. 鉴于**雇主和承包商**将按照**争端裁决协议书一般条件**第 6 条的规定，支付这些酬金和其他付款，**成员**承诺，根据本**争端裁决协议书**担任**DAB**（裁决员）的职务。

5. 鉴于提供这些服务，**雇主和承包商**共同并各自承诺，按照**争端裁决协议书一般条件**第 6 条向**成员**付款。

6. 本**争端裁决协议书**应受 .... 法律管辖。

签字人签字：	签字人签字：	签字人签字： ....
在下列证人在场下	在下列证人在场下	在下列证人在场下
代表**雇主**签字	代表**承包商**签字	**成员**本人签字
见证人：	见证人：	见证人： ....
姓名：	姓名：	姓名： ....
地址：	地址：	地址： ....
日期：	日期：	日期： ....

DISPUTE ADJUDICATION AGREEMENT

[for each member of a three-person DAB]

Name and details of Contract ....
Name and address of Employer ....
Name and address of Contractor ....
Name and address of Member ....

Whereas the Employer and the Contractor have entered into the Contract and desire jointly to appoint the Member to act as one of the three persons who are jointly called the "DAB" *[and desire the Member to act as chairman of the DAB]*.

The Employer, Contractor and Member jointly agree as follows:

1. The conditions of this Dispute Adjudication Agreement comprise the "General Conditions of Dispute Adjudication Agreement", which is appended to the General Conditions of the "Conditions of Contract for Construction" First Edition 1999 published by the Fédération Internationale des Ingénieurs-Conseils (FIDIC), and the following provisions. In these provisions, which include amendments and additions to the General Conditions of Dispute Adjudication Agreement, words and expressions shall have the same meanings as are assigned to them in the General Conditions of Dispute Adjudication Agreement.

2. [*Details of amendments to the General Conditions of Dispute Adjudication Agreement, if any. For example:*

    In the procedural rules annexed to the General Conditions of Dispute Adjudication Agreement, Rule _ is deleted and replaced by: " ... "]

3. In accordance with Clause 6 of the General Conditions of Dispute Adjudication Agreement, the Member shall be paid as follows:

    A retainer fee of .... per calendar month,
    plus a daily fee of .... per day.

4. In consideration of these fees and other payments to be made by the Employer and the Contractor in accordance with Clause 6 of the General Conditions of Dispute Adjudication Agreement, the Member undertakes to serve, as described in this Dispute Adjudication Agreement, as one of the three persons who are jointly to act as the DAB.

5. The Employer and the Contractor jointly and severally undertake to pay the Member, in consideration of the carrying out of these services, in accordance with Clause 6 of the General Conditions of Dispute Adjudication Agreement.

6. This Dispute Adjudication Agreement shall be governed by the law of ....

SIGNED by: ....   SIGNED by: ....   SIGNED by: ....

for and on behalf of the Employer   for and on behalf of the Contractor   the Member in the presence of
in the presence of   in the presence of

Witness: ....   Witness: ....   Witness ....
Name: ....   Name: ....   Name: ....
Address: ....   Address: ....   Address: ....
Date: ....   Date: ....   Date: ....

争端裁决协议书

合同名称和内容 ....
雇主名称和地址 ....
承包商名称和地址 ....
成员名称和地址 ....

鉴于雇主和**承包商**已签订**合同**，并希望共同**聘请成员**为由三人共同称作的"**DAB**"的一员，
[并希望成员担任DAB 主席职务]。

雇主、承包商和**成员**共同达成**协议**如下：

1. 本**争端裁决协议书**条件由**国际咨询工程师联合会**（FIDIC）出版的《**施工合同条件**》1999年
   第 1 版所附 "**争端裁决协议书一般条件**"，及下列条款规定组成。这些规定包括对**争端裁决协议书一般条件**的修改和补充，其用语和措辞应与其在**争端裁决协议书一般条件**中赋予
   相同的含义。

2. [对**争端裁决协议书一般条件**的修改的细节(如果有)。例如：

   在附在**争端裁决协议书**的一般条件后的程序规则中，删去规则 — — — ，代以下文："…"]

3. 依照**争端裁决协议书一般条件**第 6 条，应向**成员**支付如下：

   每个日历月的聘请费 ....
   加上每日酬金 ....。

4. 鉴于**雇主**和**承包商**将按照**争端裁决协议书一般条件**第 6 条的规定支付这些酬金和其他付
   款，**成员**承诺，按本**争端裁决协议书**所述，担任共同作为**DAB**的三人中的一名成员的职
   务。

5. 鉴于提供这些服务，**雇主**和**承包商**共同并各自承诺，按照**争端裁决协议书一般条件**第 6 条
   向**成员**付款。

6. 本**争端裁决协议书**应受 .... 法律管辖。

签字人签字：............   签字人签字：............   签字人签字：............

在下列证人在场下   在下列证人在场下   在下列证人在场下
　代表**雇主**签字   　　代表**承包商**签字   　　**成员**本人签字

见证人：............   见证人：............   见证人：............
姓名：............   姓名：............   姓名：............
地址：............   地址：............   地址：............
日期：............   日期：............   日期：............